Removal Aftershock

Removal

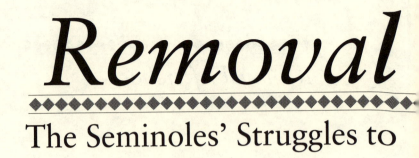

The Seminoles' Struggles to

Aftershock

Survive in the West, 1836–1866

Jane F. Lancaster

THE UNIVERSITY OF TENNESSEE PRESS / KNOXVILLE

Library of Congress Cataloging-in-Publication Data

Lancaster, Jane F., 1940–
    Removal aftershock: the Seminoles' struggles to survive in the West.
1836–1866 / Jane F. Lancaster.
         p.   cm.
    Includes bibliographical references and index.
    ISBN 0–87049–845–2 (cloth: alk. paper).
    ISBN 0–87049–846–0 (pbk.: alk. paper)
    1. Seminole Indians—Removal. 2. Seminole Indians—History—
19th century. 3. Seminole Indians—Government relations. 4. Indian
Territory—History—19th century. I. Title.
E99.S28L35   1994
973'.04973—dc20   94-129
                                    CIP

In memory of those Seminoles who suffered and died
In honor of their descendants who survive today

For
Phil and Fonda

Contents

Figures

Maps

Tables

Preface

Although Native Americans have a special place in the history of the United States, Indian historiography is far from being comprehensive. Throughout the centuries of Indian-white relationships, all branches of government have devoted attention to the relevant issues. Legislative hearings and acts, court cases, treaties, and wars involving Indians have been prominent in America's past, but the omissions in historical writings are both numerous and obvious. Until very recently, high school and college history textbooks gave little attention to Native Americans. The inhabitants of Indian Territory, especially, were generally excluded or mentioned only briefly in those accounts, whereas cavalrymen and cowboys were discussed at length. As a result, much of the realities of the relations between the United States and Native Americans have remained unknown or misunderstood, and Native American historiography is poorer for such omissions and imbalances.

The impact of the policies of the government of the United States on the Indian minority has been well studied for certain selected periods and areas. Among these well-covered periods is the Removal Era of the early nineteenth century, during which thousands of Indians were cleared from east of the Mississippi River, to make land available for white settlement, and sent to the western prairies. The resulting suffering, deprivations, and deaths of large numbers of Indians have been vividly portrayed in both scholarly literature and the popular media.

Although the removal years have received a great deal of attention, there has been little interest in the history of the tribes during their first decades in the West. Yet the difficulties of adjusting to a new land with a different climate, combined with the inability of the federal government to administer properly its Indian policies, produced as much hardship and suffering among the Indians as did removal itself. Conditions were harsh during those first decades on the prairies, and each tribe faced its own problems. Furthermore, those decades were historically important, because federal Indian policies of the time had a marked impact on later relations between the United States and the native populace.

The United States government's promotion in the early nineteenth century of the necessity of sending the Indian tribes east of the Mississippi River to lands west of that river, where they could develop toward civilization safe from encroachment from white settlers, was one of the greatest misjudgments and shortsighted policies ever instituted by that government. This idea of preserving westward lands for Indian tribes had begun initially with the British, who in various treaties had set aside lands west of the different boundaries for the Indians. Later, President Thomas Jefferson and other national leaders promoted the idea, and some historians believe Jefferson had this in mind when he made the Louisiana Purchase in 1803. Nonetheless, by 1830, when removal to Indian Territory was enacted by the Congress, the plan was obsolete. The West was changing dramatically and could no longer afford safety and security for thousands of uprooted Indians from the East. A more credible reason for such an extensive undertaking was Andrew Jackson's theory that the Indians should be cleared from the East to allow whites to densely settle the borders of the country so that it could more easily be defended from international aggression. Whatever excuses are used to justify moving the Indians from the East to the West, numerous uncertainties awaited the immigrants west of the Mississippi River.

During the first decades after removal of the southeastern tribes, the territory and its environs were replete with tension, which complicated life more for the Indians. Although the United States government, in preparation for the thousands of Indians coming from the East, had negotiated a few peace treaties with several of the more hostile tribes in the West, much unrest existed not only among the different Plains tribes, such as the Comanches, the Kiowas, and the Pawnees, but also between them and the migrating Indians. In the summer of 1836, as more militant Indians were scheduled to arrive from the East, fear of an Indian uprising in the territory was so great that the governor of Arkansas was asked to have militia ready for service on the Arkansas frontier. The Cherokees were also thought to have had war plans against the United States in the 1830s. For several years, the Osages were a threat to peace with the tribes on the Plains as well as with others in the territory. Such issues as unclear land boundaries, disputed hunting grounds, different cultures and customs, and lack of a common language often led to outbreaks of hostilities between the tribes.

On the perimeters of Indian Territory, whites created a more disturbing atmosphere. To the south, the Texans fought and won their independence from Mexico, established the Texas Republic (1836), and became a part of the United States (1845). As the white settlers rushed in, they clashed with the Indians there and either wanted them out of Texas or wanted their aid in fighting the Mexicans. The Mexicans, on the other hand, worked among Indians in Texas and the territory, trying to incite their attacks on the Texans. Finally, after the Mexican War, the Mexican Cession (1848) added vast lands stretching to the Pacific Ocean with numerous Indian tribes to the jurisdiction of the United States, as did the Oregon Territory (1846) in the Northwest. With the new territories came an influx of white settlers, spurred on by the available land and gold and silver discoveries, who crossed Indian Territory, causing disturbances with the tribes there.

To the north of the territory, the slavery issue was becoming explosive, as it was throughout the nation. After the Kansas–Nebraska Act (1854) allowed settlers to determine whether to have slavery, hostilities erupted between the pro and anti forces, which led to many acts of violence, deaths, and the descriptive phrase "Bleeding Kansas." Many blacks, both slave and free, lived among the immigrant tribes; therefore, the slavery issue created tension among the tribes as well. On the territory's eastern border were the Arkansas slaveholders, who often dipped into the area, pretending to capture runaways. The Arkansas whites accused the territory of being a haven for runaways. Moreover, they complained about having thousands of Indians on their western border and were successful in having troops from Fort Gibson moved to Fort Smith for their protection for one brief period.

Consequently, several thousand eastern Indians were located in the West during one of its most volatile periods. Thrown between the hostile and pacific tribes on the west, the demanding whites on the east, the feuding anti- and proslavery settlers to the north, and the Mexican and Texas agitators to the south, in reality the eastern Indians could have little feeling of security. During these first decades, most available troops had been required for the Second Seminole War (1835–42), the Mexican War (1846–48), the Third Seminole War (1855–57), the Civil War (1861–65), and various skirmishes with both Indians and whites. As a result, the War Department, which controlled Indian affairs until 1849, had no forces large enough to police the West in order to promote a sense of security among the immigrant tribes. Less than three thousand forces guarded the entire western frontier in the early 1830s. Therefore, at various times, the Indians themselves held intertribal peace congresses in attempts to improve the relations among the tribes and to promote peace in their new homeland.

Besides the internal and external problems of Indian Territory, the Five Civilized Tribes took major problems to the West. Before leaving the East, treaty and nontreaty factions had developed between those favoring removal, who signed treaties with the United States, and those who opposed leaving the East. The divisions in the large Cherokee tribe led to the assassination of several Cherokee leaders in the early months after their arrival in the Indian Territory and caused difficulties for several decades thereafter. Moreover, the small Chickasaw tribe was unhappy with its quasi-submergence in the larger Choctaw tribe, and the small Seminole tribe resented the same situation with the much larger Creek tribe.

The history of the Seminole tribe in the West during the three decades after 1836 is suggestive of the hardships encountered by all of the tribes so relocated. Uprooted from their homes in Florida and transported to

Indian Territory over a period of some years, these Native Americans found themselves in a strange new world. They had lived in a land of "summer, game, fish, clear waters, and orange groves." Varieties of fish and wild game, abundant crops and numerous livestock produced on fertile farm and pasture lands, and the ever-present kunti root had assured the Seminoles of a bountiful food supply. Moreover, some of the Indians owned slaves, who performed much of the manual labor. The mild climate, abundant food supplies, and slave labor afforded the Seminoles a life-style far different from that which they would find in the West. Unfortunately for the Indians, white settlers coveted their land, so in the first half of the nineteenth century, treaties with the United States mandated that the Seminoles leave the homes and life-styles they had known and relocate.

When they settled in the Western Territory, known as the "wild wilderness," the Seminoles encountered severe climatic and other environmental conditions that contrasted sharply with those of their native Florida. Both winters and summers presented extremes unknown in Florida. Winter temperatures plunged to ten degrees below zero, and ice, snow, and hail were common. The winter of 1845–46 was one of the worst on record. A few years later, during the Civil War, several Indians either froze to death or lost arms and legs to frostbite. The summers brought droughts, searing heat, and plagues of insects. The droughts were especially severe in the 1850s. Moreover, food proved to be in short supply and difficult to obtain. Fish and game were less abundant, citrus fruit nonexistent, and farm crops yielded less but required more labor. The territory was rich in mineral and timber resources, but they were of little use at the time. In short, the Seminoles' new homes in the West provided little of the security and freedom from care and want that they had known in the East. To survive they had to adopt a radically different life-style.

The Seminoles' most difficult struggle in their first years in the West was a constant battle to maintain their tribal identity and retain their tribal lands by avoiding submergence in the much larger Creek tribe, a development that some treaties seemingly required. In the late 1830s, the bulk of this small tribe found itself in this unsettling new land, where it had to begin a survival struggle for tribal identity and land. The problems between the Creeks and the Seminoles in the East prohibited any possible quiet merger of these tribes in the West. A major portion of the Seminoles were "runaways" from the Creeks who had become Seminoles at different intervals over the years. Nonetheless, as early as the 1820s, Andrew Jackson established the idea that the Seminoles should be moved onto Creek lands. According to early records, some Creeks themselves wanted the Seminoles included in their western homeland. Further complicating the already precarious situation, a Creek chief, considered a foe in the East, had settled on the area designed for Seminole settlement.

Hundreds of Seminoles under Chief Micanopy refused to go to their assigned western district among the Creeks or to locate farther west near the hostile Plains tribes. For months they hovered around Fort Gibson, where they suffered from shortages of food, clothing, and shelter while they depended on the government and traders for dire necessities. As they loitered, smallpox and measles epidemics added to their misery.

Placating the Seminoles was probably the only alternative the federal government had, because it could not have afforded a Seminole war in the West among thousands of other Indians while the Second Seminole War continued in Florida. A few government officials in Washington, such as Commissioner of Indian Affairs Thomas Hartley Crawford, Secretary of War Joel Poinsett, and President Martin Van Buren acted on the tribe's behalf and in 1839 made available another land district and appropriations, which in reality prevented the extinction of the Seminole tribe during its initial period beyond the Mississippi River.

By the 1840s, however, the Seminole tribe was still spread over parts of Cherokee and Creek lands, resenting its lack of secure land and independence as a nation. Although the United States government in the treaty of 1845 provided still another assigned area for the tribe, as well as assuring the provisions promised in the 1832 treaty, it gave no permanent tribal or land security to the Seminoles.

In the midst of the struggle for tribal and land separation from the Creeks, and as the United States became more embroiled over the slavery issue, the Seminoles found themselves entangled in serious developments with regard to the blacks, both slave and free, who lived among them.

White and Indian slaveholders harassed the blacks, causing many of them to believe that the Seminoles could not protect them. Some blacks chose to locate around Fort Gibson and sought protection from the military. After the United States government ordered the blacks returned to the Seminoles, a few distraught Seminoles allied with some blacks, and both left Indian Territory and sought freedom in Mexico. Providing a military colony there, they received land grants in return for their services in the Mexican army.

While this group lived in Mexico, those Seminoles in Indian Territory under head Chief John Jumper continued their fight for separate tribal status. They offered to induce the Florida Seminoles to come west in return for tribal independence. In mid-1853, the Seminoles wrote President Franklin Pierce, pleading to be made a nation separate from the Creeks. A couple of years later, their subagent wrote that "their nationality swept away, their country under the control of another tribe, their annuity miserably small, no provisions for schools or any other species of improvement; no incentive of any character whatever—how could they improve?" Finally, after twenty years in the West, the government officials, as well as the Creeks, agreed that the Seminoles should have tribal independence and their own land. The treaty of 1856 gave them that status with more than 2 million acres of land. Nonetheless, as the Seminoles were slow to move onto their new district because of its proximity to the hostile Plains tribes, they were snared by the white man's war—a war that swept through the Indian Territory and probably caused more destruction, proportionately, to the territory than to anywhere else in the nation.

At the outbreak of the Civil War, the Federals neglected the territory, evacuated the troops from in and around the area, and moved the headquarters of the Southern superintendency from Fort Smith to Kansas. The Confederates moved in, established an Indian bureau, negotiated treaties with the tribes, annexed Indian Territory, gave the Five Civilized Tribes three territorial representatives to the Confederate Congress, and promised to fulfill the provisions of earlier U.S. treaties. Although the Seminoles and other Indians in the West wanted to avoid this war, they were drawn into the conflict and eventually divided into loyalists and rebels.

The loyalist Seminoles, with several thousand others, fled to Kansas during the terrible winter of 1861–62, where most of them suffered for the duration of the war from a lack of provisions and shelter while illnesses such as mumps, diphtheria, measles, smallpox, frostbite, consumption, and pneumonia raged among them. One observer wrote that the Seminoles' condition was "beyond the power of any pen to portray." Several months later, when the Union regained control of Indian Territory, the rebel Seminoles fled to the Red River area, where they faced hardships similar to their northern counterparts. During the war, the homes and lands of both were ravaged by robbers, murderers, guerrilla bands, and both Federal and Confederate forces.

The southern Seminoles' participation in the war was the excuse the United States used to demand a portion of their tribal lands that had been granted in the 1856 treaty. This land was needed for loyal tribes from Kansas, where whites demanded their removal, and for tribes elsewhere. Consequently, in 1866, the Seminoles sold their entire district of more than 2 million acres for fifteen cents an acre and paid fifty cents an acre for 200,000 acres ceded by the Creeks. Finally, after five different assigned districts in thirty years, this former Florida tribe could make somewhat more permanent plans with regard to its western homeland.

Accounts of the Seminoles' activities in the West between 1836 and 1866 are few and widely scattered. Historians have studied in depth the Seminoles' wars with the United States in Florida, but they have devoted little attention to the tribe's struggles in the West to maintain tribal identity on their own lands, struggles that extended over a period of thirty years. The lack of book-length studies of the tribe also suggests the problem of integration that plagues Indian historiography. A number of useful articles in such periodicals as the *Chronicles of Oklahoma* treat various aspects of the Seminoles' western activities. Books on the Five Civilized Tribes by Arrell Morgan Gibson, Angie Debo, Grant Foreman, and others provide solid but limited information on matters discussed in this work. The few accounts in print on both the eastern and western Seminoles include Joshua Giddings's *Exiles of Florida* (1858) and Daniel Littlefield's *Africans and Seminoles: From Removal to Emancipation* (1977), works that deal especially with the Seminoles' relations with blacks. Charles Coe's *Red Patriots: The Story of the Seminoles* (1898) and Edwin C. McReynolds's *Seminoles* (1957) are general histories of both segments of the tribe, but they devote relatively little attention to the tribe's early years in the West.

This book focuses on this hitherto neglected era in Native American history and places the Seminoles in their correct historical position as a Native American tribe. By examining the Seminoles' adjustments during their first decades in the West in light of federal Indian policy, it concludes that after thirty years of struggles, caused largely by the faulted policies of the federal government, these Indians were a "stricken, divided, and beggared people scattered over hundreds of miles." For this tribe, the federal government's program of placing it in a western land away from white settlers, where it could be nurtured toward civilization and Christianity, was not only a shortsighted policy but also an illogical and inhumane one. Without the stubbornness and determination of these early tribal members, no western Seminole tribe would have existed in 1990. Truly, the mere survival of the early Seminoles earned them special distinction as a tribe.

Acknowledgments

If this work merits any acclaim, it is largely because of the teaching and guidance of a small core of historians in the Department of History at Mississippi State University. Professor Roy V. Scott deserves accolades for his patience, empathy, and encouragement while I was his doctoral student and for his later readings and critiques of parts of this manuscript. The expertise of Professor William E. Parrish in western history, his diligence as second reader, his guidance as department head and later assistance with this work have been of great value. Professor E. Stanly Godbold, Jr., taught the importance in writing of presenting the "forest before the trees," helping me to see the importance of and the need for broad concepts in historical writings. Professor John F. Marszalek instilled an invaluable analytical approach to the writing of history without which I would be unable to operate as a historian. Without the contributions of each of these professors and of other members of the department, as well as of Peggy Bonner, departmental secretary, the tasks of historical research and writing would have been more difficult.

While pursuing my research in Oklahoma, Georgia, Florida, North Carolina, and Washington, D.C., I came into contact with many efficient and courteous archivists, librarians, and government officials. At the University of Oklahoma, Curator Jack Haley and librarians Daryl Morrison and Nathan E. Bender of the Western History Collections offered useful advice and provided copies of needed materials. Sarah Erwin, librarian at the Thomas Gilcrease Museum Library at Tulsa, made available copies of materials that would have been difficult to obtain elsewhere.

At the National Archives in Washington, Robert Kvasnicka recommended several leads to various sources, while Mary Ann Hawkins of the Federal Archives Branch in East Point, Georgia, made those sources available. These primary materials provided much of the heart of the book.

Several Native Americans, including Seminoles, a Choctaw, and a Cherokee, made Indian history come alive and provided timely information. Dwayne Miller, Seminole chief of the Thomas Palmer Band, recounted his people's story, and Floyd Harjo, a former Seminole nation chief, contributed unprinted information about the Seminoles' Mexican land. Other Seminoles at the Wewoka agency were cordial and responsive. Their superintendent, Choctaw George Goodner, answered questions, made phone calls, and helped locate material that otherwise would have escaped me. Cherokee Dennis Springwater, area tribal operations officer at Muskogee, agreed to an interview that yielded a vast reservoir of facts essential to any study of the Seminoles. Karen Ketcher, a secretary in his office, was equally helpful.

Others who were especially helpful include Martha Irby and her staff at the interlibrary loan office of Mitchell Memorial Library at Mississippi State University. Phyllis McCorkle typed the manuscript promptly and accurately. Bobby and Patricia Stilwell of Vienna, Virginia, extended gracious hospitality. My family, Harwell, Phillip, and Fonda, deserve special acknowledgment for playing a secondary role to Clio for the past several years and for listening to endless conversations about the Seminoles. My gratitude also goes to my publishing family at the University of Tennessee Press, especially to Acquisitions Editor Meredith Morris-Babb, to Acquisitions Assistant Kimberly C. Scarbrough, and to Managing Editor Stan Ivester, whose promptness and efficiency have been noteworthy. Finally, without the interesting and unusual Seminole Indians, I would have had less motivation to complete a manuscript. Therefore, a special salute goes to the Seminoles in Oklahoma and in Florida.

Removal Aftershock

1

From the East to the West

After the United States gained control of Florida in 1819, the estimated five thousand Seminole Indians there encountered unprecedented changes. The treaties of 1823, 1832, and 1833 forced these Indians, many of whom were Creek "runaways," to experience a change of location, a reduction of their territory, poverty, and, eventually, war against gradual removal to the West. In compliance with the United States Indian removal policy, between 1834 and 1859, groups of Seminoles, with some of their black slaves, were moved beyond the Mississippi River. Conditions there were harsh, and the new Bureau of Indian Affairs, inundated by problems associated with the implementation of its removal policy, had made no satisfactory arrangements for the new arrivals. A sense of security came to the Seminoles only after the tribe had relinquished title to the Florida Peninsula, endured thirty years of frustration beyond the Mississippi, and agreed following the Civil War to accept a reduction in its allotted lands in Indian Territory from 2,169,080 to 200,000 acres. The Seminoles' problems coincided with Spain's cession of Florida to the United States in 1819; over the next few decades, most of the tribe was gradually moved west.[1]

Efforts to clear Indians and blacks from Florida gained momentum in the early nineteenth century in correlation with the rise of the slavery issue. The Seminole settlements had become heavily populated with slaves who had fled the United States to freedom in Spanish Florida.[2] Also living among the Indians were blacks either born under their control, purchased from whites, or captured on raids in Georgia and Alabama. Considered independent, slaves only in name, most of these blacks lived securely in separate communities, where they farmed, hunted, fished, and paid an annual tribute of stock and produce to the Seminoles.[3] Separating the runaways from those blacks the Indians owned was almost impossible, because both blacks and Indians had escaped from the southern colonies, especially South Carolina, since the early 1700s. The blacks settled in the rich bottomlands of the Apalachicola and Suwannee rivers, where some owned plantations; they populated such communities as Mulatto Girl, King Hejah, and Big Hammock. Their knowledge of English, Spanish, and Indian languages made them useful to the Indians as advisors and interpreters.[4]

The Seminoles, considered runaways themselves, were of various ethnic, political, and linguistic backgrounds. These Indians evolved as an identifiable group after they migrated into Florida and absorbed the remnants of Indian tribes there. By the later 1700s, the English had named them Seminoles, from the Muskogee or Creek word *simanoli,* for "runaway" or "wild." (The terms *Muskogee* and *Creek* also came into use in the eighteenth century.) The Seminoles who migrated into Florida throughout the eighteenth and early nineteenth centuries were largely from the Upper and Lower Creek towns of the vast Creek Confederacy that spread over much of Georgia and Alabama. The Creek nation itself was a "melting pot" of different ethnic groups that by the 1830s included more than twenty-four thousand Indians. The traditional founders of the Creek Confederacy—the Cowetas, Kasihtas, Coosas, and Abihkas—came originally from the West, and during the Removal Era the argument was that they should return to the West. Historian J. Leitch Wright, Jr., uses *Muscogulges* to refer to both the Creeks and Seminoles who eventually scattered over the southeast. They are perhaps better identified through two broad divisions of the same language family—Muskogee and Mikasuki (the latter also spelled Miccosukee, it refers to both a form of the Hitchiti language and a tribal group).

The Seminoles filled a vacuum that had been created by the near annihilation of Florida's aboriginal population, which had included tribes such as the Calusas of the southeastern coast, the Tequestas of extreme southern Florida, the Jeagas from the Jupiter Inlet area, the Ais of farther north, the Timucuans in northern Florida and part of Georgia, and the Apalachees near the Tallahassee area. The reduction of these groups began after their first contact with Europeans, which was probably Ponce de León's visit in 1513. Diseases such as smallpox, typhus, measles, and influenza took a large toll, and possibly one-half of the Indians died during the winter of 1612–13. The exploits of the Spanish military and missionaries and raids by Indian allies of the Europeans reduced further Florida's native population. Many of those who survived suffered from restrictions and punishments meted at the missions established by the Jesuits and Franciscans. Moreover, the Spanish sent expeditions to burn towns, behead leaders, and destroy societal structures when Indian chiefs opposed them. By 1656 Florida's aboriginal survivors were "disarmed and powerless."

Years later, the Spanish encouraged Indians from the Lower Creek towns to occupy land vacated by the aboriginals. The Spaniards wanted to create a buffer zone between Spanish Florida and the advancing English settlements. The offer attracted the Lower Creeks, who sought to avoid possible enslavement in the English colonies as well as the domination of the Upper Creeks. These Upper Creeks, or Muskogee speakers, who lived along the tributaries of the Alabama, Coosa, and Tallapoosa rivers in Alabama had subjugated the Lower Creeks, mostly Hitchiti or Mikasuki speakers, who were situated in towns along the Chattahoochee, Flint, and Ocmulgee rivers in Georgia.

The Hitchiti speakers, such as the Oconees, Sawoklis, Okmulgees, and Apalachicolas, had arrived in Florida by the mid-1700s. The Oconees, who became the nucleus of the "true" Seminoles of Florida, had moved from the Oconee River near Milledgeville, Georgia, to the Lower Creek territory about 1715. Three or four decades later, they went southward to the Alachua Prairie in north Florida. The Oconees furnished the early titular leaders of the Seminoles—Cowkeeper, Payne, Bowlegs, and Micanopy.

Over the years, border tension and other international problems caused more Lower Creeks, Upper Creeks, and other Indians to go to Florida. At the close of the Creek War with the United States (1813–14), a large migration of Upper Creeks increased the Indian population in Florida by an estimated two-thirds. These Muskogee speakers literally surrounded and overwhelmed the Hitchiti speakers. Other Upper and Lower Creeks went to Florida after the beginning of the Second Seminole War, but the migrations ceased as the Creeks of Alabama and Georgia were evacuated to the West in the 1830s. Nonetheless, by the early 1800s, the Seminoles in Florida were a blend of numerous tribes, including the Yamasee, Yuchi, Mikasuki, Koasati, Oklawaha, Apalachee, Jeaga, Guale, Hitchiti, Chiaha, Chilucan, and others, as well as blacks, zambos (persons of mixed African and Indian ancestry), mulattoes, and a few hundred Spanish Indians. The Mikasuki speakers were described as the most hostile toward whites, and though smaller in number, provided the majority of the resistance leaders.[5]

This amalgamation of Indians and blacks near the southern border of the United States kept the plantation owners of Georgia and Alabama worried. The Spanish, however, accepted these groups and placed no restrictions on their privileges.[6] In 1792, when a United States agent went to negotiate for the return of slaves living among the Seminoles, he received no official recognition by the Spanish.

The security of the Seminoles and the blacks was jeopardized in the early nineteenth century. Between 1811 and 1813, there were many border incidents between the Georgians and Indians. Some Georgians anxious to reclaim runaways entered Florida hoping to wipe out the Seminoles; they were repulsed. By February 1813, the Seminoles of north-central Florida faced starvation after volunteer and regular American forces had destroyed several hundred of their towns, hundreds of bushels of corn, and had dispersed large numbers of their horses and cattle.[7]

A few years later, several hundred free blacks with a garrisoned fort, called the Negro Fort, in the Apalachicola River valley caused slaveholders along the southern frontier to fear for their property and personal safety.[8] Major General Andrew Jackson, commander of the U.S. Army's Southern Division, wrote Mauricio de Zuniga, the Spanish commandant at Pensacola, that if the fort were not removed, it would be destroyed. In 1816, Jackson had Fort Scott built on the west bank of the Flint River. The necessity of moving supplies freely along the Apalachicola River to Fort Scott was the excuse Jackson used to destroy the Negro Fort that summer. After the fort had been destroyed and about three hundred blacks killed, the Mikasukis under Nea Mathla's leadership threatened to annihilate the whites if they crossed the Flint River.[9]

When hostilities between Indians, blacks, and U.S. citizens led to attacks in which several soldiers under Lieutenant R. W. Scott, as well as women and children, were killed and scalped, Secretary of War John C. Calhoun sent more troops to quell the disturbances. In December 1817, Andrew Jackson was ordered to Florida to bring the Seminoles under control; he informed President James Monroe of the desirability of taking the area for the United States. Most of the military action occurred west of the Suwannee River, whereas between 1812 and 1813 it had been east of the river. By 28 May 1818, Jackson, who had several hundred Creeks fighting with him, had secured St. Marks and Pensacola and had directed troops to take St. Augustine.[10]

In October 1818, in a letter to George W. Campbell, United States minister to Russia, Jackson stated that he was ordered to put a "speedy end" to the Seminole conflict, adding that the frontier reeked with the blood of America's women and children. Spain's inability or refusal to prevent Indians and former slaves from raiding settlements in the United States caused him to "take much action on his own."[11] As a result of Jackson's leadership, the First Seminole War ended with parts of Spanish Florida under U.S. military control. During the war, Seminole towns in northern and central Florida were devastated, fields and cattle were destroyed, and several slaves were abducted.[12]

The United States' acquisition of Florida depended greatly on Jackson's personal goals of gaining for his country the rich agricultural land of the Indians and of capturing runaway slaves.[13] Jackson wanted the Indians out of Florida; his actions almost guaranteed their future eviction. After his campaign, Seminoles became wanderers; they delayed making crops. Consequently, Jackson's actions inflicted severe hardships on the Florida Indians.[14]

The Florida issue created considerable controversy in Washington. Secretary of War Calhoun, with responsibility in Indian affairs, criticized Jackson's Florida expedition. Secretary of the Treasury William Crawford suggested returning Florida to Spain, because he claimed that waging war with a friendly nation violated the Constitution. Jackson, however, had the support of President Monroe and the defense of Secretary of State John Quincy Adams, who took the position that Jackson's conduct was justified because he was pursuing the Seminoles.[15]

The Spanish king, Fernando VII, considered Jackson's activities in Florida as an outrage upon his honor and dignity, so he ordered suspension of ongoing diplomatic negotiations regarding Florida until the United States gave a satisfactory explanation. On 26 November 1818, Adams wrote George W. Erving, the minister plenipotentiary of the United States at Madrid, and presented a full vindication of Jackson's operations. He stated that "the neglect of Spain to perform her engagements of restraining Indians from hostilities against the United States, and by the culpable countenance, encouragement, and assistance given to those Indians, in their hostilities, by the Spanish government and commandant at those places" gave the United States the right to demand that Spain punish the officers responsible and pay for the losses.[16]

The United States and Spain settled their differences at Washington, D.C., on 22 February 1819, with the Adams-Onís treaty in which Spain ceded eastern and western Florida to the United States. Thereafter the status of the Seminoles and the blacks began to deteriorate rapidly. Although Article Six of the treaty stated that the inhabitants of the territories should be eventually incorporated into the nation with "enjoyment of all the privileges, rights and full immunities of the citizens of the United States," the transfer of control resulted in unprecedented changes for the Indians.[17]

Andrew Jackson became territorial governor of Florida in 1821 and was unsympathetic toward Seminole land claims. He established the idea of reuniting the Seminoles and Creeks by insisting that the best policy was to move the Seminoles to Creek country. Jackson thought Indians should simply be ordered to relocate without negotiations.[18] He directed the Seminole chiefs to take the tribe to a certain area of the peninsula, and United States commissioners stipulated that the tribe must stay a certain distance from the coast.[19]

The Seminoles faced other problems. Their new agent, Captain John Bell, was suspended for conduct unbecoming for an officer, and their sub-agent, Jean Pénières, died.[20] Pénières had advocated removing the Indians and blacks to another territory, because he considered reenslavement of the blacks impractical. Other complications came when frontier slaveholders dipped into Florida to capture slaves who often belonged to the Seminoles. When the chiefs complained to Washington, they received no reply.[21]

These unsettling circumstances created a poor background for any negotiations and further diminished Seminole trust in the United States. Within three years after the official signing of the treaty with Spain, however, the United States and the Indians concluded the Treaty with the Florida Tribes of Indians (the Treaty of Camp Moultrie), in which the Seminoles relinquished title to the bulk of the Florida Peninsula in exchange for a greatly reduced area of land east of Tampa Bay. At Moultrie Creek near St. Augustine on 18 September 1823, thirty-two Seminoles signed the agreement consisting of ten articles. Commissioners William P. Duval, James Gadsden, and Bernard Segui signed for the United States. The Indians' location on the peninsula underwent significant changes, although six chiefs (Nea Mathla, John Blount, Tuski Hajo, Mulatto King, Emath Lochee, and Enconchatimico) signed an additional article that allowed them to remain in their old settlements in the vicinity of the Apalachicola and Chattahoochee rivers as long as they continued to occupy and improve the land. Moreover, the chiefs had to submit names of those under their control to the superintendent or agent of Indian affairs in Florida. No other persons were to be allowed in the settlements without permission from the officials. In 1823, this left 214 men under control of the six chiefs.

Although the treaty stated that the Seminoles sought the protection of the United States, and Articles Three through Six guaranteed that protection and barred trespassers from their areas, the land was gradually taken from them. Such provisions as those providing for a year's rations of meat, salt, and corn; forty-five hundred dollars for abandoned lands;

Nea-Math-La, or Nea Mathla. *The United States considered Nea-Math-La head chief of the Seminole delegation at the negotiations for the treaty of 1823. He was one of six chiefs allowed to remain in their old settlements near the Apalachicola and Chattahoochee rivers. This chief and a few other tribal leaders visited officials in Washington in 1826. Sources indicate that he eventually moved out of Florida into southern Alabama. Courtesy, National Anthropological Archives, Smithsonian Institution.*

two thousand dollars for transportation; and five thousand dollars annually for twenty years could in no way compensate the Indians for the hardships brought by the land change. Moreover, Article Seven required their diligence in returning runaway slaves and fugitives from justice.[22]

Accepting a smaller territory brought suffering to the Seminoles. They had previously claimed almost 24 million acres, which included "all of Florida south and east of the Old Spanish Road, less certain areas. The Old Spanish Road ran from St. Augustine west to its intersection with the perimeter of an earlier Pensacola purchase, and thence around the eastern edge of that perimeter to the Gulf of Mexico."[23] Prosperous and familiar with the fertile lands of northern Florida, the Indians appealed for relief after a portion of the tribe moved to the Tampa Bay area, which by comparison was poor, miserable, unhealthy, and inaccessible to good water. Their appeals were answered with the demand that they relocate in the West.[24]

Thus, the Treaty of Camp Moultrie generated numerous conflicts between the Florida Indians and the United States. The annuities promised in the 1823 treaty often were withheld to compensate slave owners for alleged losses from Seminole raids and for runaways. As the number of whites increased along the southern frontier, the number of escaping slaves multiplied proportionally, and the demands of Georgia slave owners grew. These problems, combined with poor farmland, brought starvation to the Seminoles.[25] By 1829, they were being referred to as the "starving Florida Indians."[26]

While the Indians tried to deal with the basic changes resulting from their first treaty with the United States and from U.S. control, the United States faced a major challenge in administering national Indian policy. The Office of Indian Affairs, located in the Department of War, was in its infancy. Although Secretary of War Calhoun administratively created the office in 1824—one year after the Treaty of Camp Moultrie—it was 1834 before Congress officially established it.[27] By 1830, when removal had become the dominant policy, the office had the responsibility of transferring the Indian tribes, including the Seminoles, from the East to west of the Mississippi River. Justification for such a policy sprang in part from arguments that the contiguity of white settlements destroyed

Tuko-See-Mathla, or Tokose Emarthla (John Hicks). A leading Florida Seminole whose name is listed on the treaties of 1823 and 1832. He made the trip to Washington with Nea-Math-La's delegation in 1826. Some recognized him as head chief briefly after Nea-Math-La left Florida. Courtesy, National Anthropological Archives, Smithsonian Institution.

Indian character. According to the commissioner of Indian affairs in 1832, unless the government rescued the Indians, they would become extinct. Consequently, a policy of "transferring their residence, and congregating their tribes, in domains suited to their condition" was instituted. Further, it was hoped that the Indians could become as "enlightened as the Picts of England and the Vandals and Goths of Continental Europe [and] remain standing monuments of savage habits and heathenish darkness, subdued and irradiated by the light of knowledge and the sun of Christianity."[28]

The Seminoles became a major target for removal after Indian-white relations deteriorated further as a result of the seizure of Seminole slaves by whites.[29] Pressure mounted on the Seminoles to go west, and their chiefs were offered bribes.[30]

After ten years of U.S.-Seminole discord, on 9 May 1832, at Payne's Landing on the Oklawaha River, Commissioner James Gadsden negotiated what became the Seminole removal treaty. Fifteen chiefs and headmen signed this agreement, which stated that the Seminoles would go west "to a country more suitable to their habits and wants than the one they at present occupy." Seven trustworthy chiefs (Jumper, Foke-Luste-Hajo [Hadjo or Harjo], Charley Emathla [often written as Emarthla], Coa Hadjo, Holati Emathla, Ya-ha Hadjo [Yaha Hajo], and Sam Jones), agent Major John Phagan, and interpreter Abraham were to examine the land offered. Moreover, the Seminoles were to reunite on land of the Creeks and be readmitted to the privileges of that tribe. These provisions prefaced the seven articles. Although the treaty stated that the Indians should be satisfied with the land in the West and the disposition of the Creeks, it was binding on all signers. Article One relinquished Seminole title to lands occupied in Florida and mandated their westward migration. The Creeks would receive an additional allotment of land in the West, the amount to be determined by the number of Seminoles making the move.

This treaty's provisions for the Seminoles, as those of the earlier treaty, were minimal. Upon the tribe's arrival, they were to receive $15,400 for the land relinquished and its improvements; blankets and homespun frocks for each of the warriors, women, and children; an annuity for a blacksmith to extend ten years beyond the term stipulated in the Treaty

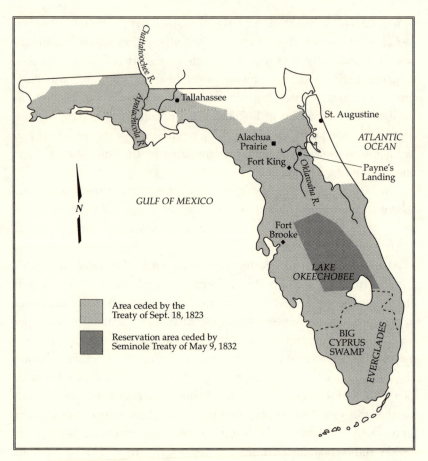

Map 1. *Seminole Land Ceded by 1823 and 1832 Treaties*

of Camp Moultrie; three thousand dollars annually for fifteen years; money or cattle to replace losses; as much as seven thousand dollars in claims for allegedly stolen slaves; and subsistence for up to one year. The Indians were given three years to relocate. Those living in the Big Swamp southwest of St. Augustine and those outside established boundaries were to go in 1833; two other groups were to follow in 1834 and 1835.[31]

The United States considered the treaty of 1832, called the Treaty with the Seminoles (or the Treaty of Payne's Landing), a major victory. That same year, Commissioner of Indian Affairs Elbert Herring reported that "the Seminole Indians having sustained much suffering for several preceding years, through the failure of crops, occasioned by the inundation of their lands, and from other causes, felt disposed, under the privations of the past winter, to seek a better fortune in a kinder soil." Colonel James Gadsden was subsequently commissioned to negotiate a "provisional treaty" with the Seminoles. This treaty required that the tribe relinquish title to its Florida territory and locate west of the Mississippi River among the Creeks. According to Herring, the document would become obligatory after a delegation of Seminole chiefs examined the western land and considered it favorably.[32]

The following October, Gadsden made yet another treaty with the Apalachicola band at Tallahassee. Signed by John Blount, O Saa-Hajo (Davy), and Co-ha-thlock-co (Cockrane), this treaty took the land located along the Apalachicola River in the vicinity of Tuski Hajo's improvements. This treaty was most unusual, because it required that the 256 Indians involved should go west "beyond the States and Territories of the United States of America" by November 1833. It granted a year's extension if necessary. The chiefs who signed and their warriors received three thousand dollars and were to get an additional ten thousand dollars upon their removal. Their annuities provided by the 1823 treaty were to continue.[33]

In accordance with the terms of the Treaty of Payne's Landing, a delegation of Seminoles accompanied by Agent Phagan traveled west to examine the Indians' future homeland. A Creek chief later reported that some Creeks had told the delegation that because at one time in the East the Creeks and Seminoles had been one people, they would settle where

Tulcee-Mathla, or Tulce Emathla. Another chief who represented the Seminoles in Washington in 1826, he was from the area near Chocachatti where branches of the Alachuas lived. Courtesy, National Anthropological Archives, Smithsonian Institution.

they would again be one people when the Seminoles moved west. He claimed that the Seminoles agreed.[34] But Plains Indians, such as the Comanches, Kiowas, and Wichitas, stole horses and packs while the delegation hunted buffalo with the Creeks. These depredations led the Seminoles to doubt the government's ability to protect their tribal sovereignty in the West.[35]

Nevertheless, United States commissioners, Montfort Stokes, Henry L. Ellsworth, and John F. Schermerhorn, continued the plans for the Seminoles' migration by arranging the Articles of Agreement and Convention with the Creeks in February 1833. One of its objectives was the establishment of boundary lines that would "secure a country and permanent home to the whole Creek nation of Indians, including the Seminole nation who are anxious to join them." Article Four stipulated that the "Seminole Indians of Florida . . . shall also have a permanent and comfortable home on the lands hereby set apart as the country of the Creek nation." The commissioners were to select the land for the Seminoles, where they would live by themselves as constituents of the Creeks.[36]

Six weeks later, on 28 March 1833, the same commissioners concluded a treaty with the Seminole delegates. It stated that the Indians had examined the land designated for them and were satisfied with it. The area assigned lay "between the Canadian river and the north fork thereof, and extending west to where a line running north and south between the main Canadian and north branch, will strike the forks of Little River, provided said west line does not extend more than twenty-five miles west from the mouth of said Little River." The Seminole delegates further agreed that their nation would begin removal as soon as the government made the necessary arrangements. The Indians requested and the commissioners recommended that Agent Phagan handle their removal. The seven Indians who signed the treaty included signers of the 1832 treaty or their representatives.[37]

Much confusion evolved from the Seminoles' action in the West. One delegate, Jumper, later reported that the Indians thought they were only signifying their approval of the land and that they would decide on removal after returning to Florida.[38] The leaders of the Seminole council in

Yaha Hajo. His name is listed on the removal treaty of 1832. Yaha Hajo was also one of the seven influential chiefs selected to go to the West to examine the Seminoles' lands and whose name is listed on the treaty made at Fort Gibson in 1833. Courtesy, National Anthropological Archives, Smithsonian Institution.

Florida refused to accept the treaty of 1833, claiming that the delegates had no right to make it.[39] Yet the government and the Creeks seemed determined to reunite the two tribes. In 1834, Secretary of War Lewis Cass received a delegation of Creeks who informed him their tribe would be disappointed if the Seminoles failed to settle with it. But the new Seminole agent, Wiley Thompson, knew the Seminoles objected to this proposal for several reasons, including the fear of the loss of their slaves to Creeks.[40] Moreover, Jumper informed Thompson that his people did not want to go among people in the West who stole horses and packs.[41]

While the Seminoles faced this crisis, the Office of Indian Affairs underwent changes as it continued to implement its removal policy. Efforts at becoming more efficient reduced appropriations and led to a reduction of the number of Indian agents. Agents received instructions to curb the giving of gifts and to distribute only provisions. Nevertheless, the War Department reported that the Indians had become a degraded and wretched vanishing race among whites, requiring the government to institute its policy of protection and perpetuation. This policy called for the Seminoles to leave Florida, and a number were expected to remove in 1834.[42] However, only the 256 Apalachicolas under John Blount left that year, and they settled, as mandated by the treaty, on land outside the United States near the Trinity River in Texas.[43]

By early 1835, President Andrew Jackson and Agent Thompson informed the other Indians that their removal was imperative. Jackson urged them to go west peacefully and promised that they would receive a year's provisions. He also stated that military forces had been ordered to Florida in case the young men refused to emigrate, adding that "should you listen to the bad birds that are always flying about you, and refuse to move, I have directed the commanding officer to remove you by force."

To implement this order, on 23 April 1835, at the Seminole Agency, Wiley Thompson presented an agreement for the Seminoles to sign. Chiefs and subchiefs of the Seminole tribe had to acknowledge the validity of the treaties between the United States and the Seminole nation made at Payne's Landing on 9 May 1832 and at Fort Gibson on 28 March 1833. Moreover, the chiefs and subchiefs had to freely and fully assent to the treaties' provisions and stipulations.[44] Eight principal and an equal number of subchiefs signed the agreement, but five others, including Principal Chief Micanopy, refused. Thompson removed the names of those who rejected the agreement from the list of chiefs. His action brought reprimands from Washington, and he was told that agents were to refrain from deciding who were tribal chiefs.[45]

After this meeting, Seminole resistance mushroomed. The Indians bought war materials and clashed with whites outside Indian boundaries. In late December 1835, Agent Thompson and four others were killed in an Indian attack led by Osceola (Asseola), who gained a reputation as the major leader of resistance. Seminole chiefs Micanopy, Jumper, and Alligator and their warriors attacked two companies under Major Francis L. Dade while they marched from Fort Brooke to Fort King. Only three of the 102 soldiers survived the attack, and they died later from their wounds.[46]

These attacks proliferated into the longest and most costly of the Indian conflicts of the United States—the Second Seminole War. The United States lost an estimated fifteen hundred men and spent from $30 to $40 million in the affair.[47] The Indians used no more than an estimated 1,500 to 1,660 warriors, whereas some twenty to forty thousand Americans saw service over the seven-year struggle.[48] William Tecumseh Sherman, a young officer in the war, probably evaluated it correctly when he reported it as a mismanaged, ill-commanded, and confused conflict.[49]

Although the Indians' refusal to accept treaties and agreements with the United States led to the outbreak of hostilities, an important underlying cause was the desire by the United States to remove the fugitive slaves as well.[50] Seminole expulsion was an effort to solve the black problem as much as the Indian problem.[51]

In early 1835, Florida territorial governor Richard K. Call, inspired by friends in Tallahassee, wrote President Jackson to ask permission for whites to buy 150 blacks from the Seminoles. Call noted that such action would eliminate one impediment to the Indians' removal, because black influence with the Indians remained high and the blacks violently opposed leaving the peninsula.[52] Two months later, the acting secretary of war, Carey A. Harris, wrote Agent Thompson that the president

Asseola, or Osceola. Asseola was a major resistance leader against removal to the West and in October 1837 was captured under a white flag of truce in an attempt to talk with General Thomas S. Jesup. Imprisoned at Fort Moultrie, South Carolina, he died there of quinsy and malaria and was decapitated by the doctor in charge. Courtesy, National Anthropological Archives, Smithsonian Institution.

thought the Indians could be induced to remove by selling the slaves. This action also would prevent capture of the slaves by Creeks in the West.[53]

To complicate further the position of the blacks and the later relations between the Creeks and the Seminoles in the West, Major General Thomas Jesup concluded an agreement with the Creek chief Opothleyahola and other Creeks to use between six hundred and one thousand Creek warriors in the war with the Seminoles. Jesup promised the Creeks the Seminole plunder, including the seizure of their slaves. The Creeks were to receive twenty dollars for each of the plantation slaves who were returned, $31,900 for debts, and pay for their soldiers.[54] Consequently, the struggle eventually opened the territory to white settlement;[55] it also created the roots of turmoil in the West.

The U.S. government had hoped for no resistance or delay in removing the Indians. In December 1835, James Erwin and Daniel Greathouse received a government contract to provide supplies and transportation for the Seminoles expected to emigrate. These men gathered an estimated five hundred bushels of corn, five wagons of fodder, fifty beeves, and several teams at Rock Roe on the White River in Arkansas, where a large group of Indians was expected. Unfortunately, no Indians arrived, and Erwin and Greathouse suffered heavy losses.[56]

Several months passed before the arrival of the first group of Florida Indians in Indian Territory. This party of friendly Seminoles, led by Chiefs Holati Emathla and Foke-Luste-Hajo (Black Dirt) and supervised by Lieutenant Joseph W. Harris, who escorted it from Florida via New Orleans, reached Little Rock, Arkansas, on 5 May 1836. When Harris described these Indians to Secretary of War Lewis Cass in July 1836, he said they had been reduced to a wretched condition in Florida. Hated and despised by their fellow countrymen for not resisting removal, they had also lost everything. For more than a year, most of them had wandered about after having their cabins and other property destroyed by their brethren. Exposure, fatigue, privation, and persecution reduced their numbers and made their condition wretched.[57]

After their arrival at Little Rock, these Seminoles faced an additional month of misery and agony. They disembarked from their steamboat at McLain's Bottom on 9 May. Lieutenant J. Van Horne took the group with a few wagons of Indian goods—blankets, shirts, corn, bacon, other treaty provisions, and about twenty horses they had bought—to Seminole country, a distance of 127 miles. A severe outbreak of measles had spread from twenty to seventy-eight of them between 9 and 13 May. The accompanying doctor feared the epidemic would attack them all, because the Indians refused his prescriptions, bathed in the cold river water, and camped in filthy surroundings. The "neighbors" also complained about the Indians destroying the timber, so Van Horne issued four days' rations and began the journey despite the sickness. He kept a daily journal in which he described hardships the Indians endured: the constant rain, lack of roads, flies, sickness, and death. On 15 and 16 May, Van Horne reported that he had on his hands from 130 to 150 sick Indians. Some were placed in wagons; others too sick to travel were left behind to die. Ten days later, after continuous rain, the whole country was a quagmire, and each wagon had to be dragged by ten or twelve yoke of oxen. The rain soaked the exhausted Indians, and under these conditions the disease spread. By 28 May, at least twenty Indians lay dying in their own filth; the odor tainted the air in the camps. From one to four died daily. The wife and daughter of Chief Foke-Luste-Hajo died on the trip from McLain's Bottom to the Seminole district.

Although the Indians had guns, tomahawks, and knives, which they constantly displayed, they were not violent and seemed to respect Van Horne. Van Horne indicated, however, that he had to force them from camp each day, and that "positive mutiny" occurred at times. After the interpreter and issuing agent applied for discharges because of sickness, Van Horne's assistance came from a civilian and a doctor under contract to accompany the group to the Canadian River. Although Van Horne had difficulty without an interpreter, he no doubt had the confidence of the Indians. After Chief Holati Emathla died and was buried one and a half miles from the Canadian River, they asked Van Horne to name his successor. Having been with them such a short time, he refused, and they selected Eneah Thlocko [possibly also spelled Ne-ha-tho-Clo].

The death of Holati Emathla, whom Van Horne described as a good person, but cool and crafty, left his people brokenhearted. Considered the anchor of his band's future hopes, the Seminoles loved and cherished

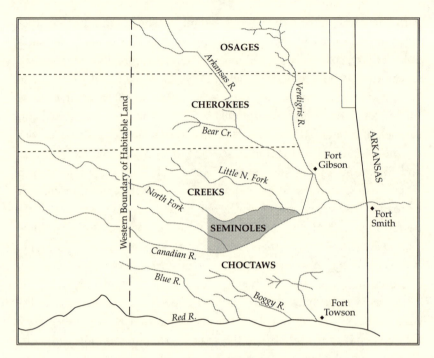

Map 2. The Western Terrritory, 1834

him. His was the "directing and controuling Spirit that guided this little band along its mazy path—his the hand that bound them with the friendly tie and which watchfully held each link together—and his the heart at which the deadliest shafts were levelled." Joseph W. Harris thought the United States owed the chief a debt of gratitude, one that his bereft family and people should receive.

After years of confusion in Florida and an exhausting trip west, these Seminoles—from 300 to 320 of an estimated 407—reached the location that the United States government had designated by 5 June 1836.[58] About six weeks later, Harris described them to Lewis Cass as poor and destitute. Many had lost their children or their parents, and "feeble in health and discouraged in heart amongst strangers and in a strange land;—and finally, without a warm and liberal friendship, and fostering protection from our government—how little of promise has their future prospects."[59]

For this group of Seminoles and those to follow, the first decades under U.S. control brought contraction of their land, starvation, loss of the Florida territory, war, and gradual removal to an unknown land. The future decades for those in the West and those left behind held further uncertainties and hardships that were allayed only by the Seminoles' strong will to survive. Several months lapsed before other Florida Indians were forced westward.

2 *Among the Creeks and Cherokees*

Those Seminoles who went west between 1836 and 1842 entered into an area that had not been prepared for them and was poorly administered by the United States. Moreover, Indian Territory had become a melting pot of confusion as thousands of transplanted eastern Indians suffered from intratribal factionalism and intertribal disputes. Immediately, the Seminoles found themselves in a dispute with the Creeks over land, while also beset by a lack of provisions, unfulfilled treaty promises, and fraudulent claims for their slaves. Soon droughts, crop shortages, and a smallpox epidemic overwhelmed them. The tribe would have become extinct without the intercession of Commissioner of Indian Affairs Thomas Hartley Crawford after October 1838.

Crawford, who had been made aware of the Seminoles' plight by the acting superintendent of the Western Territory, William Armstrong, sought to obtain for the Indians new appropriations, a change of assigned land, and their own subagent. He also advised against taking their slaves. The commissioner's responsible actions, which were atypical, resulted from his desire to build the Seminoles' confidence in, and reduce their hostility to, the federal government. Much of their animosity had developed because they refused to forfeit tribal identity and be absorbed by the more numerous Creeks.

Even those Seminoles who arrived in the territory in 1836 and complied with the government's mandate by settling near Little River on land allotted to them in Creek country had to battle to survive.[1] Chief Foke-Luste-Hajo and his warriors had fought for the United States in the Second Seminole War and were described as unwavering in their faith in and defense of the nation. This party settled in the first Seminole town, Foke-Luste, on fertile soil in the assigned territory, but it arrived too late in 1836 to plant crops. Within five months, as these Seminoles suffered from disease and died, their number dropped from the estimated 300 to 320 who arrived in May to 265 by September. The poor harvests of 1837 led them to consider moving farther west in search of better hunting grounds.[2]

Under the circumstances, the Seminoles, in addition to other tribes such as the Choctaws, Creeks, Osages, Quapaws, Senecas, and Senecas and Shawnees who had been located far in the interior, became dependent on the government and traders to meet their needs. The government annuities became crucial to the Seminoles' very survival.[3]

According to the government's policy, the agent responsible for each emigrating party of Indians was required to notify the disbursing officers in the West to prepare for their arrival. Officers accompanying the groups were also to keep the western officials updated on their traveling progress; the incoming tribes were to receive good quality provisions. But distribution of the annuities and other financial matters presented problems. The Indians often mismanaged the payments of money they received. Moreover, as goods, both high quality and shoddy, flooded the territory, the tribes often pledged their annuities to traders and thus became heavily indebted and desperate. To eliminate such problems, the principal disbursing agent for the Western Territory, Captain Jacob Brown, suggested in 1837 that each tribe have its own agent and interpreter. These officers would be paid according to the number of Indians served. Brown recommended that a Seminole agent receive $750 yearly and the agents of the larger Cherokee, Choctaw, and Creek tribes $1,500. The agents of smaller tribes and interpreters for larger tribes would receive $500. Brown also asked for the appointment of regular paymasters to handle the Indian funds. This policy was adopted for the larger tribes, but the Creek agent served the Seminoles until 1842 when they got their own subagent.[4]

Foke-Luste-Hajo, or Black Dirt. Foke-Luste-Hajo's name is listed on the treaties of 1832 and 1845, and his representative is given on the treaty of 1833. It also probably appears on the treaty of 1823 as Fahelustee Hajo. This chief, one of the first to arrive in the West (1836), had the first town in the new western district, Foke-Luste, named for him. National Anthropological Archives, Smithsonian Institution.

The Office of Indian Affairs had failed to establish an efficient and organized system of administration in the territory for the Seminoles and the other Indians who came from the East. But Commissioner of Indian Affairs Carey Allen Harris seemed so overburdened with his duties associated with Indian removal that efficiency was almost impossible. These duties included removing the Indians in "New York, Ohio, Indiana, Illinois, Michigan, and Wisconsin . . . in Georgia, North Carolina, Tennessee, Alabama, Mississippi, Florida . . . to new homes southwest of the Missouri River."[5]

Therefore, the Office of Indian Affairs had the responsibility of forcing more Florida Seminoles to move west. On 6 March 1837, two days after Martin Van Buren became president, Major General Thomas Jesup, commander of United States forces in Florida, negotiated the "Capitulation of the Seminole Nation of Indians and their allies." By the terms of this document, Chiefs Jumper, Holahtoochee (Davy), and Yahaloochee, representing Principal Chief Micanopy, agreed to cease hostilities and to proceed west immediately with their entire tribe. Until the fulfillment of the agreement, federal authorities could hold Indian hostages. Jesup agreed in Article Five that the Seminoles and their allies who came in peacefully would be "secure in their lives and property, that their Negroes, their bona fide property, shall accompany them to the West; and that their cattle and ponies shall be paid for by the United States at a fair evaluation." Yahaloochee and his people, who were to come in immediately and soon to be followed by the others, would receive subsistence in camp and for twelve months after arrival in the West. The provisions of the Treaty of Payne's Landing were guaranteed. Twelve days later, at Fort Dade, Micanopy signed and confirmed the eleven articles in the capitulation. Some Seminoles had consented to such terms earlier, after the battle of Hatcheelustee Creek on 27 January 1837. They claimed they were tired of fighting and that their families were suffering.[6]

After a lapse of several months, two groups of Seminoles numbering 1,069, headed by Chief Micanopy and transported on the steamers *Renown* and *South Alabama,* arrived at Fort Gibson. Their move was supervised by John G. Reynolds, a lieutenant of marines and a disbursing agent.[7] The Seminoles who disembarked at Fort Gibson were cold, hungry, and destitute refugees from the swamplands of Florida who had spent weeks or months in camps at Tampa or New Orleans, where they were often harassed by slave dealers and subjected to other indignities.

Mustered for provisions at Fort Gibson, those Indians and blacks aged fourteen or older received a full allowance, whereas those younger than fourteen got a half-ration. An enrolling agent or subagent kept a roll, revised monthly, of heads of families in each tribe, along with the number of individuals in each family. Seminoles who received subsistence in the West in 1838 numbered 1,651, making a daily outlay of $131.14.[8]

After reaching Fort Gibson, Chief Micanopy and other Seminoles refused to leave the area when they learned that Creeks occupied the district intended for them. They camped along the southern bank of the Arkansas River about two miles south of Fort Gibson. Micanopy subsequently held a council with the Creeks to discuss where the Seminoles would locate. Upper Creeks under Chief Opothleyahola had settled on the Seminoles' allotted land after the Seminoles delayed their removal from Florida. Because the land allotment for both tribes included 13,140,000 acres, this part of the small Seminole tribe had no intention of settling among the powerful Creeks, who numbered between eighteen and twenty thousand. They wanted land away from the Creeks.

The resentment between the Seminoles and Creeks foreclosed any quiet merging of the two tribes. The Seminoles were for the most part "runaways" from the Creek nation. Groups had left the Creeks throughout the eighteenth century. In 1814 Andrew Jackson had defeated the Creeks and forced them to cede two-thirds of their land to the United States. Later many Creeks who had fought against Jackson, referred to as "Red Sticks," and their slaves had migrated to Florida. They resented those Creeks who had aided Jackson and contributed to their loss.

The Creeks had incited Seminole hatred in other ways. They signed the Treaties of New York and Colerain, in 1790 and 1796, respectively, and agreed to yield the blacks among them to their owners, including those among the Seminoles in Florida. Moreover, in the Second Seminole War, Chief Opothleyahola, who now lived on the Seminoles' western land, had agreed to furnish between six hundred and one thousand Creeks to fight for the United States against the Seminoles.

Micanopy. A principal Seminole chief, he went West in 1838, where he held that title until his death in late 1848 or early 1849. Micanopy's complete refusal to be dominated by the Creeks helped assure western Seminole tribal permanence. Courtesy, National Anthropological Archives, Smithsonian Institution.

Micanopy, who controlled a large number of blacks, feared settling near Opothleyahola for other reasons. Both of these men had been powerful and wealthy in the East. But Micanopy, a fat, short Indian who weighed about 250 pounds and was probably near forty years of age, lacked Opothleyahola's strong leadership ability. Micanopy had much influence among his people because of age and wealth, but he supposedly had little talent. Opothleyahola, cool and cautious and with talents of a superior nature, understood his people's sorrows and aspirations. Micanopy and the other Seminoles still had several other reasons for refusing to settle among the Creeks.[9]

The condition of the Creeks themselves, no doubt, alarmed the Seminoles. They were divided into two factions, with hatred, jealousy, and discord so intense among them that the governing officers had to exert much effort to prevent bloodshed and to achieve any friendly agreement. Drunkenness, gambling, carousels, and frolics were common, and prostitution and poverty were problems as well. This was the assessment that Creek agent James Logan remembered several years later about his first meeting with the Creeks in 1838.

Three months after arriving in the West, the Seminole chiefs declared that they found the allotted land acceptable, but they still refused to locate among the Creeks, who, they feared, would treat them as "dogs." Pointing out that secure land had been promised them, they argued that no other tribe could rightfully claim their district.[10] At the same time, they dreaded going farther west because of the danger from wild Plains Indians.[11] A stalemate remained concerning the Seminoles' location.

In 1838, while more than a thousand Seminoles were camped near Fort Gibson, a severe outbreak of smallpox struck the Seminoles, Creeks, Choctaws, Cherokees, and Chickasaws and took precedence over the question of land. Reports to authorities in Washington depicted the Seminoles' pitiful condition. Without tools to build cabins, destitute of clothing, and in need of blankets, they also suffered from the smallpox outbreak. Moreover, because of a drought, provisions were required for large numbers of hungry Seminoles, Quapaws, and Osages. General Matthew Arbuckle wrote the adjutant general concerning the Seminoles, and a junior officer, who had observed their desperate condition, reported on their plight.

Fortunately, Commissioner of Indian Affairs Thomas Hartley Crawford, a lawyer from Pennsylvania, was a careful and devoted public official. Although he favored Andrew Jackson's removal policy, he wanted to bring efficiency to the supervision of the Indian Territory. He also wanted the Indians civilized. With unusual administrative ability and foresight, he worked to promote better communications between the Indian Office and its western agencies. Realizing good relations were essential in controlling the Indians, the commissioner sought the respect of the influential chiefs.

Consequently, he initiated immediate action to ease the Indians' distress. He informed Secretary of War Joel Poinsett on 14 December 1838 that smallpox raged among the Five Civilized Tribes and on the upper Missouri. Although the spread of the disease had been limited somewhat by precautionary measures and some lives had been saved, the Indians seemed apathetic, arousing fears that the disease might destroy them. Hiring physicians to vaccinate them appeared the government's only recourse. These doctors were to receive about six cents for each vaccination. Crawford asked Poinsett for five thousand dollars to finance the project. The secretary forwarded the recommendation to H. L. White, chairman of the Senate Committee on Indian Affairs, and to John Bell, White's counterpart in the House of Representatives. The funds were made available, but the vaccinations, carelessly done, accomplished little.[12]

Meanwhile, Commissioner Crawford continued to act on other issues on the Seminoles' behalf. Realizing that a Seminole-Creek merger would prove fatal to the Seminoles, he proposed a plan to provide them with a new location. In reporting to Secretary of War Poinsett, Crawford stressed that the treaty of 1833 contemplated a separate location for the Seminoles adjoining the Creeks, although the primary objective remained tribal reunion. He stated that it would not be consistent "with our relation to them to allow them to remain where they are and perish for although they have been receiving subsistence it must soon stop." Crawford indicated that because of their severe privations, the Indians appeared indifferent to planning their future. Unused funds amounting to $195,250 for further removal and subsistence for the remaining Florida Seminoles could only be applied for those purposes. He therefore recommended asking Congress to overrule certain treaty provisions to allow for a different location and to provide new appropriations.

The Treaty of Payne's Landing (1832) also remained inapplicable for those in the West because of continuing hostilities with the Seminoles in Florida. Only annuities to the friendly emigrants under a law of 4 June 1836 and blankets sent in September 1838 helped the Indians in their distress. No appropriations existed to relieve their physical needs, including clothing for the winter. Crawford estimated that ten thousand dollars would keep the Indians alive and prepare them for locating farther west in the spring. He added that provisions in the treaties of 1823 and 1832 allowed for tools to build cabins and for supplies of agricultural implements and cattle. Crawford's request for aid for the Seminoles was thus simple—legal authority to change their location and to provide an appropriation for them.[13]

On 15 January 1839, Secretary of War Poinsett presented the commissioner's report to President Van Buren. Showing genuine concern, Poinsett stated that "humanity, as well as sound policy, requires that the wants of those people should be promptly attended to; and it appears but just, as they are obstinately opposed to unite with the Creeks, that they should be provided with an independent tract of country west of the Mississippi." The next day, Van Buren laid the information from Poinsett and Crawford before the Senate, emphasizing the "propriety of setting apart a tract of country west of the Mississippi for the Seminole Indians, so that they may be separated from the Creeks, and representing the necessity of a small appropriation for supplying the immediate wants of those who have been removed." He asked for "early consideration and favorable action of Congress."[14] Within a month, Congress passed an act to provide for the "location and temporary support of the Seminole Indians removed from Florida." The president was authorized to find a suitable location west of Missouri and Arkansas. A sum of ten thousand dollars was to support the Seminoles until such relocation occurred.[15]

In accordance with the new act, Acting Superintendent of the Western Territory Armstrong and General Arbuckle undertook to arrange for a new location still on Creek lands but where no Creeks lived. The area selected lay between the Deep Fork of the Canadian River and the Arkansas River and was sufficiently large for the western Seminoles and for later migrants from Florida.

The Seminoles who relocated found the area suitable, but several of the Indians refused to move and remained in the Fort Gibson area on Cherokee lands. Those who lingered around the fort until their year's subsistence was depleted and thus delayed the move onto the new land required additional aid.[16]

To promote a speedy adjustment and to teach those Seminoles who had changed location to support themselves, the government furnished agricultural implements and laborers to assist in planting crops. A blacksmith shop equipped with a striker and a stock of iron and steel was made available. Due to the Indians' late arrival, however, the corn harvest fell short, and they received subsistence for a year after the move. Armstrong reported that the Indians maintained a "bad feeling," resulting largely from the presence of the blacks, who, Armstrong felt, were indisposed to work and influenced the Indians greatly. He expected a few, particularly Alligator, who had refused to move to the new area, and his friends, to return to Florida. Yet despite the problems, the new land assignment, coupled with the appropriation of ten thousand dollars, temporarily satisfied some Seminoles and enabled them to avoid tribal extinction.

Commissioner Crawford also supported better handling of Indian funds to promote tribal advancement of the Seminoles and others. He hoped to redeem the "interesting race [Native Americans] from the slavery of bad habits and the degradation of vice, and the inclination for both." He added that with the first stone of the foundation laid, "the height of the superstructure is in the womb of time." After an act in 1838 prohibited military officers from disbursing funds, Crawford suggested that carefully selected district pay agents be appointed to handle the money.[17]

In March 1840, Crawford reported on the Seminoles' condition to members of Congress. He stated that the $15,400 to be paid the Seminoles on arrival in the West was in the hands of the western disbursing agent. In compliance with instructions of March 1839 and with the Indians' consent, half of the fund was to be used to build cabins, to cultivate and fence ground, and for other improvements. This arrangement was partly carried out, but the disbursing agent, Captain M. D. C. Collins of the United States Army, died a defaulter to the government and apparently had misused some of the Seminole appropriation. The 2,511 Seminole emigrants (407 emigrated in 1836 [listed as 1837 in the record], 1,851 in 1838, and 253 in 1839) did get blankets and frocks, however, and other provisions. Crawford concluded that the government's liberality with Seminoles was exceeded with no other tribe.[18]

Concerned with placating the western Seminoles, Crawford attempted to eliminate other causes of frustration. He advocated appointing a subagent for them. Upon completion of settlement in the new district, their small annuity was to increase by three thousand dollars, which was to be distributed by the Creek agent. However, Crawford thought the Seminoles should have a resident subagent to protect their interests and to become influential with them. A "turbulent, ill-conditioned race" with its malignant qualities exacerbated, the Seminoles would never incorporate peacefully with the Creeks. Consequently, they should be conciliated to persuade them that "we [United States] mean them well, and will do justice in the way most conducive to their interests." If left isolated, their improvement would proceed slowly, but a qualified subagent could serve a useful purpose to the government and to the tribe. Although Crawford knew of no obstacles in the treaties to the appointment of a subagent, if necessary the Seminoles and Creeks could abrogate their reunion and annuities. Several months later, in 1842, a subagent was appointed making another victory for the Indians largely because of Crawford's intercession.[19]

Some Seminoles, including the shrewd and mannerly Chief Alligator and several hundred others who refused to go to the Deep Fork area and remained on Cherokee lands north of Fort Gibson, suffered hardships and sought Crawford's attention as well. Alligator claimed that General Jesup's promises of a gun for him, and an agent, as well as plows, hoes, axes, kettles, and protection for his people in their new country remained unfulfilled. Crawford reported to Secretary of War John Bell that those Seminoles received none of the items because they refused to relocate.

Crawford declared that although he knew nothing of Jesup's promises, Jesup should be contacted to satisfy Alligator's faith in the fidelity of the government.

The Cherokees allowed these Seminoles to live on their land because of sympathy for them, given their pitiful condition. In addition, the Cherokee leader John Ross had been instrumental in getting the rebelling Florida Seminole leader Osceola to surrender under a flag of truce, assuring him of the credibility of the United States government. After Osceola's imprisonment and subsequent death, the Cherokees felt some responsibility for this turn of events and for the surviving Seminoles.[20]

Considerable unrest existed among the individual Cherokees as well as between the tribe and the United States. Whites in Arkansas had agitated for the removal of Fort Gibson and caused much of the Cherokee dissatisfaction. As early as 1838, Arkansas settlers worked to have Fort Gibson moved onto Arkansas soil. They thought their border needed heavy protection from the thousands of Indians moving into Indian Territory. Most military authorities wanted to retain the fort in its old location to protect the Indians who came from the East. For a while the troops went to Fort Smith. The Cherokee agent had to move his agency seven or eight miles eastward. Indian Bureau officials forbade traders at Fort Gibson to buy from or sell to the Indians. Instead Arkansas settlers brought their goods to sell at the fort. Thus the Cherokees, Creeks, Osages, and Delawares lost their market, and the Indians, including some wealthy ones, also lost their major source of supplies.

These factors, combined with the warring between Cherokee tribal factions that had resulted in the murder of several key leaders, suggested the possibility of a Cherokee–United States war. The Arkansas and Missouri governors prepared somewhat for an outbreak. The Creeks were asked to organize companies and regiments for possible use by the United States if hostilities ensued. Reports warned that John Ross sent "wampum and warlike talks" to the Seminole and Creek chiefs in an attempt to arouse hostility to the United States. Alligator and about one hundred warriors visited Ross, but conflict was averted. Despite these uncertain conditions, most of that party of Seminoles remained in Cherokee country for several years.[21]

Whereas the Seminoles on Cherokee lands were concerned with war and supplies promised but not delivered, that part of the tribe settled in the new location above the Creeks, between the Arkansas River and the Deep Fork of the Canadian River, by 1840 wanted their Florida brethren to quit fighting and join them. They had made insignificant progress, yet they now asked the government to send a delegation to explain to those in Florida that they had not perished in a barren land. Commissioner Crawford and other officials hoped that the dispatching of such a delegation would speed the end of the expensive and difficult war in Florida. Consequently, in compliance with the desires of the Seminoles, Western Superintendent Armstrong and United States Army Captain John Page received orders to prepare a delegation of a few Seminoles and Creek chiefs, "best effected to the United States," and one or two Choctaws to make the trip to Florida to meet with the Seminoles there.[22] On 2 November 1840, a healthy and cheerful delegation of Seminoles and Creeks, led by Chiefs Holahtoochee and Nolose Ohola and accompanied by Page, arrived at Tampa Bay after a month's trip. The *Niles National Register* reported the delegation was prepared to explain that "milk and honey flow[ed] in every river, creek and bayou in Arkansas, and that deer and turkeys, ready cooked, follow[ed] in their trails, crying eat me, eat me." Though the group met with representatives of most clans on the peninsula, the war continued until 1842.[23] Secretary of War Poinsett requested an appropriation of fifteen thousand dollars to defray expenses of the delegation.[24] Members of the Indian delegation received two dollars a day. Records of Congress list other expenses of the deputation (see table 1).[25]

In February 1841, Congress also appropriated $100,000 to pay Florida Indians who surrendered and agreed to removal. Several of the prominent Seminole leaders received thousands of dollars for valuable and special services in promoting removal. E-cho-e-math-tic and Cosa Tustenuggee each received five thousand dollars to emigrate, and Coacoochee (Wild Cat) accepted three different sums totaling about eight thousand dollars for his assistance. By 18 June 1842, almost ninety-eight thousand dollars had been used.[26] A total of 934 Indians emigrated between April 1841 and April 1842 (see table 2). With the 2,968 who arrived before April 1841, the number of Florida emigrants who had been transferred from the East to west of the Mississippi by mid-1842 was an estimated 3,902.[27]

Wild Cat emigrated with a party in the fall of 1841. He had been a major resistance leader since 1837 and was one of the most colorful and active of the Florida Seminoles. He would become the same among the western Seminoles.[28] As he prepared to depart Florida, he expressed vividly the Indians' reluctance to leave their homeland. Standing among the weeping Seminoles on a vessel in Tampa Bay, he told General William Jenkins Worth: "I am looking at the last pine-tree of my native land. I am about to leave Florida forever; and I can say that I have never done anything to disgrace the land of my birth. It was my home. I loved it as I loved my wife and child. To part from it, is like separating from my own kindred. But I have thrown away the rifle; I have shaken hands with the white man, and I look to him for protection."[29]

But the whites had difficulty protecting the Seminoles and the several hundred blacks who had emigrated with them. Between 1838 and 1843, an estimated five hundred persons of African descent went west with the Seminoles. These included runaway slaves, freeborns, and blacks bought or stolen by the Seminoles. Several of them had been associated with the Indians as "allies or vassals" for fifty years or more. A few had married Indians. The "international pressures" had forced a unique relationship to develop between the two races, which, prior to removal, seemed to be based largely on "political and military expediency." After arriving in the West, however, the blacks' status was cloudy. In Florida, General Jesup had promised the Seminoles the security of their property in the West; he included the blacks. Moreover, those blacks who surrendered were to have guaranteed security in the West. But several Creeks who fought with the United States in the Second Seminole War had captured blacks. According to the agreements made for their service in the war, they could keep those blacks captured except the plantation slaves for whom they had received money. Yet some blacks captured by Creeks were shipped west with the Seminoles. The Creeks, without having had the blacks in possession, sold some of them to whites. Lieutenant John G. Reynolds, who supervised the largest group of blacks and Indians who

Table 1
Monies Paid to Send Delegation of Seminoles and Creeks to Florida, 1840–41

1840

July 20—Emma Luchee—For notifying chiefs to meet in council at Fort Gibson	$ 10.00
October 11—Jonas Bigelow—For passage of 17 (Seminole delegation) from Fort Smith to Little Rock. $12 each	240.00
October 17—Steamboat *Cherokee*-For passage from Little Rock to New Orleans. $30 each	510.00
October 18—J. W. Smith—For transportation of same from United States barracks to New Orleans	2.70
October 19—Hide and Goodrich—For same from New Orleans to Tampa Bay—$15 each	255.00
October 19—John H. Mills—For subsistence, etc. while in New Orleans waiting to go to Tampa	18.07
October 19—Joseph Jewell—14 pairs of brogans for the delegation—$1.50 pair	21.00
October 19—J. K. Walden and Co.—For shirts, feathers, etc.	31.50
November 9—Everlett and Brown—Tobacco, soap, stationery	31.13
November 21—John B. Allen—Tobacco, knives, tin cups	9.80
December 31—Captain John Page—For expenses from Washington via Fort Gibson to Tampa Bay between June 5 and December 31, 1840	252.25

1841

May 31—Captain John Page—Expenses at Tampa Bay and Fort Brooke January 1–May 3, 1841	147.50
June 21—Captain John Page—Transportation of baggage from Tampa Bay via Tallahassee to Washington—1,092 miles 10 cents a mile	109.20

Table 1, continued

June 21—Captain John Page—Postage	3.75
July 1—Antonio—Services as express to notify chiefs to meet in council at Fort Gibson	10.00
December 5—Thomas Black—For interpreter to delegation to Florida. August 1 to November 23, 1840—$2.50 daily	287.50
December 15—Na-Cosa-tustenuggee—For services as delegate, October 1, 1840 to Apr 19, 1841—$2 daily	402.00
December 15—Par-sark-e-ho-la	402.00
Cho-shuk-ne harjo	402.00
Is-sis-siko	402.00
Tom-a-ho-lakta	402.00
Antonio	402.00
Ne-cosa	402.00
Ya-ho-la	402.00
Cotse-tustenuggee	402.00
Hotkla-pa-yee (October 1, 1840 to June 3, 1841)	492.00
Kloth-lo-harjo	492.00
Cappet-sa-chop-ko	492.00
Hok-pis-harjo	492.00
Tus-te-ne-coo-chee (October 1, 1840 to November 12, 1841)	816.00
December 20—A. Harris—Blankets, calico, shrouding, handkerchiefs, knives, tobacco	262.69
December 21—Arthur Dudney—For ferrying delegation across the Arkansas	8.25
December 31—Hart, Labatt, and Co.—Shawls, shroudings, tobacco, provisions	118.46
Total	**$8292.80**

Reported to the secretary of war by W. B. Lewis of the Treasury Department on 2 June 1842.

SOURCE: U.S. House, *Expenditure in 1841—Florida Indians, etc.* H.Ex.Doc. 247, 27th Cong., 2d sess., 1842, pp. 2–3, 12.

Table 2

Seminole Indians Emigrating from Florida, April 1841–April 1842

Date	Number Emigrating
April 1841	210
May 1841	11
May and June 1841	196
October and November 1841	197
February 1842	226
April 1842	94
Total	934

SOURCE: T. Hartley Crawford to John C. Spencer, 12 May 1842, Report Books, roll 3, vol. 3: 171.

went west in 1838, tried to keep the blacks with their Indian masters as instructed by General Edmund P. Gaines. He found it difficult, especially when whites, such as General James C. Watson of Georgia, demanded the blacks they bought from the Creeks.

Commissioner Harris had informed Reynolds when to deliver the blacks sold by the Creeks to the whites. When Reynolds and his group reached Arkansas in 1838, he asked the governor of that state for military aid in seizing the blacks claimed by the whites. The governor refused his request and insisted the matter should have been settled in Florida because it incited the Indians just as they reached the frontier. Reynolds then asked for assistance at Fort Gibson; no one accommodated him.

Several hundred blacks eventually entered Indian Territory with the Seminoles. They attempted to maintain their own Florida life-style in their separate villages. The Creeks continued to claim ownership of several of the blacks and objected to the separate concentrations of slaves on their land. With such an ambiguous background, problems between these two groups were bound to continue.

Although useful to the Indians as farm workers, from the beginning, federal officials regretted allowing the blacks to accompany the Indians westward. They exerted great influence over the Seminoles and reportedly set a bad example for other slaves. The closeness to the slave state of Arkansas caused anxiety, and fears mounted that they would provide a refuge for runaway blacks and become a den of thieves. Later reports declared that runaway blacks from Louisiana and Arkansas had taken refuge in the Seminole black town along the Deep Fork of the Canadian River. Whites thought this "hive" should be broken up because it was impossible to recover a slave from the group. Still, because a large number of the Seminole blacks had fought in the Second Seminole War, their relations with the Indians remained strong. Ohio congressman Joshua Giddings concluded that the Seminoles had never regarded the blacks with more favor than when they arrived in the West.[30]

Yet claims of ownership of blacks by Creeks generated controversy. The danger of the Creeks oppressing the Seminoles by seizing their blacks became grave. Often the Creeks claimed that the Seminole slaves had escaped from them before or during the Second Seminole War, had been captured with the Seminoles, or had surrendered under a proclamation of some commanders in Florida. By 1842, the necessity of dealing with the Creek claims became crucial.[31]

Whites also continued their demands for some of the blacks. General Watson reasserted that in May 1838 he purchased several blacks belonging to Creek warriors who served in the Second Seminole War. Commissioner Crawford first considered having agents take the blacks because they reportedly were not controlled by the Seminoles. Hoping to improve the Indians' attitude, however, Crawford later refused to honor Watson's claims for the slaves because of the difficulty in determining which were Seminole blacks. He recommended reimbursing Watson for the 103 blacks involved.[32]

After other whites made claims for blacks who had lived among the Seminoles for forty or fifty years, Chief Micanopy appealed to the government for assistance. Commissioner Crawford reported that such claims only produced trouble, and although the Indians derived little from that "species of property," forcing surrender of the slaves would incite the Indians at an inopportune time. Crawford advised using caution in handling all claims for blacks living among the Seminoles.[33] The black problem was even more complicated because the Seminoles were so scattered.

Most Seminole chiefs had attempted to isolate their bands in the West to avoid being superseded by other chiefs. A common practice in Florida, this method of settling, coupled with the ambiguous land issue, caused several major groupings to appear on the Creek and Cherokee lands. The largest portion of the tribe (1,098), under Halpatter Tustunuggee (Alligator) and Holahtoochee, located on Cherokee lands from nine to fifteen miles north of Fort Gibson; the second largest group (827), under Principal Chief Micanopy, had settled in the new district on the Deep Fork, ten to forty miles southwest of Fort Gibson; Concharte Micco took 479 to a point twenty miles south of the fort; Black Dirt headed 360, the first party in the territory, who had settled on Little River; and Wild Cat had a small party three miles south of the fort. Others settled near Park Hill on Cherokee land.[34]

Consequently, bringing unity to the scattered tribe was of extreme importance when the Indian Department provided a subagent for it in 1842. The new official, John McKee, a native of Kentucky, arrived at Fort Gibson on 12 April, almost three months after his appointment. With little education and limited knowledge of bookkeeping, he had difficulty supervising the Indians' annuities and other compensations as well as handling the communications with the federal government.

Yet while he served the Seminoles, he probably had the most influence with his tribe of any agent assigned to the Five Civilized Tribes. The Seminoles, depicted as the "most forlorn, pathetic, and least advanced of the Five Civilized Tribes," lacked any semblance of education. Micanopy had opposed the school provided in the treaty of 1823. In 1826, he, Nea Mathla and other Seminoles told Americans that the Great Spirit did not want them to read or write. Some Seminole leaders objected to making "red children" into "white children." Consequently, the chiefs had difficulty dealing directly with Washington and relied heavily on the subagent. With the tribe scattered over Creek and Cherokee lands, the subagency became the only symbol of unity.

According to direct orders from Superintendent Armstrong, McKee was to establish an agency on Seminole property that would provide the

tribe with a headquarters and persuade the Indians to farm. McKee succeeded in neither. The subagent was also warned to watch the Seminoles
diligently, because some of them had recently bought lead and powder at
Fort Smith.

One of McKee's few accomplishments was his attendance at an intertribal congress called by the Creeks and held on the Deep Fork River in
May 1842. This council was held specifically to promote peace and understanding among the tribes and to regulate intertribal trade. Some
twenty-five hundred Seminoles, Creeks, Choctaws, Chickasaws,
Caddoes, Delawares, Shawnees, Quapaws, Senecas, Pawnees, Osages,
Kickapoos, Wichitas, Kitchees, Piankeshaws, Towockennys, and
Isterhutkeys (white men) attended and camped in a two-mile circumfer-
ence. Their fires and temporary shelters dotted the woods and the prairies. The Indians consumed twenty thousand pounds of beef, ten barrels
of flour, and meal in proportion. The congress had a positive influence
on the prairie Indians and raised the prestige of the Creeks as peacemakers. Because of their civilized habits and association with the whites, the
importance of the immigrant Indians grew among the native tribes.

The whites who attended the congress, including Creek agent James
Logan; General Zachary Taylor; Superintendent Armstrong; James L.
Alexander, clerk to the Upper Creeks; W. G. Jacobs, clerk to the Lower
Creeks; and Seminole subagent McKee, apparently impressed the Indi-
ans. Logan, who spoke Kickapoo, Shawnee, and other Indian languages,
played a helpful role, allowing several tribes to communicate.[35]

Attending an intertribal congress failed to remove the stains brought
to Subagent McKee's months of service. The dishonesty and corruption
that were so rampant among western officials of the Indian Office struck
McKee as well. Accusations against him ranged from overcharging the
government for corn and beef to recording inaccurate numbers of rations
and other purchases. Superintendent Armstrong learned that McKee tried
to profit from government employees in his agency and that he was involved in a multitude of other corrupt activities. The subagent also failed
to make an annual report to the commissioner of Indian affairs. In October 1842, after denial of a furlough permitting his return to Kentucky, he
resigned and became a wagon and forage master in the territory.

According to some secondary sources, other officials and residents in the territory often faced similar charges. Superintendent Armstrong was accused of going to the West with a twenty-thousand-dollar debt and accumulating forty thousand dollars above that in a few years. His salary was fifteen hundred dollars a year. George W. Clark, who acted briefly as subagent for the Seminoles after McKee's resignation, gambled every night and bet hundreds of dollars, although his pay was three dollars a day. Other influential citizens were associated with heavy gambling.[36] Several officials found it difficult to extend honest contracts for Indian supplies to traders.

Despite the corruption among some white officials in the West, the Seminoles managed to survive the early years. A smallpox epidemic, provision shortages, and a drought caused suffering. The failure of the Florida delegation, inapplicable treaty stipulations, fraudulent slave claims, and the failure to provide separate land brought disappointments. Yet with Commissioner Thomas Hartley Crawford's intercession, appropriations eased the Seminoles' difficulties with diseases and lack of food and clothing. His support also produced a more suitable land arrangement, supervision of tribal funds through their own subagent, and certain safety from slave claims. Thus the Seminoles' strong will to survive and the concern of Commissioner Crawford combined to enable the Indians to maintain their tribal identity during the first five years beyond the Mississippi. Unfortunately, the western Seminoles still faced a future filled with anxiety and frustrations.

3 Divided We Stand

Thomas L. Judge, a long-time federal employee who took charge in January 1843, faced a monumental task as he supervised the Seminoles during the next two and a half years. The tribal divisions, need for complete separation from the Creeks, the Seminoles' lack of education, and their continued misuse of readily available whiskey required that a strong government official promote their welfare. Fortunately, Judge had sympathy and support for these Indians and began working to unify the tribe. The subagent also hoped to make education available and to settle the dispute with the Creeks. Initially he planned to gather the tribe on the assigned Creek land about fifty miles from Fort Gibson. Within two years he had built an agency and blacksmith shop there. By the end of his service, the Indians had gained a separate land where they were congregating.[1]

In 1843, Judge found a variety of conditions among the Seminoles. Micanopy and his followers, who had settled in log cabins on the Deep Fork River in accordance with the government's provision in 1839, seemed to have a comfortable subsistence. They had livestock and raised rice, potatoes, and other vegetables on rich fertile soil, and had fenced seven or eight hundred acres of corn. The blacksmith stayed busy sharpening the ploughs, wedges, troughs, and other farming implements. (Be-

sides the blacksmith, whose annual salary was $600, by 1844 Judge re-
ported that he had employed a striker with an annual pay of $240, an
interpreter, Abraham, who received $300, and a teacher, John Bemo, with
a salary of $600.) Blacks contributed most of the labor. Tribal leaders
reported they were content, but they sought to strengthen the tribe and
to attain an "equal footing with other nations." Although they had a
blacksmith, iron, steel, blankets, and an annuity, they lagged behind the
Choctaws and Chickasaws, who owned cotton gins, grist mills, and saw-
mills.

Some Seminoles in other locations faced starvation when their annuities expired after 1843. Those with chiefs such as Alligator and Wild
Cat who suffered in Cherokee country also remained resentful and suspicious. In reality, the western environment, so different from Florida
with its abundance of fish and game, forced the entire tribe to forsake its
traditional life-style. Thus, the climatic adjustment increased the uncertainties until the Indians adapted to the new mode of living.[2]

Despite hardships that stemmed from problems of adjustment, the
Seminoles impressed Subagent Judge favorably. The men, devoted to their
women and children, used most of the annuities to clothe them. No cases
of infidelity were reported. The subagent called them "high minded,
open, candid, and a brave people" and declared that if they received a
"tithe of the aid and assistance that other tribes are the subject of, their
advances toward civilized life would be second to no tribe." The next
year Judge reported that among "the poor, neglected, and despised Seminoles, there is as much honor and integrity as among any, though they
[the other tribes] may be far in advance of them in the habits of civilized
life." The tribe had some troublesome members, but Judge indicated that
without interference by whites, fewer problems would exist.[3]

During Judge's first months as Seminole subagent, the Seminoles demonstrated their desire to improve their conditions in the West by participating in another intertribal council. This congress, called by the Cherokees, took place at Tahlequah in June 1843. Wild Cat, Alligator, and ten
others represented the Seminoles at the four-week affair. Three or four
thousand Indians—men, women, and children from eighteen tribes—
gathered on the Cherokee council ground. About thirty cabins housed

the delegates, while the unofficial observers, who also witnessed the events and ate the beef, camped over the plains in "true Indian style."

Each group of delegates, from tribes such as the Seminole, Creek, Chickasaw, Peoria, Wichita, Chippewa, Shawnee, Delaware, Ottawa, Osage, Seneca, and others, was accompanied by Indians waving eagle feathers and playing ancient native music. The groups met at the foot of a flagstaff bearing a white flag painted with crossed pipes and locked hands, the Indian symbols of peace and friendship.

The days' activities involved much fellowship, with handshaking, pipe smoking, feasting, and dancing. Business usually proceeded slowly because the speeches were interrupted continuously in order for all to understand them. Displays included belts of wampum, beads, and pipes given to the Cherokees and other southern tribes since 1781. The Senecas had sent some of these items to the Cherokees and others to encourage them to "walk with them upon the white path of friendship."

The congress adjourned after the delegates signed a treaty of eight provisions. The tribes agreed to maintain peace and friendship and to pursue farming, manufacturing, and other peaceful endeavors. Hoping to suppress the use of "ardent spirits," they called for a ban on liquor from the territory. Despite their concern, the sheriff of the district and his squad destroyed about seventeen hundred gallons of whiskey while the tribes met. Of major importance was the commitment that no nation would consent, without the other tribes' approval, to "sell, cede, or in any manner alienate to the United States any part of their present territory."[4]

Because the Seminoles were actively involved in "civilized endeavors," Judge and Commissioner Thomas Hartley Crawford thought they should be educated. Crawford agreed to send Seminole John Bemo to begin teaching his people in the West. Bemo claimed to be a nephew of Osceola who at an early age had been carried to sea by a Frenchman. He eventually came into contact with a minister in Philadelphia who sponsored his education. Afterward Bemo wanted to rejoin his people and share his knowledge. The minister made such a request to Commissioner Crawford, who sent the young man of "irreproachable conduct" to the western Seminoles. Crawford also suggested building a plain log house, on the most economical plan, where Bemo could teach. If funds permitted, a replacement could give more advanced instruction after Bemo taught what he knew.

By August 1844, Bemo reported to Subagent Judge that he had opened his school at Prospect Hill on 15 March. Forty students came; only fifteen boys remained when the pupils learned that no board was provided. Bemo noted that several parents wanted their children educated but thought a midday meal should be provided. It was too far for the children to carry their "Oscof lead for dinner." Bemo concluded that he would have more pupils if he provided food. Nonetheless, he seemed pleased with the Seminoles' attitude and response to his teaching. Large congregations, mostly blacks, went to hear him preach once or twice a week. Some Indians living close to the school began to adopt the manners and dress of whites.[5]

In 1844, one teacher-preacher serving a tribe of more than three thousand scattered Indians and the efforts of the 1843 congress failed to curb the misuse of alcohol among the Seminoles. The idleness and frustration faced by many Seminoles did little to reduce their demand for liquor, which continued in the West as it had existed in Florida. Because illegal whiskey flooded the Indian Territory, it was readily accessible to most Seminoles and became a major obstacle to the tribe's advancement. Some army officers had wanted the arriving Seminoles to go directly to their new lands without stopping at Fort Gibson, where they could buy whiskey.

The government had struggled for years to keep liquor out of Indian Territory. The Indian Intercourse Act of 1834 and previous laws mandated control of such traffic. Troops at Fort Gibson had patrolled the Arkansas River to prevent whiskey shipments from reaching the immigrant Indians. They also moved to various other points, including Fort Smith and Fort Coffee, in an attempt to make their efforts more successful. Owners of some fifty to seventy whiskey shops situated along the western border of Arkansas sold their product without restrictions. If the Indians had no access to whiskey brought by boats or wagons, some "brewed" their own. Usually, traders and merchants tried to have whiskey available when the Indians received their annuity payments. White men married to Indian women dispensed liquor claiming to be exempt from United States laws. Some Indians even smuggled in their own liquor from Texas and Arkansas.

Drunkenness became common among the Indian tribes. Men, women, and children fell victims to misuse of intoxicants, and several Indians died from excessive drinking. The Cherokees drank less whiskey than most other Indians, but they brought it to their country and sold it to the Creeks. Consequently, the Seminoles were not alone in their heavy drinking in Indian Territory.[6]

In 1844, one traveler visited a Seminole camp a half-mile from Fort Gibson and saw two hundred men, women, and children of the most miserable appearance. Most of the men, still inebriated from a "drunken frolic," refused to let a thundershower the previous night disrupt their dancing. The women, also participants, waited until the men sobered up and required no care before they began their frivolities. This practice had developed in Florida because the Indians wanted someone sober at all times.

Chief Micanopy and other chiefs drank excessively. At times Micanopy was accused of having more interest in the "contents of his bottle" than in the education of his people. In April 1844, Micanopy, Alligator, Wild Cat, and their braves, squaws, and dogs went to hold council with Judge Richard Fields in the Cherokee country. Micanopy carried an empty bottle. Gopher John, the black interpreter, explained that Micanopy was drowsy, and "something was produced to quicken the old gentleman's faculties," after which the other chiefs partook.

Micanopy and his associates complained to Fields about their Creek relations, lack of tribal unity, and his loss of control as the head chief. According to the chief, the band near Fort Gibson held council without his consent and invested the tribe's subagent with power to negotiate with the government.

Apparently Micanopy's party greatly respected Fields. An influential Cherokee, Fields had gone to Florida in 1837 with his tribe's delegation to induce the Seminoles to emigrate. It was probably this same Fields who headed a group of three hundred Cherokees living in Texas in 1822. In 1844 he was described as an intelligent merchant who lived in a two-story home, a sign of distinction, about seven miles from Fort Gibson. When the Seminoles wanted his advice, Fields recommended they send a delegation to Washington.[7]

Subagent Judge, well aware of the Seminole tribal divisions and of their disputes with the Creeks, had worked for months to settle the explosive situation. Seeking tribal unity, he had attempted to get those Seminoles on Cherokee lands to go to the assigned district, but they had refused. They still resented any Creek domination and feared the Creeks might take their slaves. Judge held a council with the Seminoles and Creeks in October 1843 and firmly stated that the Seminole slaves should be secure. Afterward a few Seminoles living in Cherokee country agreed to move to the North Fork of the Canadian River if land was available.

In reality, Judge knew the Seminoles, Creeks, and Cherokees would never concur on laws concerning blacks. He also knew that the blacks with the Seminoles on both Creek and Cherokee lands were bound to cause trouble. The Creeks had instituted stricter laws regarding blacks. In addition to prohibiting them from living in separate villages and keeping arms, it was now illegal to have preaching by them or for them. The Cherokees also had passed a law in December 1842 forcing free blacks, except those freed by Cherokees, from their territory. Therefore, in an effort to get the Seminoles out of Cherokee country, Judge had recommended the suspension of their annuities. Because so much discord existed, he suggested the possibility of settling the Seminoles on neutral ground west of the Cherokee nation.[8]

Some Creeks and Cherokees opposed having the Seminoles settled among them. The Creeks argued that the circumstances of those Indians had changed materially since they first agreed to accept them. The prolonged war in Florida had created a "turbulent and predatory spirit" that raised the likelihood that the Seminoles would become troublesome neighbors. Moreover, the Creeks had received no compensation for the land the Seminoles occupied. Most Cherokees supported settlement of the Seminole-Creek controversy because of the marauding habits and destitute condition of the Seminoles on their land. The Cherokee council urged the Seminoles to move to their designated lands because of their drinking, indolence, and thievery. With a multitude of such conflicts, it was "perfect folly" for the government to designate boundaries for Indian tribes living in such close proximity without demanding respect for them.[9]

As early as October 1843, Judge wrote Commissioner Crawford about the Seminole-Creek animosity over land, blacks, and other issues. In November, Crawford recommended that a commission be formed to determine a suitable course of action; Secretary of War James M. Porter approved such action the following month. Several months lapsed before a commission was established in April. It consisted of the Chickasaw, Cherokee, and Creek agents with the Seminole subagent and was chaired by Superintendent Armstrong with instructions to mediate with the Seminoles and Creeks.

The commission's greatest challenge was persuading those Seminoles on Cherokee lands to relocate. They still feared the Creeks would dominate them and take the blacks among them. The Seminoles and Crawford agreed that they should retain ownership of their blacks. The Creeks were directed to refrain from taking the blacks who moved with the Seminoles to Creek country without approval from the president of the United States. Crawford continued to maintain that Creek claims to the blacks should be disregarded, but this had little immediate effect on the Seminoles in Cherokee country.[10]

Crawford hoped both the Seminoles and Creeks would concede to certain stipulations. He thought that the Creeks, because of their large number, should extend their laws over both tribes. These ordinances could be changed to meet the two tribes' needs. He also wanted the Creeks to refrain from taking property brought from Florida by the Seminoles. Because it was imperative that they eventually settle in Creek country, Crawford wanted the Seminoles to "come to terms" with the Creeks.[11]

It was also imperative that their economic condition be addressed. Wild Cat, who had been in the West less than three years, was distressed about the plight of his tribe. He expressed his feelings in a letter printed 30 March 1844, in the *Arkansas Intelligencer*. The editor prefaced the letter by expressing sympathy for Wild Cat and his people, because of the "pitiable condition" that their conquerors had forged upon them. The chief wrote, "Our poor little children—they are crying like wolves, hungry, cold and destitute!"[12]

Wild Cat had found western life disappointing in other ways. Earlier that month a Mr. Wilkins, who was traveling through the territory, had approached Wild Cat and asked him to join a "menagerie" that he was forming of Osages, Cherokees, and Seminoles to exhibit in the East. Wild Cat, no doubt insulted, agreed to go if he could display Wilkins on alternate days, with each keeping his receipts.

Shortly thereafter Commissioner Crawford turned his attention to the Seminoles' economic distress. The western disbursing agent had misused the $15,400 appropriated for the Seminoles according to Article Two of the treaty of 1832. With that money wasted, no annuities after 1843, and subsistence stopped, the tribe had no financial assistance available from the government. Therefore, Crawford asked that Congress make a new appropriation of the same amount stipulated in the 1832 treaty. This sum applied to the "bold manly race would allay discontent, soften their feelings, [and] ameliorate the suffering of those truly unfortunate people." He also wanted the secretary of war, William Wilkins, to insist that the commission act immediately to settle the Seminole-Creek unrest.[13]

In 1844, Subagent Judge stressed to the commissioner that the greatest dissatisfaction of the western Seminoles arose from the fact that they had "no land to call their own" and they objected to becoming constituents of the Creeks.[14] The Seminoles considered themselves an oppressed minority with few rights to govern themselves. According to Judge, they wanted to be permitted to concentrate on the North Fork of the Canadian. While they remained scattered over Creek and Cherokee lands, they interfered with other tribes' possessions; this condition also prohibited their advancement. Because it was unlikely that the Seminoles would yield without some changes in the allotted land, new arrangements, or force, would have to be used.[15]

Judge had met much resistance when he tried to get the Seminoles on Cherokee lands to migrate to their assigned district. He had recommended that their annuities stop in an effort to force their removal. None of his actions had worked. Instead, Wild Cat, Alligator, and two subchiefs decided to go to Washington and ask for title to the land they occupied. This delegation also included the influential Cherokee merchant Richard Fields, who supplied them. They probably thought he could be persuasive in helping them obtain land in the Cherokee nation.

While in Washington in the spring of 1844, Wild Cat's group voiced other concerns about their status in Indian Territory to government officials. They opposed having to settle among the Creeks, and they disliked Judge. Moreover, the delegation asked about the government's failure to supply them with implements.[16]

Judge informed the commissioner that the chiefs who lived on Cherokee land rather than on their assigned land were not representative of the tribe. Several other Seminole chiefs who opposed Wild Cat's delegation had sent Judge to Washington that spring with full power to act for them. Moreover, Foke-Luste-Hajo, Halleck Tustenuggee, Pascofar, and others signed a statement that condemned Wild Cat's group. Those chiefs who protested had full confidence in Judge and believed that Wild Cat had been advised by people who did not have the Seminoles' best interests at heart. Wild Cat and his delegation did more than meet with Washington officials. According to the *Arkansas Intelligencer* they visited a bar in Pittsburgh, where they imbibed alcoholic drinks and where Tiger Tail made a speech. They also met with a Reverend Orson Douglas in Philadelphia.

Apparently, a few Cherokees wanted some Seminoles to stay in their country and began promoting their cause. One Cherokee wrote the *Arkansas Intelligencer* and complained about Judge. He implied that Judge had prevented the Seminoles from sending their own chiefs with him to represent them at the White House. Other charges against Judge were many: he managed the tribe's affairs without consulting his superiors in Washington; he induced the Indians to give him unlimited power of attorney to obtain a treaty; he prevented the Seminole chiefs from visiting Washington, citing the president's busy schedule, and he failed to represent those Seminoles on Cherokee lands. Moreover, the idea of negotiating a treaty originated with Judge instead of with the Seminoles. If a treaty provided funds for the Indians, Judge would use them as he pleased. Consequently, according to this Cherokee, these poor Seminoles would get justice only when there were better appointments in the Indian Office.[17]

Some Seminoles, therefore, hoped that the proposals of Wild Cat's delegation would prevail over those of Subagent Judge. They also wanted the commissioner of the Bureau of Indian Affairs to conduct an investigation that would prove that Judge's papers regarding power of attorney for all the Seminoles were obtained fraudulently with the assistance of a black of poor reputation and a trader in Indian Territory. This Indian thought Judge wanted to become Creek agent and feared his powerful friends might help him succeed.[18]

Creek agent J. L. Dawson, who had recently vacated his position, also caused problems for Judge. Dawson, described as a gambling addict who had been involved in several get-rich-quick schemes, and two others had murdered a trader. He then fled to Texas. Prior to his departure, he had caused some "despicable whites" in Creek country to talk injuriously about Judge. These verbal attacks began after Judge discharged Dawson's relative, the Seminole blacksmith, for loose and immoral conduct.[19]

Despite the adversities faced by Judge in managing Seminole affairs, he defeated the attempts by Wild Cat's delegation to gain land in Cherokee country. The subagent, however, failed to persuade Indian Bureau officials to move that portion of the tribe to the Seminole district.[20]

Wild Cat and his delegation faced a disturbing situation when they returned from Washington to the Cherokee country. Their people, forced from their homes by flooding from the Arkansas and Grand rivers, were encamped on the prairies near Fort Gibson. Because they had lost their possessions, even the corn growing and in storage, about 295 reported to the subagent that they stayed alive by eating berries and begging. Judge requested and received from the commandant at Fort Gibson half-rations for eighteen days for these Indians. Judge also suggested moving the group to Creek land on the south side of the Arkansas and furnishing rations until they were established in a suitable location.[21]

Judge's and Wild Cat's delegation persuaded officials in the Indian Bureau that the Seminoles wanted complete separation from the Creeks. If given land on the Creek allotment, the Seminoles asked that it be restricted to Seminoles and kept under their jurisdiction. Crawford realized that only a treaty between the United States, the Seminoles, and the Creeks could produce such results. He agreed that the Seminoles' desires should be met, and he wanted the commission to be authorized to set aside a separate district for the Seminoles. Although Crawford hoped the transaction could occur without any payment to the Creeks or any extraction from the Seminoles, he felt the commissioners should know that the Seminoles would receive the $15,400 as promised earlier. If absolutely necessary, with the Seminoles' approval, part of that fund could be presented to the Creeks.[22]

On 15 June 1844, Secretary of War Wilkins approved Crawford's request to give the Seminoles separate land under their own jurisdiction. Crawford notified Armstrong and the other commissioners to negotiate with the two tribes for a separate land for the Seminoles. This action came despite an earlier letter from several Creek chiefs, including Roly McIntosh, Ufallo Hadjo, and Benjamin Marshall, who voiced their disapproval of such a settlement. The commissioners, nonetheless, had full authority in reaching a satisfactory arrangement among the Indians. Moreover, the officials could allow for moderate compensation for property losses, temporary rations, and a small appropriation for the Seminoles' removal. If the Indians demanded payment for abandoned property, the treaty should include for such claims five thousand dollars, of which twenty-five hundred would be divided equally among heads of families in the West. The balance would provide agricultural implements. Crawford instructed Acting Superintendent Armstrong to concede to limited funding for removal and temporary rations.

Expenses of the commission had to be kept to a minimum, with no funds available to ease the negotiations. The officials received compensation only for traveling expenses. Crawford stressed that the Seminoles' removal from Florida had cost huge sums of money and that the pending removal resulted from their refusal to locate on assigned lands. Because the Indians would not be moving a long distance, he suggested using wagons only for transporting the sick and baggage.[23]

The agents and their tribes had different motives for wanting a treaty. Pierce M. Butler, a former governor of South Carolina and lieutenant colonel in the United States Army, had served as Cherokee agent throughout the early 1840s. He defended those Cherokees who wanted the Seminoles off their land because of their marauding activities. Moreover, the quasi-free status of the Seminole blacks was a threat to the Cherokees who maintained a slave code similar to that of white southerners. Thus, the Cherokees who had suffered from the Seminoles' intrusions and their agent wanted the Seminoles to have another district.

But the Creek and Seminole agents had other concerns. Creek agent

James Logan of Arkansas knew the Creeks opposed having the Seminoles concentrated in one locality. However, if Creek laws prevailed, the Creeks could possibly force the Seminoles to merge with them. Subagent Judge hoped that a separate district would allow the Seminoles opportunities to improve.[24]

The treaty, signed by the commission and the Indians on 4 January 1845 allowed the Seminoles, who had caused the government "so much trouble," to locate on any area of Creek land where they would be contented. Expressed clearly in the preamble, the treaty's purpose was to "reconcile all difficulties respecting location and jurisdiction, to settle all disputed questions which have arisen, or may hereafter arise, in regard to rights of property, and especially to preserve the peace of the frontier, seriously endangered by the restless and warlike spirit of the intruding Seminoles."[25]

The treaty provided separate funds for both the Seminoles and Creeks. The former tribe was to receive $15,400 and an annuity of three thousand dollars for fifteen years as provided in the treaty of 1832, two thousand dollars in goods for the same period, and one thousand dollars for agricultural implements for five years. The Creeks received an additional three thousand dollars for education for twenty years.

The Seminoles wanted to settle near the Little River, where rations and subsistence would continue for six months after moving there. Those in the West who refused to move within the allotted time period were barred from sharing in the treaty's benefits. An amendment added to the document in May extended the time limit to twelve months for those in Florida who would relocate.

The treaty had major flaws, however, and laid the foundation for ten more years of disagreement between the Seminoles and Creeks. It failed to provide complete separation of the two tribes. Although permitted to settle in separate communities in Creek country where they could make their own town regulations, the Seminoles were still subject to laws made by the Creek council. The Seminoles had permission to participate in the Creek council but later failed to do so. They had complete separation from the Creeks only regarding monetary policies. Northern and western boundary lines were also to be marked to avoid encroachments by either tribe on others. The president was to rule on property disputes. The Seminoles did gain a separate land, but it was still on Creek territory where Creek laws prevailed.

A majority of the chiefs and headmen of the Seminoles (twenty-two) and Creeks (forty-two), who were described as friendly, frank, and businesslike, ratified the Treaty with the Creeks and Seminoles of 1845 despite its weaknesses. The chiefs were among several persons at the formal signing, which included army captains, three interpreters, and other witnesses. Two minor amendments added later were ratified by fifteen Seminoles and twenty-one Creeks. President James K. Polk signed the treaty on 18 July 1845.[26]

Wagons soon passed through Cherokee country under contract to remove the Seminoles to the new Creek district. John Coheia (Gopher John), regarded by some as the chief of the Seminole blacks, was hired to use his wagon and three yoke of oxen to help move them. He assisted in settling the blacks in the lower valley of Little River. Because the House of Representatives adjourned before the Senate ratified the treaty, and Congress made no appropriations, those who contracted to move the Seminoles were unpaid for fifteen months. The next Congress appropriated twenty-six thousand dollars for subsistence for the Seminoles during their removal to the Little River area and for six months thereafter and provided funds for the required goods and agricultural implements.[27]

In compliance with the treaty, most, not all, of the Seminoles relocated in an area about eight miles north of Little River. For a time they seemed reasonably contented, at least more than at anytime since their migration from Florida. Their new land, composed mainly of prairie but with adequate timber, seemed adaptable to growing grain, especially corn, and to raising livestock.

The Seminoles, who usually emigrated west with a headman with whom they located, had settled in several towns or bands, called *tal'was* or *tulwas,* divided according to Hitchiti (Mikasuki) and Muskogee languages. Consisting of log cabins, towns of various sizes were scattered a few miles apart and were a transferred feature of the Florida habitat. Although the nation held control of the land, each family cultivated from one to five acres near a water supply, which might be in a bottomland a half-mile from the cabin. Seminoles were expected to marry within the band and to live in a general locale; however, if they moved, they maintained membership in the town of birth.

Each town was a political subdivision of the Seminole nation. A general council had supervisory control over the entire nation and selected a principal chief and an assistant who served for life unless they retired or were impeached. The council consisted of a majority of the headmen, including three members from each band, the *meko* or *mico* (band chief), the *heniha* (assistant chief), and the *tustanugy* (war leader). With the approval of the principal chief, they passed tribal laws that could not conflict with the enactments of the Creek council. Wild Cat acted as counselor to Chief Micanopy, and five other chiefs, Tusse Krai, Octi-archee, Pascofar, Echo-emathla, and Passuckee-Yoholo, formed the executive council. Most contact between the towns resulted from the tribal council meetings and the Green Corn dances.[28]

Within the towns, the Seminoles had a matrilineal clan system that regulated most aspects of family and social life and also tended to have Muskogee and non-Muskogee linguistic divisions. Clans such as the Wind, Bear, and Bird were considered true Muskogee, whereas those of Deer, Tiger, Fox, and others were usually non-Muskogee, although exceptions did occur. Originally members of a clan were thought to be descendants of a common animal or simple ancestor. Clans could adopt outsiders, and in the East some zambos had been considered free and clan members as well. When visiting another town, clan members stayed with members of their own clan.

Because the Seminole children belonged to their mother's clan, they were educated and disciplined by a member of her family. Although she might apply the switch, the father abstained from any corporal punishment of his children. When children misbehaved, the mother's brother or another male clan member chastised them and occasionally used a needle to "dry scratch" their forearms or legs. This uncle selected suitable spouses from other clans for the nieces and nephews. Clans also delegated punishments for adultery, murder, and other crimes, and when an offender escaped, another clan member was held accountable.

Religion was an important part of town and clan life. The town chiefs served as religious leaders, and each town had its own sacred rituals. The Seminoles believed the Master of Breath was the supreme god in the heavens, and that other main gods in the sky were thunder, lightning, and the sun. It was imperative to keep harmony between the sky, earth, and the underworld—the three components of the cosmos. The religious realm included other supernaturals in shapes ranging from little humans, to unusual animals similar to cows, deer, and bears, to forms with human and snake features.

The Green Corn festival, or Busk Ceremony, held every year when the green corn ripened, was the most sacred event of the religious year and took place at the town's square ground or ceremonial center. In the center of the square ground, a sacred fire of four logs was built and was presented to the sun, the "giver of life" to maize, the Seminoles' most important food. Ceremonies usually lasted several days, during which the Indians tried to maintain the goodwill of the animal spirits and to purify the sacred fire and themselves. It was also a time for delegating Indian names and assigning clan seats. A man might have three or more names—a name given at birth based on physical traits or his clan, a war or hunting name, and a civil or religious name. Besides *mico, heniha,* and *tustanugy,* other titles or names assigned included: *yahola* (one who officiated at rituals), *imala* (an advisor or assistant), *hillis haya* or *kila* (medicine man), *shaman* (prophet), and *hadjo* (warrior).

The festival began with a stomp dance and included a variety of others dances, such as the women's Ribbon or Sun Dance. The ladies appeared in Florida fashions, with long skirts made of rows of patchwork and tight bodices covered by capes of gauzy material, beads, earrings, and shells around the lower legs, and silver hair combs with multicolored ribbons flowing almost to the ground. The men's attire included the Florida-style patchwork jackets with blousy sleeves. The festival ended following more dances, several sessions of taking medicine, a pole ball game, and a feast. When the sacred logs had burned, the Indians took the coals to the fires at the various camps and the new year began.

Besides the Green Corn festival and the different dances, ball games were social gatherings. The men and boys played intertown stickball games that were sometimes quite dangerous. Men opposed the women in single pole ball games often played before the all-night stomp dances. With the ball games, the Green Corn festival, and other dances, the Seminoles were active socially in their towns and clans.[29]

The Seminoles, with several other western tribes, encountered continuing difficulties arising on the frontier as they tried to maintain their traditional cultural features. The decade of the 1840s was a turbulent one in Indian Territory. With so many Indians from the East thrown between the white settlers and the wild Plains tribes, problems inevitably arose. The uprooted Indians continued to fall prey to marauders such as the Comanches, Pawnees, and Kiowas. In addition, Mexican agents still resentful of Texas independence, stalked the Indian Territory trying to incite attacks on Texans. The army commanders at Forts Gibson, Towson, Coffee, Wayne, and Washita, with the Indian agents and tribal leaders, were kept busy with the threats to peace.

Consequently, the Creeks, considered by some in the territory as the foremost peacemakers on the frontier, called an intertribal congress in May 1845 after assuming that the United States military protection was inadequate. This congress included delegates from the Seminole, Creek, Choctaw, Chickasaw, Shawnee, Delaware, Piankeshaw, Osage, Kickapoo, Quapaw, Peoria, and Caddo tribes. Termed the most successful of the Indian congresses prior to the Civil War, it brought peace between the Kickapoos and the Chickasaws and Choctaws. The Indians discredited the Mexican agents. In the speeches, the delegates advocated a pan-Indian unity and a socioeconomic fusion. Fifty-two Seminoles led by Micanopy and Wild Cat attended the sessions and heard speakers plead that they avoid spilling one another's blood.

Even at this early date, two months before President Polk signed the treaty of 1845, Cherokee agent Butler took note of the Creeks' attitude toward the Seminole delegates. When the Seminoles arrived on 16 May, they "took their seats quietly and modestly in rear of the Creeks." Butler concluded that the Creeks would hold a "tight rein" on the Seminoles after the official approval of the treaty.[30]

After working to secure a separate land allotment in Creek country and participating in the intertribal congress, the Seminoles lost their sub-agent. Although Judge had promoted the tribe's unity, education, and

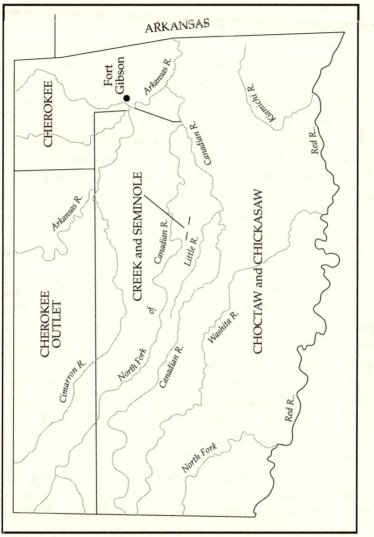

Map 3. Seminoles' location according to treaty of 1845.

general progress, there were a variety of complaints against him. Super-intendent Armstrong suspended him on 9 June 1845, claiming that Judge gave unauthorized rations to the Indians who moved near the agency. Apparently Judge had given contracts to A. H. Olmstead rather than to Matthew Leeper, whom Armstrong preferred. Moreover, Joseph Carter, an agency blacksmith Judge had fired, complained to the Office of In-dian Affairs that he drank excessively, used funds for his personal ben-efit, and served as a puppet for traders in Seminole country.[31] John Bardwell, one trader licensed in the Cherokee country, had come into conflict with Judge in October 1844 after trading with the Seminoles. Bardwell claimed Judge was "notoriously known" in Indian country and was "in collusion with a licensed trader in Creek country, with whom he lives and by whom he thrives." Bardwell said Judge prevented him from being paid for goods he sold to the Seminoles so Judge's friend could be paid.[32]

Judge responded to the accusations against him by denouncing Armstrong. He claimed the superintendent had sided with Alligator, Wild Cat, and members of other tribes against the rest of the Seminoles. Armstrong, although described as very honest, was himself unable to avoid some corrupt traders in extending contracts and was also accused of "accumulating money" very rapidly.[33] Such charges of irregularities among Indian officials in the West were numerous.

Regardless of the many charges of irregularities, Judge brought some improvement to the Seminoles between 1843 and 1845. He had assumed responsibility for a starving, dissipated tribe that suffered from major in-ternal division. In a land with a strange environment, deficient in game, the Seminoles also had worried about the disturbances on the frontier. Furthermore, after the threat of complete Creek domination, the Semi-noles had demanded land away from the Creeks. By the time Judge left the tribe in June 1845, a semblance of tribal unity had begun to appear, and the treaty of 1845 had provided the Seminoles another land district and new, though limited, funds to supply certain needs for several years. Although these short-term improvements brought little permanent satis-faction to the western Seminoles, their tribal identity remained intact as they endured further hardships in the late 1840s.

4 *A Subagent's Dilemma*

Marcellus M. Duval supervised Seminole affairs in the West between July 1845 and November 1852. He took charge after Gideon C. Matlock served a brief period following Thomas Judge's removal in June of 1845. Duval faced troublesome times during his more than seven years as subagent of a poor, uneducated, and scattered tribe that was dissatisfied with its relationship with the Creeks. By 1849, the uncertain status of the Seminole blacks caused part of the tribe and some blacks to leave the territory.

Although Duval brought much experience to his office, having served as postmaster at Fort Gibson and as a clerk to Cherokee agent Pierce Butler, he brought little general improvement to the Seminoles. Lacking the sympathetic understanding of his predecessor, he considered the Indians lazy. When they wasted their annuities, he called them "worthless and depraved." As the years passed, Duval's slave-state background and his perhaps improper interest in the Seminole slaves tainted his tenure as subagent and eventually caused his removal.

Duval established his headquarters near Little River about two and a half miles from the Seminole council house and approximately a hundred miles from Fort Gibson. From his one-room log house, he maintained contact with his superiors and other whites by dispatching a rider or going himself to the nearest post office, which was at Fort Gibson. Loneliness and discomfort were the lot of Duval and most other Indian agents as they endured the isolation, rough terrain, bad weather, and long hours associated with the duties of working among the Indians. Nonetheless, control of large sums of money—the annuities—as well as rule over Indians and blacks apparently made these positions attractive.

Duval's job demanded effective management because the Seminoles were still scattered. Several members of the tribe lived among the Creeks near the North Fork of the Canadian River about fifty miles from Little River. Others stayed on the Deep Fork, about sixty miles away, on Elm Creek, a distance of seventy-five miles, and in Cherokee country. Duval expected more Seminoles to move closer to the nucleus of the tribe in the vicinity of the council house just north of Little River.

In addition to supervising a scattered tribe, Duval was working with Indians who had to struggle to survive. In 1845, the late crops and a drought, combined with the inconveniences of relocation, dimmed hopes for the Seminoles' immediate progress. The subagent suggested allocating payments and rations at different intervals in order to prolong their benefits. He also recommended providing less beef and more corn for the tribe.

Even the Seminoles in the Little River country were discontented. They argued that the government's treaty promises to "give them a country in exchange better adapted to their habits of life" remained unfulfilled. Instead, they lived on land lacking sufficient game and water and with a colder climate that required more effort to live.

As the Seminoles continued their struggle to survive in the West, Subagent Duval reported that their watchwords, "Live as you please, but die brave," reflected the attitude that gave them the spirit to endure. Duval also stated that each male Seminole yearned for the opportunity before his death to proclaim, "I'm a man and a warrior, and not afraid to die." The Seminoles' identity, faith, and pride in their heritage helped them to prevail over a multitude of hardships that came in the late 1840s. Government neglect, rivalry with the Creeks, disputes concerning blacks, and trouble with trespassers failed to alter the Seminoles' resolute determination to survive in their western homeland.[1]

The Indians found the climate harsh as the "blasts of winter" swept across the prairies. With its low temperatures, the winter of 1845–46 reportedly was one of the most severe in the West and caused considerable suffering. The adverse weather, combined with the Indians' late arrival in their new district in the spring of 1845 and government subsistence for only six months, supplied in accordance with the treaty of 1845, had rendered them almost destitute by January 1846. A few Seminoles cooked slippery elm bark for a corn substitute. They survived in this fashion for six months until Duval used their annuity credit to purchase corn.

The tribe, however, worked sufficient land and raised enough good crops in 1846 to maintain themselves throughout the remainder of that year and into the next one. Because they were supplied with an adequate stock of agricultural tools, farming prevailed. Each town had a field in common, but there were also individual fields. Corn and vegetables—sweet potatoes, rice, beans, and goober peas—became mainstays. Duval soon described them as being agriculturists comparable to almost any tribe on the border. Some Seminoles hunted to supplement their supplies of food because each man owned a rifle. With these agricultural and local hunting activities, the Indians succeeded in easing somewhat their economic problems. With sufficient food they appeared healthy, and their birthrate increased.

The Seminoles lived simply, although somewhat better than in previous years. Their cabins were usually equipped with one or two stools, a pestle and mortar, hominy baskets, two or three pots or kettles, and "sofkee" (corn soup) spoons. A beef hide placed in a corner for a bed completed their furnishings.

The subagent had expected trouble between the Seminoles and Creeks. None developed immediately after the Seminoles relocated. Some tribal members seemed quiet and friendly, leading Duval to conclude that the Indians' impression of the United States and its policies had changed after Wild Cat's delegation went to Washington and learned the strength of that nation. This lesson had been left unclear by the Florida War according to the subagent. The Seminole tribal members acknowledged the supremacy of the Creek general council, although they maintained self-government in their towns.

Displaying their honesty, the Seminoles paid their debts, without coercion, with the $12,600 they received from the government as compensation for abandoned improvements in Florida. They did ask for blankets, linsey-woolseys, and other cloth the women and children needed. The cost of the large quantity of stroud they required was exorbitant. The Indians needed and wanted the money the government had promised them in earlier treaties. Therefore, Duval knew they would require "much care" by the government. He added that they never blamed God for their misfortunes.[2]

Although the Seminoles had been in the western territory for almost ten years, they still lacked organized religious and educational instruction. Their attitude toward education and Christianity was understandably apprehensive. Before moving West, some Seminoles believed Americans wanted to educate them in order to convert them. The Indians at that time thought missionaries were rivals to the town leaders. Moreover, they thought they might destroy the Indians' souls, clans, and religious rituals. Without doubt, the suspicious attitude of the Florida Indians had resulted largely from their poor relationship with the Spanish missionaries during the preceding centuries and, more recently, with the American missionaries in the South.

One missionary reported to Creek agent James Logan in October 1846 that upon visiting the Seminoles in the southwestern part of the Creek nation, he learned the Seminoles expected the government to take the initiative in educating and Christianizing them. "Some of their principal men, when asked if they would like to have schools and preaching among them, replied that they did not know; but supposed that if it was good for them their Great Father, the president, would send it to them." Therefore, Christianity was neglected and even rejected because the "proper authority" failed to send it.[3]

The neglect of education among the western Seminoles continued between 1845 and 1849, although the new commissioner of Indian affairs, William Medill, actively promoted education and improvement for the Indian tribes in general. Medill, who was born in Delaware and became an Ohio lawyer and United States congressman, received his appointment from President James K. Polk in October 1845. The commissioner adopted several policies of his predecessor, Thomas Crawford, and worked vigorously to advance the Indians' progress toward the civilization of whites, to curb the liquor traffic, and to reform abuses in Indian trade. His tasks became more difficult as the nation's Indian population expanded with the acquisition of new territories in the Southwest and Northwest. Moreover, between 1846 and 1848, large numbers of whites moved to the West, causing more difficulties between whites and Indians. Medill had some success in getting the Indian Intercourse Act passed in 1847. It provided imprisonment for whiskey sellers, payment of annuities to family heads rather than to tribal chiefs, and semiannual payments to tribes whose other funds were excessive. Moreover, traders could not claim tribal funds for the debts of individual Indians. Medill stressed the importance of educating the Indians to reduce problems with them. Yet during his administration, the Seminoles faltered because of their lack of educational opportunities.[4]

Because the Seminoles had received no formal instruction in the West except through John Bemo's school, they relied heavily on the use of the bilingual black interpreters. The blacks liked to use their linguistic talents to keep control over the Indians. One black named Abraham served as an interpreter for Chief Micanopy and the subagent. Abraham had been influential in various negotiations between the United States and the Seminoles. Another black interpreter named Cudjo served the Seminole chiefs as late as 1845. John Horse, or Gopher John, translated for the Seminoles in the Cherokee nation between 1843 and 1845 and later at Fort Gibson, when the blacks took refuge there. Because of the Seminoles' lack of education, the blacks had every opportunity to control the Seminoles' communication with the different subagents and with other federal officials.[5]

The lack of education and religious instruction seemed a minor problem compared to the jealousy and rivalry that smoldered between the Seminoles and Creeks. Because the Seminoles were scattered over Creek lands (the majority was on Little River in the southwestern corner of the nation and on the edge of the adjoining prairies), some of the Seminoles were afraid that the Creeks would attempt to extend their laws entirely over them. Conversely, the Creeks felt uneasy about the Seminoles' attitude toward obeying laws of the Creek council as mandated by the treaty of 1845. Initially, Duval thought the Creeks would treat the Seminoles fairly, but soon the Seminole-Creek controversy was simmering again. Difficulties stemmed from the old problems associated with the Creeks' assistance to the United States in the Second Seminole War, from hatred created during the tribes' original separation several decades earlier, and from the question of the ownership of the Seminole blacks.[6]

The uncertain status of the blacks caused the Seminoles the most trouble in the late 1840s. When the Seminoles moved to the new district in accordance with the treaty of 1845, the blacks tried to establish the same arrangements they had had with the Seminoles in Florida and when they had first arrived in the West. They settled in separate groups and lived in cabins with furnishings similar to the Indians. They did most of the work in getting the Indians settled. The blacks also farmed and paid an annual tribute of produce to the Indians.

But these blacks failed to reestablish the same relationship that had existed between them and the Seminoles. Instead, after the Creeks and whites stepped up their slave raids, they became greatly disturbed. They began to distrust the Seminoles' ability to resist the Creeks, especially when slave traders promised them one hundred dollars for each black. Likewise, the Seminoles had lost confidence in the blacks as interpreters, because the government had failed to keep its promises to them. Some Seminoles even sold free blacks. Consequently, many of the blacks turned more and more to the military officials at Fort Gibson for protection.

In 1845, General Thomas Jesup had visited Fort Gibson and had left a list of blacks that he considered free according to his information from the Second Seminole War. Some blacks hastened to prove that they were free. Many had come to the West with scraps of paper with information about their surrender recorded by various officers. They gave these to the agent or to the commander at Fort Gibson to record. A few blacks bought their freedom, and others simply had their statements about their freedom recorded. Shortly after May 1845, black leader Gopher John and the commander at Fort Gibson, Colonel Richard B. Mason, made an unsuccessful trip to Washington and asked officials to allow the blacks to return to Florida.[7]

Their uncertain status resulted largely from the promises made to the blacks by General Jesup during the Second Seminole War. Jesup, a Virginian who had lived in Ohio, served as commander of the United States forces in Florida between 1836 and 1838. He attempted to prevent any slave hunting during the Second Seminole War that would have prolonged the removal of the Seminoles. The commander refused to make the soldiers capture runaways; he ordered the taking only of blacks who were Seminole allies.[8] In the capitulation of 1837, Jesup promised that the blacks or allies of Seminoles who surrendered would have their security guaranteed in the West. He also promised that the Indians could keep their bona fide property, including slaves. When runaways, freeborns, and blacks captured or bought by the Seminoles settled together in the West, it became impossible to determine which were legally free.

The commander at Fort Gibson, Colonel Mason, wanted the army to protect those Seminole blacks who had papers declaring their freedom. General Matthew Arbuckle, now commander of the Seventh Military Department at Fort Smith, agreed with Mason. After the blacks of various categories turned to the army officials for protection, their dependence on the Indians diminished.

By 1845, the majority of the Seminoles' black men, including several with their families, had taken refuge around Fort Gibson. Sixty or seventy blacks got jobs helping construct the stone buildings there. Other blacks continued to farm and raise herds in their villages on the Little and Deep Fork rivers. The estimated three hundred Seminole blacks were divided geographically as well as legally.

In 1846, Jesup wrote Arbuckle that he had succeeded in getting the blacks' case before President James K. Polk to determine whether they should live in separate villages or go to another country. According to the treaty of 1845, the president was to decide the contested property cases of the Indians. Polk consulted Jesup and learned that in Florida Jesup had promised the black chiefs Auguste and Carollo that the blacks could settle in separate villages as part of the Seminole nation in the West; they were to have the protection of the United States.

Jesup also wrote Secretary of War William L. Marcy that most blacks had either surrendered or were captured; owners had given up very few.

Because the blacks had gained their freedom, Jesup hoped it would be insured by United States protection. The general considered the blacks a personal responsibility and intended to raise the matter before Congress if the president and the War Department refused to defend them.[9]

Meanwhile, the new commander at Fort Gibson, Colonel Gustavus Loomis, continued his predecessor's protective handling of the blacks living around the fort in compliance with General Arbuckle's orders. He provided religious instruction for them, and several tried to learn to read the Bible. Moreover, when the blacks were without jobs after the completion of the construction work at Fort Gibson, Loomis issued small quantities of food to them.

The generosity extended the blacks by Commanders Mason and Loomis displeased Subagent Duval. He had worked vigorously to have the blacks restored to the Indians. Duval had informed Commissioner Medill that the Indians wanted their dispute with the blacks settled. Duval declared that if the blacks were not Indian property, they should be removed from Indian Territory.

Duval and his brother had an interest in the blacks for other reasons. With an Alabama background, they supported slavery and wanted to get possession of some Seminole slaves. In early 1848, the Seminole chiefs sent Duval's brother, William J. Duval, to Washington to represent their slave interests before federal officials. The brothers used this service later to establish a claim for about a third of the Seminole blacks.

In the spring of 1848, the Creeks also sent a delegation to Washington to discuss the status of the blacks. The Indians presented a grim picture of the Seminole blacks at Fort Gibson and on Little River. They described them as worthless thieves who encouraged slaves from surrounding areas to join them. Moreover, because the blacks were under laws of the Creek council, that tribe needed to be clear as to the blacks' official status.[10]

President Polk, a slaveholder who had wrestled with the troublesome Seminole slave problem for two years, referred the matter to Attorney General John Y. Mason, another slaveholder from Virginia. Mason, serving an interim term between those of two northerners, Nathan Clifford of Maine and Issac Toucey of Connecticut, decided the blacks were the property of the Seminoles and must return to their towns in Indian Territory. He saw no need for the government to protect them. Polk approved this policy on 8 July 1848.[11]

In accordance with this decision, General Arbuckle sent Brigadier General William G. Belknap to Fort Gibson to supervise the return of the blacks to the Seminole chiefs. Although trouble was expected, the transfer went smoothly. On 2 January 1849, the Indians regained control of about 260 blacks. More than half of the 260 were still at Fort Gibson, whereas the others had filtered back to Seminole country or had stayed in their settlements on the Deep Fork and Little rivers. A few were at the North Fork and Arkansas rivers. The blacks were told that they could continue to live in their towns and that they would not be sold. The Seminole chiefs gave the impression that they would treat the blacks kindly. The military authorities instructed the blacks to complain to their agent if they were bothered and to defend themselves against slave hunters.

The blacks became rebellious after they were returned to the Indians' control. They violated Creek laws, especially in regard to the carrying of weapons. Although the chiefs instructed the blacks to settle fifteen miles north of the agency, Gopher John and a majority of the group located about thirty miles from the agency and proceeded to conduct themselves as though they were "independent of Indian authority." They considered themselves free because the government officials tried to keep them in a semifree status "even after the rule that they belonged to the Seminoles." Settled in villages mostly at Deep Fork and Wewoka, they began farming and flatly refused to be separated. The Creeks, who were unhappy with armed blacks living in their country, were encouraged by whites and Cherokees to disarm the blacks and enslave them.[12]

Subagent Duval wanted the blacks disarmed because the Seminole council had agreed to deliver them to their owners. He also feared Creek reactions to the blacks' violation of their laws. Taking the blacks' weapons would have benefited Duval directly, because he and his brother claimed ownership to a third of them for their earlier efforts on the Indians' behalf.

Therefore, the subagent wanted the government to use troops to disarm the blacks. Acting superintendent of the Western Territory, John

Drennen, wrote General Arbuckle on 20 July 1849 to ask that he act on
Duval's request. Lieutenant Franklin Flint, acting assistant adjutant general at Fort Smith, informed Drennen that control of the blacks should
have begun with their departure from Fort Gibson. Moreover, sending
troops was impossible because of a cholera epidemic and high water.
Flint, however, did fear that the use of troops might be necessary later.

Flint complained to Drennen that most of the problems in Indian
country stemmed from whites, but he blamed the Seminoles for some of
the disturbance. Although the Seminoles were told at Fort Gibson not to
sell the blacks, Flint was convinced that they wanted them disarmed in
order to do so. Arbuckle thought the Seminoles could handle the situation with the blacks. He did agree, however, that it would be difficult to
reduce the blacks to slavery again after they had spent three years at Fort
Gibson expecting to receive their freedom. If they were disarmed, they
would be easy targets for speculators. Thus, General Arbuckle offered to
send a discreet officer to talk to the blacks about peaceful cooperation.
Duval refused Arbuckle's offer, probably because he feared it would im-
pede his efforts to take control of several of them.[13] Arbuckle concluded
that because the Indians sold the blacks for the "merest trifle," they valued them less than they pretended.

Nonetheless, Drennen regretted that Arbuckle was unwilling to use
force to disarm the blacks. He thought that otherwise the Seminoles and
Creeks would take their weapons. Drennen also noted the inconsisten-
cies in the government's policy regarding the blacks. If they were declared
to be Seminole property and they rebelled, the government, according to
Drennen, should protect the Indians. But Arbuckle maintained his belief
that the Seminoles could handle the matter.[14]

Subagent Duval dealt with other pressing matters in 1849. Rain
caused the crops to be late, and the Indians devoted little attention to
livestock. Moreover, they continued to use whiskey in "large quantities"
and still had no school in operation. In addition, an estimated fifteen hundred to two thousand whites who passed near the agency en route to
California that spring allegedly stole ponies from the Seminoles. As the
whites passed, they simply drove off with the "crowd" the Indian ponies
they found on the range. The whites had usually departed before the In-

dians discovered the animals were missing. The situation became more complicated when the Seminoles sold ponies they had stolen possibly from other Indians. Duval spent two months, April and May 1849, visiting the different parties en route to California to discuss the problem with them.[15]

While Duval worked with the numerous problems as Seminole subagent, Commissioner of Indian Affairs Orlando Brown complained about the cumbersome and inefficient organization of the Indian Office. Major changes occurred in the administration of Indian affairs when Zachary Taylor became president in March 1849. The Office of Indian Affairs was transferred from the War Department to the newly created Interior Department. The first secretary of the interior, Thomas Ewing of Ohio, put his own men in office and tried to keep a tight control over Indian affairs. Brown, a political appointee from Kentucky, simply carried out Ewing's orders. They both supported education and protection for the Indians.

Under the new system, officials in the field still reported to the commissioner, but that officer now submitted his reports to the secretary of the interior rather than to the secretary of war. The negotiation of treaties, distribution of annuities, and supervision of Indian trade fell to the Interior Department, whereas the protection of the frontier and agency posts remained the responsibility of the military. But the shortage of officials in the field—five superintendents, nine agents, and twelve subagents—caused Brown to complain; later, more agents were hired.[16]

Commissioner Brown, with President Zachary Taylor and Secretary of War George W. Crawford, also acted to promote the removal of the remaining Florida Seminoles.[17] The Floridians had continued to agitate for the expulsion of the Indians and to complain about Indian depredations. Governor William D. Moseley told the General Assembly of Florida as early as 1845 that he was disappointed with the government's failure to enforce the Treaty of Payne's Landing, which provided for complete Seminole removal. Secretary of War Crawford suggested to Secretary of the Interior Ewing that a delegation of western Seminoles go to Florida to urge removal of the "wildest and fiercest remnant of a tribe which have [*sic*] been distinguished for their ceaseless opposition to . . .

civilization."[18] With a Seminole-white conflict in Florida developing again in 1849, rumors of Indians killing whites spread in Washington and could have led to war.

Fortunately, President Taylor had firsthand knowledge of the Florida Seminoles as he had served as commander of the United States forces in the Second Seminole War between May 1838 and April 1840. While in Florida, he refused to take the captured blacks away from their Seminole owners or to force them into slavery. Later, when he commanded the Second Military Department in the West, he treated the Seminoles fairly. Now as president, Taylor remained calm, preferring to rely on reason and reconciliation. He rejected whites' demands to call out the Florida militia. Taylor's careful efforts in postponing a tragic Third Seminole War have remained unappreciated. One biographer of Taylor cites the president's action in the Florida crisis as one of his main domestic achievements.[19]

Rather than declare war, government officials decided to send another delegation to Florida. By 23 May, Subagent Duval reported to Lieutenant Flint at Fort Smith that the Seminole council had agreed to this and proposed selecting five to twenty Indians with two or three interpreters for the mission. The western Seminoles wanted their Florida tribal members to join them. Three Seminoles, Chiefs Jim Jumper, Wild Cat, and Alligator, sent a letter to General Edmund Gaines from the Seminole agency on 23 May. They said they were a poor tribe—"living just to get along. As much as to say almost dead, yet we want to see our brothers very much, as we love one another." They added that they had separated from the Florida Indians only because the whites forced them to do so.[20]

Subagent Duval informed Commissioner Brown that he believed a western delegation could "remove the Florida Indians cheaper than the military." He thought, however, that if the Indians described the country to the Seminoles in Florida as they did to him, the delegation might fail. Duval was at Fort Gibson gathering supplies to deliver to the Seminole council when he received instructions from Brown regarding the Florida delegation. He left immediately for the agency to meet with the Seminole council to elect delegates. Duval also sent for Wild Cat, who was on a trading expedition at Fort Smith.

But Wild Cat had other business besides trade at Fort Smith in September 1849. He, Alligator, George Cloud, and fifteen Seminole warriors visited General Arbuckle at Fort Smith to complain about Subagent Duval. These Indians were disturbed about Duval's claim to ninety of the blacks. The subagent felt that he and his brothers, William and Gabriel, deserved the blacks because they had worked so vigorously to get them restored to the Indians. According to the Indians, the subagent sought the aid of the Creeks in seizing the blacks and threatened to withhold the Indians' annuities unless he got them. Their head chief, Jim Jumper, approved Duval's actions, and, without the owners' consent, promised him the blacks. Wild Cat supported the blacks. He said that he had no problems with those armed blacks who settled in the Seminole district. He approved having them live in separate towns. They needed their weapons to kill game to feed their children because they were poor. He objected to having to submit to Creek laws, especially those regarding blacks. General Arbuckle told the Indians to take their complaints to Superintendent Drennen.[21]

Duval later reported that Wild Cat tried to delay the appointment of the delegates to Florida. Duval thought he probably wanted a large sum of money, which was "true to his character," because he wanted "to rule and make himself felt." The subagent believed Wild Cat to be motivated more by his own ambition than by hostility to the government. Duval, who also thought Wild Cat's opposition resulted from Arbuckle's efforts to discredit the subagent, was determined to crush Wild Cat's resistance. He learned later that Wild Cat's group had attempted to send a "talk" to the Florida Seminoles to delay their acceptance of removal. This would have given Wild Cat an opportunity to make money on a "treaty" and to gain control over his people. Wild Cat was accused of wanting the Florida Indians to send for him and others in the spring of 1850 so that they and the Florida chiefs could make a treaty for land south of the Rio Grande. Settlement in that new country was expected to free them from Creek or U.S. control and possibly enable them to influence some prairie tribes.[22]

After a few weeks' delay, Duval informed Commissioner Brown that the Seminoles were to meet him on 16 October 1849, when they would leave the North Fork of the Canadian to take a steamboat at Fort Smith. Creek agent Philip Raiford was to supervise Seminole activities during Duval's absence. Duval and the group waited on the North Fork for Halleck Tustenuggee to join them. The subagent made Tustenuggee head of the group because he wanted his people united and because Duval had great respect for Tustenuggee's honesty and integrity.

Halleck Tustenuggee had changed his attitude after he arrived in the West. This six foot tall Mikasuki Indian, with a smooth delicate face and genteel manners, had been considered one of the most fierce and bloody of the Florida Indians. He had killed his own sister when she favored surrendering to the United States. Tustenuggee evidently liked power. At the close of the Second Seminole War, he claimed to control all the Indians in Florida. When he and his band of forty warriors and eighty women went west in July 1843, he said, "I have been hunted like a wolf, and now I am sent away like a dog." Nonetheless, upon leaving the peninsula, he told the commander of the United States forces in Florida, General William Jenkins Worth, "I have given you my hand, and now my heart, in friendship, and what I have said shall be done." Duval thought this Indian would be more effective than any other western Seminole in promoting removal of the Florida Indians as several of his Mikasuki brethren were among those remaining in Florida.[23]

The subagent was pleased with the eleven delegates. Besides Halleck Tustenuggee, they included: Holata Micco, Tustenac Chopco, Noke Sucker, Cho-Co-Tustenuecoochee, A-Hallec-Harjo, all Mikasukis; Tar-Co-Se-Fixico, Cot-Chu-Chee, Cot-Char Fixico, Tallahassees; Hotulke Harjo and Albuttachee, Hitch-ity Alachuas, and the two interpreters, Jim Factor and Joe Riley.

Their journey to Florida was uneventful. After traveling via Fort Smith on the steamer *St. Francis,* they arrived at Van Buren, Arkansas, on 26 October. They were in New Orleans by 3 November and left there three days later on the propeller driven *Ashland.* After arriving at Fort Brooke, Florida, on the tenth, the delegates hunted deer and collected roots before they went to talk to their Florida brothers.[24]

Getting a group of Florida Indians to emigrate took considerable effort and created controversy. Duval accused the commander of the United

States forces in Florida, General David E. Twiggs, of trying to control the Seminole delegation. By January 1850, Duval had received no instructions from the Indian Office. Consequently, General Twiggs took the primary role in persuading the Indians to emigrate.

The government provided a sum of $100,000 in gold for Indian removal, so General Twiggs was able to make a generous offer to the Indians. He included transportation to the West, subsistence while en route and for twelve months thereafter, blankets and dresses for the women, and compensation for abandoned livestock. He was also willing to give different amounts of money to each Indian who agreed to relocate. In spite of the offers of Twiggs and the efforts of the western Seminoles who visited the various chiefs, only ninety-six Indians agreed to move to the West. Others hesitated because of the Seminole-Creek controversy in the West and because of the simple desire to stay where they were. In the end, however, no more than an estimated 250 to 260 Indians remained in Florida after the group of ninety-six departed.

Those who agreed to remove included men, women, and children under Chiefs Kapiktsootsee and Cacha Fixico. They left New Orleans on 19 March 1850, westward bound on the steamboat *Cotton Plant* and under the supervision of Brevet Major R. S. Garnett. The western delegation returned with them. According to War Department instructions, the Indians were transported as ordinary deck passengers on a clean boat with an assistant surgeon in charge of their health care. They received provisions from the commissary in addition to items bought on the fresh market. For protection, the Indians put their large amounts of money in the ship's safe.

When this party reached Fort Smith on 31 March, the majority chose to travel overland to the Seminole district rather than by river boat via Fort Gibson. Overland transportation was scarce, but an army officer secured six of the ten or twelve wagons at Fort Gibson to haul the Indians' baggage. The Seminoles left Fort Smith on 2 April and made a journey of 120 miles to Seminole country. By the tenth, most of the group had reached a trading house some twenty miles from the Seminole agency. There they deposited the baggage. Under the circumstances, Garnett thought they stood the trip well.

According to Garnett's original instructions, if the Seminole subagency had made no provisions for the new arrivals, he was to make arrangements for rations for two months. Each daily allowance was to consist of one and a half pints of corn and a pound of beef. A gallon of salt went with every one hundred rations. Garnett, who took flour from Fort Smith and bought meat along the way, attempted to supply the rations until the Indians reached their destination. He learned that neither the Seminole subagency nor the Western Superintendency had instructions regarding provisions for the emigrants after their arrival. When the superintendent felt unauthorized to feed the group, Garnett acted according to previous instructions. He contracted with Charles Johnson of Fort Smith to supply Chief Kapiktsootsee and the other Seminoles their rations for two months. Garnett left for New Orleans on 13 April, where he made his report to Major W. W. Mackall at Tampa Bay on the twenty-second.[25]

When Duval returned from Florida to his subagency in April 1850, he found that the situation regarding the blacks had become worse. Wild Cat and Gopher John had left for Mexico with a group of Indians and blacks. Duval immediately blamed the departure of Wild Cat's party on Arbuckle's failure to disarm the blacks; he accused the general of "aiding and abetting" Wild Cat. Moreover, Duval declared that Arbuckle had encouraged Gopher John to take the free blacks to Mexico where he could become a "great man."

The principal chief of the Creeks, Roly McIntosh, claimed that the blacks had so violated Creek laws that some action was imperative. In July, armed Creeks, Cherokees, and whites went near Wewoka to capture some blacks. When the Seminoles learned they planned to attack the black town, they decided to defend it. Subsequently, Brevet Captain Frederick T. Dent of the Third Infantry warned Duval and the Creeks that if a Seminole-Creek war ensued, United States forces would intervene. After some Creeks moved to the north side of the North Fork of the Canadian River, five of them held a council with the Seminole chiefs and Duval. The Seminoles, probably fearing retaliation by the United States forces, agreed to help the Creeks take the blacks. A combined force seized about 181 blacks and delivered them to the Creeks six miles from the black town. Gabriel Duval took several, claiming them as attorney fees for his deceased brother. Meanwhile, another 180 blacks defied their pursuers and fled to Texas.[26]

Consequently, after five years of Duval's supervision, the Seminoles and their blacks had undergone one of their most tumultuous periods in the West. Unhappy with their location, the government's allocations, and their relationship with the Creeks, the Indians also had lost their close relationship with the blacks. As the Seminoles entered the 1850s, they faced two more years of Duval's supervision. Several Seminoles with some blacks had gone to Mexico in search of the freedom they had enjoyed in Florida, and those in Indian Territory strove to maintain their tribal independence.

5 *Give Us Liberty*

In October 1849, less than two years after the Mexican War and as the slavery issue sizzled in the United States, Wild Cat led his followers out of Indian Territory and started toward Mexico. He was seeking a pleasant land without Creek denomination and with freedom for blacks, as well as one in which he might exercise his leadership. His efforts kept a portion of his tribe and some blacks in that country for about a decade. During those years, both the Indian and black men served in the Mexican army in order to maintain possession of their land. In the end, Mexico failed to meet the Indians' expectations. By 1858 they began a return to Indian Territory that was completed in 1861, although some blacks chose to remain in Mexico.

Wild Cat, the most colorful Seminole in the West, had leadership skills to serve his people in a different land. He was the son of King Philip Emathla, probably a Mikasuki and once chief of the St. John's River Seminoles in Florida. Wild Cat's mother was an Alachua and sister of the long-time head chief, Micanopy, to whom Wild Cat served as advisor. When William Tecumseh Sherman met Wild Cat in 1841 during the Second Seminole War, he found him to be energetic and intelligent. Sherman described him as about thirty, five feet eight inches in height, beautifully formed, very pleasant, and proud. General Thomas Jesup called him the most talented Seminole. Wild Cat had fought against removal until the fall of 1841 when he went west with about two hundred others. In the West, he had also fought for separation from the Creeks.

This Seminole leader had great ambitions for himself and his people. He had fully expected to become head chief of his tribe and perhaps of a confederacy of Indians in Indian Territory. At different times in the 1840s, Wild Cat and Alligator and small bands of Seminoles and Kickapoos had visited several bands of Indians in the Texas agency headed by Robert S. Neighbors. They offered those Indians gifts and tried to persuade them to emigrate to Creek country where Wild Cat probably hoped to establish control over them as chief. Neighbors obtained this information from Comanche Chief Mopochocopie who was unaware of Wild Cat's real objectives. In December 1845, Wild Cat had accompanied Cherokee Agent Pierce Butler and M. G. Lewis on a peace mission to the Comanches, and later with Halleck Tustenuggee, Octiarche, and other Seminoles made a six-week trip to the Southwest.

In 1849, Subagent Duval had learned that Wild Cat hoped to move to lands south of the Rio Grande. Some Seminoles had had an interest in Mexico for several years. A few reportedly fled there in the 1820s after the United States took possession of Florida. After the Seminoles and others arrived in the West, Mexican agents made frequent contacts with the tribes. They wanted these Indians to serve as a "counterweight" to the Americans and "untamed" Plains tribes. A Mexican emissary visited the Creeks in the summer of 1843, and rumors spread among the Seminoles indicating that the Mexicans offered land to those who would attack the Texans. Consequently, Wild Cat's idea of establishing a confederacy in Mexico was not an illogical one.

Shortly after Wild Cat failed to become head chief at Micanopy's death in late 1848 or early 1849, he decided that he could no longer live in the United States. Several Seminoles and blacks supported him because they were "tired" of being among the Creeks. Moreover, Wild Cat wanted his plans for settlement in Mexico presented to the president of the United States because he believed Billy Bowlegs and the remaining Florida Seminoles would go peacefully to land on the Rio Grande but would refuse to emigrate to Indian Territory.[1]

Coacoochee, or Wild Cat. Wild Cat was one of the most remarkable Indian leaders of the nineteenth century. He fought against removal from Florida but was shipped west in 1841. Never satisfied in Indian Territory, he resisted settling among the Creeks. Finally he led a group of Indians and blacks to Mexico, where he and others served in the Mexican army. Colonel Wild Cat died of smallpox there in 1857. Courtesy, Florida State Archives.

Before departing for Mexico, Wild Cat talked with several tribes and aroused their concern about the future plans of the United States for the Indians. According to the *Fort Smith Herald,* the Seminole leader claimed that within three years the United States intended to put the Indians in a country lacking sufficient timber and where water would be rationed. The chiefs would receive a quart a day, the women and children a pint, and others various amounts according to "rank and station." Wild Cat indicated that other chiefs were aware of these plans and hated him because they knew he intended to reveal them to the Seminoles. He refused to live in the United States under such conditions and stated his intention to go to Mexico. The Seminole leader welcomed those who wished to accompany him, hinting that those who remained could not go later.[2]

Other factors undoubtedly influenced Wild Cat to leave the United States. Jim Jumper had become the new head chief of the Seminoles. He was probably the son of the important Chief Jumper, who died en route to the West in 1838. This young Indian owned no slaves and was classified as "pro-Creek and pro-kidnapper." He was soon accused of cooperating with the subagent Marcellus Duval in taking control of the blacks. The chief promised about one-third of the blacks to the Duvals as compensation for having them returned to Indian control in 1849. Later, Jumper and the subagent supposedly were responsible for taking several slaves to Arkansas, where the Duval brothers had a farm.

Moreover, Creeks and whites continued to attack, capture, and sell some blacks, which kept their quasi-free status in continuous jeopardy. Many of the blacks, born free, believed that only death or slavery remained as alternatives in the United States, because the slavery issue was becoming more volatile in the territory. A country such as Mexico became more attractive, especially when the appeals of the blacks went unanswered by Presidents Polk and Taylor.

Consequently, Wild Cat and the black leader Gopher John combined forces and led from twenty-five to forty-five Indians, thirty blacks (including two outstanding freedmen, Abraham and Louis Pacheco), and a few Creek and Cherokee slaves to Mexico. Those slaves connected with influential Seminole families, and the half-breeds, felt relatively safe to remain in the Indian Territory.[3]

Wild Cat had a formidable counterpart in Gopher John. The two, who were about the same age, had known each other in Florida; both liked whiskey, and both had escaped from a prison in St. Augustine in November 1837 during the Second Seminole War. Gopher John, of Negro, Indian, and Spanish ancestry, was an important chief of the blacks and representative of Micanopy and Alligator in that war. After he surrendered, he acted as an interpreter and guide for the United States army and also assisted in getting several chiefs to cease hostilities against the United States. Because he had surrendered, he claimed his freedom on the basis of the promises made by General Jesup. About a year after he emigrated in 1842, the Seminole council freed him and gave him the proper emancipation papers.

Gopher John became one of the foremost blacks among the Seminoles in the West. Described as intelligent, brave, and a father to his people, this tall "ginger-colored" man associated with that faction of the tribe most hostile to the Creeks. Concerned about the welfare of his people, in 1844 he had reported on their dismal condition to the commander at Fort Gibson. The blacks had endured harassment by Seminoles, Creeks, and whites, including the sale of several free Seminole blacks. Although some blacks sought protection at Fort Gibson, where he was influential as an interpreter, by 1847 Gopher John had concluded that the blacks could no longer live securely in the Indian Territory. Although the Seminole council had earlier freed him, to erase all doubts about his status, he bought his freedom from Wild Cat. After the Seminoles regained ownership of the blacks in 1849, Gopher John and several other blacks were willing to go anywhere they could to live safely. Therefore, this unusual black leader joined the remarkable Indian leader Wild Cat in hopes of finding such a place.[4]

One night in October 1849, when their scouts reported no slave hunters in the area, these discontented Indians and blacks took their blankets, cooking utensils, and agricultural implements and started southwestward toward Mexico. The women, children, and ponies transported their possessions; the warriors, ready for combat, carried only weapons and ammunition. Several other blacks who attempted to join Wild Cat's group were overpowered at Fort Arbuckle and returned to the Seminole district. A few of them either escaped or were killed. Wild Cat's group successfully defeated those Creeks who pursued them in an effort to capture the slaves to sell to whites. According to secondary sources, the Creek war party came upon the emigrants the third day after their departure. The Seminoles and the blacks fought bravely, and the Creeks fled, "leaving their dead upon the field."[5]

The Indian and black migrants led by Wild Cat and Gopher John spent several months in Texas as they made their way to Mexico. They camped on land between the Brazos and Colorado rivers, where they planted corn and made contact with various other Indian tribes.

The Texans disliked providing homes for sojourning Indians. Tribes from the eastern and southern areas of the United States had moved into the state in large numbers in the early nineteenth century. Small groups of Seminoles, Kickapoos, and Coushattas "came to or through Texas, running like frightened game before the devastating fire of the American frontier." Those not settling in Texas usually went to Mexico. The Seminoles as well as the Creeks, Osages, Cherokees, Delawares, Shawnees, Toways, Kickapoos, and others were considered troublemakers by officials of the Indian Bureau. With the Texas Indian population reaching twenty thousand or more by some estimates, the agents found themselves constantly occupied with both permanent residents and those considered intruders. They tried to shorten the visits of the latter because they caused so much unrest among the settlers.[6]

Nonetheless, the agents found Wild Cat's ambitions interesting, and they enjoyed talking to and about this extraordinary Seminole leader. In May 1850, Special Indian Agent John Rollins met Wild Cat on the Llano River, where he headed about 250 Seminoles and Kickapoos. Wild Cat, who carried a hunting pass given him by Duval, told Rollins he had left Florida because the United States assured him a satisfactory country west of the Mississippi. Instead, he found himself among Creeks without any authority to manage his own affairs. When his complaints went unanswered, he decided to seek a more pleasant and permanent home in Mexico. He planned to offer his services to that country in return for a land grant and indicated that he intended to return to Indian Territory for other Seminoles if he succeeded.[7]

Wild Cat had made contact with several hundred Indians of different tribes by July 1850. He camped with about seven or eight hundred Seminoles, Lipans, Wacos, and Tonkawas on the Llano in West Texas. This "barbarous combination" was accused of planning to attack the Comanches, and fears arose that whites also would be killed. Some settlers feared that Wild Cat might visit Arkansas in a "hostile manner." According to the *Fort Smith Herald,* the commander there had "no man to serve even as an express rider." The *New York Journal of Commerce* reported in July 1850 that Wild Cat's group had committed some murders.

Wild Cat spent considerable time that summer attempting to assemble as large a military colony as possible.[8] He contacted Comanches, Caddoes, Wacos, and Kickapoos about joining him in Mexico. Several of the tribes were informed that he had plans to make war on Texans, to combine the Indian tribes, and to punish those who failed to support him. The Caddoes, frightened by such news, divided into small groups and moved down the Brazos River until Wild Cat returned to Mexico. On the other hand, some Kickapoos, who had left their land west of the Missouri and were living in western Creek territory near Fort Arbuckle, agreed to join Wild Cat. About two hundred young warriors accepted his offers of pay from Mexico and his promises of money and booty from the Comanches. But by the fall of 1851, these Kickapoos were persuaded by their chiefs to return to Indian Territory.[9]

Wild Cat encountered opposition when he returned to Indian Territory with two or three Seminoles on 23 September 1850 to attempt to persuade other Seminoles to go to Mexico. Subagent Duval had recommended military action against Wild Cat and the arrest of the blacks when he first learned that they had gone to Mexico. Now Duval tried to discredit Wild Cat's efforts. He thought Wild Cat's settlement south of the Rio Grande violated the Treaty of Guadalupe Hidalgo, and he accused the Seminoles of trying to cause unrest among the Lower Creeks. Wild Cat heard rumors that the Creek chief had ordered the Indian police to arrest him. An estimated six hundred Creeks went from Tuckabachee town to the Seminole district to seize Wild Cat, but he was able to escape. Although he had arrived in the territory in an inebriated condition that lasted a week, he was able to persuade a few Seminoles and blacks to join him.[10]

Duval meanwhile asked Governor P. Hansborough Bell of Texas to capture and sell the Seminole slaves who had left with Wild Cat. By October 1850, the subagent told Bell that he had dispatched George Aird, a trader, to San Antonio with a list of blacks, mostly women and children, he wanted to reclaim. Duval added that the Texas Rangers might be interested in capturing some slaves, for whom they would be well paid. He asked that the governor so inform the commanders of the military posts on the Texas frontier and at Presidio de Rio Grande. The subagent needed information about the blacks immediately after their arrest in order to obtain the Indians' permission to sell them rather than to have them returned to Indian Territory. Duval himself claimed eighteen or twenty blacks, including twelve who were with Wild Cat's family on the U.S. side of the Rio Grande, possibly near Presidio. These runaways, according to Duval, had been the property of his deceased brother. He offered to pay fifty dollars each for those delivered and confined at San Antonio.[11]

Bell reacted positively to Duval's request. By November, the governor had written Brevet Major General George M. Brooke, commander of the Eighth Military Department at San Antonio, that Duval had informed him of the "movements and machinations of the adroit warrior and arch intriguer Wild Cat." Bell feared that the Seminoles might strike the frontier of Texas. He stood ready to send a competent force into Mexico to recapture the runaways living with the Seminoles. He claimed that several citizens of the United States had asked the Mexican government to aid in seizing the slaves. In corresponding with Duval, Bell declared that General Brooke would employ all means in his command to check the movements of Wild Cat and to recover the blacks. The governor knew that settlers in Austin had a deep interest in regaining lost property and, with proper management, thought Wild Cat's objectives could be defeated.[12]

The problems that Mexicans had on their northern frontier made it an opportune time for Wild Cat to ask them for permission to settle in their country. Even prior to the Mexican War, the Mexicans had lost much property and many lives in Indian raids. Mountain tribes such as the Apaches, Navajos, and Utes, as well as Plains tribes such as the Comanches and Kiowas, had disturbed the agricultural, mineral, and ranching enterprises of large numbers of Mexicans. In the fall of 1845, the south Plains tribes had had the settlers in Coahuila, Durango, and Zacatecas "more alarmed than the nation's international crisis." They had robbed the country of horses and mules needed for transporting troops and drawing the supply trains. These Indians and the Apaches had burned thousands of bushels of grain in northern Mexico. With the other destruction, this almost brought economic ruin to the settlers.[13]

After the Mexican War, Mexicans still had serious problems with the wild Indians. In March 1850, Mexican minister Luis De La Rosa sent a note to United States Secretary of State John M. Clayton asking that the depredators be controlled in accordance with Article Eleven of the Treaty of Guadalupe Hidalgo, which stipulated that the United States agreed to "restrain all incursions of Indians from our territories into Mexico, for whatever purpose the same may be made, and when such incursions cannot be prevented, to punish and exact indemnity therefor[e], with the same diligence and energy as if they were meditated or committed within our territory and against our own people."

The Mexicans wanted a military force stationed along the border to repress the wild Indians who hindered the "progress and amity" between the border peoples. Clayton agreed that his nation should quell the hostile incursions against Mexicans by the Indians in the territory ceded recently by Mexico to the United States.[14] In December 1850, the Mexicans again raised the issue with the United States. Minister De La Rosa informed the new secretary of state, Daniel Webster, that Mexico wanted the United States to take prompt and active measures to curb the Indian incursions.[15]

Meanwhile, the Mexicans had instituted their own measures for defending the border of Coahuila by establishing military colonies there. Consequently, when Wild Cat's assemblage asked Colonel Juan Manuel Maldonado in July 1850 for land, oxen, plows, flocks, and herds, he promptly complied with the request.[16] That fall the Seminoles and Mexicans formalized their relationship. The Seminole group agreed to obey

Mexican laws, to aid in fighting barbarous Indians residing north of the Rio Grande, and to maintain peace with friendly tribes. On 26 July 1851, the Indians and blacks received a land grant at the headwaters of the San Antonio and San Rodrigo rivers in Coahuila.

The Seminoles' service pleased the Mexicans. Wild Cat and sixty warriors, one-third of whom were black, helped defeat the revolutionist José Marian Carbajal, a leader of smugglers who planned to establish an independent Rio Grande republic. From the beginning, Seminole-Mexican relations appeared amicable as the Indians and blacks conducted additional successful operations. They went with Mexican troops on desert expeditions, searched for wild tribes, and assisted citizens and troops in repulsing invaders. Wild Cat received the rank of colonel. His men were given the same pay as Mexican soldiers, and their families accepted money or beef during the men's absence. Land, booty, and unbranded animals were also rewards for service.[17]

The Indian depredations continued despite the efforts of military colonists in Mexico. Between 1849 and 1853, the Comanches and Apaches stole or destroyed much property in Coahuila and killed, wounded, or captured 375 people. The Mexican militia and military colonies were ineffective because of limited funds and the sparse population. Epidemics of cholera and fever were other problems.[18] The Mexican authorities still praised the faithful Seminoles and considered them valuable as soldiers, workers, and hunters.

But Wild Cat's colony was also a liability on the border in the early 1850s. Because the Treaty of Guadalupe Hidalgo had been in effect only a few years, a cunning chief with a strong Seminole settlement that included blacks from the United States appeared potentially dangerous. Therefore, the Mexicans provided the Indians and blacks with a different land grant, and they moved to Musquiz, a new rich land in the Santa Rosa Mountains, just northwest of Santa Rosa. It was a strategic point often visited by wild Indians. In July 1852, Wild Cat and his party received other grants in Durango and Nacimiento.[19]

Even in the different location, the activities of the Seminoles added to the tension along the Mexican-Texas frontier. Texans accused the United States government of failing to defend the border and claimed that President Santa Anna's Mexican government harbored Indians, including the Seminoles and Lipans, who raided the frontier settlements.[20]

The Texans continued to have problems with various other Indian tribes as well.[21] By May 1853, Acting Commissioner of Indian Affairs Charles E. Mix informed Superintendent Thomas S. Drew at Van Buren, Arkansas, that Texas Special Indian Agent Horace Capron had charge of a group of from three to four hundred intruding Indians, including Seminoles, Delawares, Shawnees, Quapaws, and Cherokees, recently dispatched from Texas. These Indians had settled in Texas over a period of several years. Drew was instructed to have the agents in his superintendency accept the Indians turned over by Capron to their respective agencies. They were not to return to Texas. Mix, however, had no power to provide for their subsistence on their arrival at the agencies. He did inform Special Agent Neighbors at San Antonio that an act in July 1852 appropriated twenty-five thousand dollars "for the purchase of presents and to negotiate, under instructions from the Secretary of the Interior, with the Indians in Texas who have intruded themselves into that State from the territories of the United States for their removal from that State."[22]

Wild Cat's Seminole group located just across the border in Mexico still worried the Texans. Second Lieutenant T. B. Holabird of the First Infantry reported in the summer of 1854 that the size of Wild Cat's band had been overestimated and the group's intentions misrepresented. He believed the Lipans were the culprits who were committing the depredations. That fall another army officer reported that there were 318 people, including the Indians and from fifty to sixty blacks, in the military colony near Santa Rosa, about one hundred miles from Fort Duncan, Texas. Of the 183 warriors in the group, eighty-two had enlisted in the Mexican army. Wild Cat commanded the Indian company, and Gopher John commanded the blacks. Both Indians and blacks enjoyed equal privileges and full rights as Mexican citizens. The women and children cultivated the land near Santa Rosa, where the Indians and blacks had cabins, gardens, horses, cattle, and mules.

These Indian and black soldiers obeyed military orders of a Colonel Castanedo, inspector general of the neighboring colonies. One of their duties was to guard the crossings of the Rio Grande near Fort Duncan to prevent the entry of parties that included American slave owners who intended to aid Mexican revolutionists. They were also to fight any faction opposing Santa Anna.

In February 1854, Wild Cat's band, together with others, was accused of stealing a herd of animals from settlers near Eagle Pass, Texas. One citizen followed them to San Fernando, about thirty miles from Fort Duncan, where he reported their thievery to the alcalde. Subsequently, Wild Cat explained that General Cordona was his partner in these activities, and he claimed that he could produce the agreement made between them. Therefore, he refused to relinquish the animals. This convinced the Americans that the Mexican civil and military authorities condoned the Indians' depredations.

James E. Gardner, who had lived in San Fernando, claimed that Wild Cat often came into town boasting of his "capacity to steal from the Americans." The Seminole leader claimed to be "licensed by the government of Mexico to steal from the American side of the river." When one owner attempted to retrieve thirty animals that Wild Cat had taken, Mexican authorities intervened to block him. Again in March 1854, the Indians crossed the Rio Grande, stole several animals, and returned to San Fernando. They bragged about their success to the civil and military officials and asserted that General Cordona of Coahuila approved of their actions.[23]

By 1855, raids by the Seminoles and other tribes such as the Lipans, Comanches, and Mescalero Apaches greatly affected the settlers on the Texas border. In September, William E. Jones wrote Texas Governor Elisha M. Pease that several settlers had left the southern frontier of Texas where he lived because the Indians attacked isolated families and stole their horses.[24]

The border settlers also had problems with runaway black slaves. By the 1850s, from three to four thousand fugitive slaves valued at more than $3.2 million had located in northern Mexico. The Seminole black colony included runaways from Texas, some of whom were well-educated mulattoes. The number of runaways increased after Wild Cat's group assumed its responsibility for protecting the frontier. These blacks were generally safe because Mexico refused to extradite slaves.[25]

In 1855, Texas citizens attempted to regain these fugitives. The Mexican frontier commander suggested exchanging slaves for peons, but Captain J. H. Callahan, who reportedly owned some of the Seminole blacks, wanted to recapture them. Callahan led three companies of Texans toward Mexico. With about 130 men, he reached Encino on the Leona River on 25 September. The force then moved toward Wild Cat's headquarters at San Fernando de Rosas, about forty miles from the Rio Grande. After a Mexican and Indian force almost surrounded his men, Callahan retreated to Piedras Negras, burned the village, and returned to Texas. Only the appearance of the federal forces from Fort Duncan spared Callahan's group from further Mexican attacks. Defeated in their first effort, the Texans planned other expeditions, but these failed to materialize. Nonetheless, the tension between Texans and Mexicans continued on both sides of the border.[26]

After learning of Callahan's actions, General Persifor Smith, the commander of the Department of Texas at San Antonio, took steps to prevent further excursions into Mexico. Smith heard that the burning of Piedras Negras and the "designs" on the Seminole settlement had the Indians and Mexicans aroused. Moreover, the general believed that Callahan's endeavors did not constitute "hot pursuit of a party of Indians with their plunder." Adding that the frontier settlers would suffer from Callahan's campaign, Smith anticipated "an inroad from the Seminoles to murder and scalp—not merely to steal." He was directed by authorities in Washington to prevent infractions of the law in compliance with the neutrality act of 1818. He asked Governor Pease to help suppress such actions in the future.[27]

When the Mexicans complained about Callahan's expedition, James Gadsden, United States Minister to Mexico, responded with a list of eight grievances that the United States had against their nation. One complaint concerned the enlistment of Lipans into Mexican service as well as the invitation to a "lawless band of Seminole Indians from Florida, whose chief, Wild Cat, had cooperated in the war of extermination, 'exempting in its conflagrations and murderings neither property nor the weakness of sex or infancy.'"[28]

Wild Cat apparently made several visits to Indian Territory while he lived in Mexico. On one occasion a few years after his departure, he returned with his six-month old son. Wild Cat asked the Presbyterian missionary Mary Ann Lilley to make a cloak for his baby. She complied and sewed one of plaid lindsey, which she lined in yellow flannel and trimmed with fringe. Wild Cat then returned to Mexico with his son.

Even in Mexico, discord struck Wild Cat's colony when the Indian chief Coyote (Yah-hah Fixico) and his followers as well as some blacks rejected Wild Cat's leadership. Coyote may have been from the Mikasuki, Tallahassee, or Creek branch of Seminoles. The governor of Nuevo León y Coahuila had to order the blacks and Indians to obey their Seminole leader. Still, this Seminole, who migrated to Mexico searching for land, liberty, and tranquillity for his people, had found a temporary abode in return for his group's active service against the wild Indians. The Mexican authorities considered him a daring and successful commander.

In 1857, death came to Wild Cat after he and his band returned from a scouting expedition. They camped at Alto near Musquiz, where a smallpox epidemic left fifty-three Seminoles dead. Wild Cat, in poor health that was aggravated by his excessive use of alcohol, died from the disease that killed twenty-eight women and twenty-five men. They were buried at Alto, but the Mexicans reportedly later moved the bodies. Years later one elderly Seminole black lady remembered that everyone cried when they lost Wild Cat; "he was so good," she declared.

Wild Cat's death had a great effect on the remaining Seminoles in Mexico. Although Lion succeeded Wild Cat as head chief, and others such as Nokosimala, Tiger, Juan Flores, Susano, Felipe, and Manual Flores (probably baptized Catholics) were capable leaders, the band began a gradual migration back to Indian Territory between 1858 and 1861. This return movement, prompted in part by the treaty of 1856, which gave the Seminoles complete independence from the Creeks, and in part by Wild Cat's death, gained impetus after two Seminole chiefs from Mexico visited the Seminoles in Indian Territory. They returned to persuade their people to reunite with their kinsmen.

Although the Mexican authorities regretted losing the services of the Indians and encouraged them to stay in their country, only sixty remained by 26 February 1859. Two Americans living at Santa Rosa had also

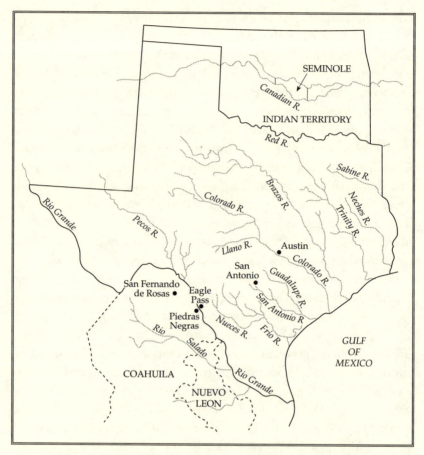

Map 4. *Indian Territory, Texas, and northern Mexico.*

worked to bring about the Seminoles' return to the United States. In March, a representative of the Seminole agent in the United States went to Villa Guerrero to persuade the Seminoles to emigrate. This effort helped lead to the removal of the remaining Seminoles two years later.[29]

Because Secretary of the Interior Jacob Thompson had authorized the return of Wild Cat's band to Indian Territory and a responsible agent was to accompany the Indians, they were allowed to pass through Texas without molestation. The Indians were permitted to take their own property, but items that belonged to the Mexicans had to be returned to the proper owners.[30] By 25 August 1861, the remaining Mexican Seminoles had gone to Texas en route to Indian Territory, where they faced more years of battles and hardships. Some blacks chose to stay south of the Rio Grande.[31]

Residence in Mexico had afforded no real peace and freedom for the Seminoles and blacks. They held their land in Mexico in return for services as a military colony. This kept the Indians embroiled constantly with wild tribes and revolutionaries. Moreover, United States officials, especially those from Texas and Indian Territory, were suspicious of the Seminoles because of the depredations from Indian raids and because of problems arising from the blacks living among them. A large number of the group died from the smallpox epidemic. Although Wild Cat had failed in his efforts to establish a confederacy of tribes in a peaceful land in Mexico, as he had earlier failed to become head chief, he had left a most remarkable legacy as an Indian leader in Florida, in Indian Territory, and in Mexico.

Those Seminoles who remained in the Western Territory while Wild Cat and his band were in Mexico also found little peace in those years. Although they continued to encounter serious problems with the Creeks as well as other tribal misfortunes, they managed to obtain complete separation from the Creeks in 1856. Neither Seminole faction, whether in the United States or in Mexico, had forfeited its stand for tribal identity.[32]

6 *Free at Last*

While a few members of the Seminole tribe lived in Mexico during most of the 1850s, those who remained in Indian Territory continued their struggle against Creek domination. By the mid-1850s, almost every official in the Indian Bureau realized that the Seminoles and Creeks had to be separated. Finally, after some twenty years in the West, the treaty of 1856 liberated the Seminoles from the Creeks and gave them their own land and tribal independence. Several factors had brought these results; the leadership of Subagent Josiah Washbourne and Seminole Chief John Jumper was one of the most important.

While the Seminoles lived in their separate district on Creek land and under Creek law, they made virtually no progress. They were described as idle, dissipated, suffering from alcoholism, and actually decreasing in number. Their relations with other tribes and whites seemed satisfactory, but their suspicion and jealousy of the Creeks remained. This distrust of the Creeks and opposition to their control had prompted the Seminoles to separate from their Creek brothers decades earlier in the East. Moreover, the Creeks had aided the United States in most of its campaigns against the Seminoles in Florida. The Seminoles also considered General Thomas Jesup's operations in the Second Seminole War, in which he had used Creek warriors, as a direct effort by the Creeks to subordinate the

Seminoles and destroy them as a nation. The Seminoles, understandably enough, found it difficult to forgive and forget the Creeks' actions

To avoid the Creeks' complete control, the Seminoles knew they must retain their own subagent. On 20 August 1851, Colonel John Drennen, superintendent of the Western Territory, sent the commissioner of the Bureau of Indian Affairs, Luke Lea, a letter from the Seminoles addressed to President Millard Fillmore. The Seminoles reported that they had heard rumors that their subagent was to be relieved, and they were afraid of having no official to represent them before the government and other tribes. They begged the "Great Father" to continue their rights as a nation and expressed opposition to being at the mercy of any tribe with different interests. The Seminoles could be neighbors of the Creeks but were unwilling to be their subjects.[1]

Because the Florida Indians had the whites aroused again, the western Seminoles saw an opportunity to benefit themselves. They offered to induce the Florida Indians to emigrate in return for their tribal independence. The twenty-five hundred Seminoles in the West thought that an increase in number would make them more powerful. However, without additional funds, any such emigration would make their condition worse. Because they received annually only three thousand dollars in cash and two thousand dollars in goods, the western Seminoles refused to promote removal of the Florida Indians without new appropriations.

Subagent Marcellus Duval agreed that another tribal delegation to Florida might be able to convince some Seminoles to come west. In 1851, he proposed to Commissioner Lea that the tribe receive additional annuities and separate status from the Creeks in return for sending such a delegation. Duval suggested that the emigrants receive subsistence for a year after removal, compensation for their abandoned cattle, hogs, and crops, traveling expenses, and the services of an accompanying physician. According to the subagent, the offering of such aid to those who emigrated seemed preferable to "hunting down" the Indians.[2]

Other officials in the Indian Bureau thought that the remaining Florida Seminoles should be removed as soon as possible. By February 1852, Commissioner Lea concluded that the removal had to be accomplished in some manner. No doubt the demands of Florida citizens influenced

Lea. A native of Tennessee, Lea was a resident of Mississippi when he went to Washington. The commissioner was concerned about the Seminoles and feared renewed hostilities would erupt between them and the whites. The attitude of the Florida legislature, the Florida congressional delegation, and the state's ordinary citizens strongly suggested such a possibility.[3]

The Indian Bureau hired a special agent, Luther Blake, to effect the Seminoles' removal. He took a western Seminole delegation to Florida in 1852, but it failed to get the Florida brethren to remove. Later that year, Blake took Florida Seminoles Billy Bowlegs, Nokose Emathla, Foschatchlee Emathla, and Chocote-Tustenuggee to Washington, where they met with President Fillmore, Commissioner Lea, Secretary of War Charles Conrad, and Secretary of the Navy John P. Kennedy. The Washington officials offered to provide comfortable transportation, payment for abandoned stock and property, and protection and support during removal. From Washington the Seminoles went to New York, where they received new clothes as a gift from the government. The Seminole delegation then agreed to work for complete removal of its tribe. President Fillmore announced that one of his objectives had been the removal of the remnant of Indians from Florida—long a "cherished object" of the government, and he now expected the Seminoles to relocate because of the promises made to and by the Bowlegs delegation.

But in early January 1853, Commissioner Lea informed Secretary of the Interior Alexander H. H. Stuart that the Florida Indians had changed their minds and now refused to leave the peninsula. This issue had, no doubt, divided the Seminoles. Rumors indicated in late 1852 that they had considered deposing Billy Bowlegs in favor of his sister, wife of Chief Assinwah (or Assunwha). Agent Blake concluded that force would be necessary and proposed that three hundred Creeks "under their own officers" be employed to search the swamps and capture the rebels. Lea reported that Floridians wanted volunteers to effect removal, but he thought such action would require an act of Congress. Lea also thought the Indians' land should be surveyed by workers under military escorts and that forces should capture the Indians and destroy their property and supplies. An agent at Fort Myers could receive and ship west those who either were captured or surrendered.[4]

President Fillmore, like his predecessors, had failed to formulate a successful policy regarding removal of the Seminoles. In January he informed Congress that two alternatives existed regarding the Florida Indians. They could be removed by force or they could abide by an agreement concluded in 1842 by which the Indians were allowed to remain temporarily in the southwestern part of the peninsula. According to this agreement made by Colonel William Jenkins Worth, no whites were allowed to settle in the area set aside for the Indians. In 1845, a neutral strip twenty miles wide was established around this district to prevent encroachment. But the Indians there still caused unrest among the whites, who in 1853 were demanding that the Indians be moved. Therefore, President Fillmore concluded that the Indians would be safer in the West than in southwestern Florida.[5]

As Lea expected, whites in Florida stepped up their efforts to bring about the removal of the Seminoles. The Florida General Assembly passed an act over the governor's veto to raise two regiments of troops and named a brigadier general to command the force. Governor Thomas Brown vetoed the bill because he thought the assembly had no constitutional authority to name a brigadier general for troops under militia regulations. Moreover, if the troops were to be a regular force, they violated the United States Constitution, which forbade states to raise armies in peacetime. The governor thus had no intention of organizing the troops. Brown, nonetheless, considered the Indians a deterrent to the prosperity of his state and wanted them removed.[6] Still, the removal of the Indians remained the responsibility of the federal government. Yet the Bowlegs band and others refused to leave Florida until the late 1850s.

While federal officials continued to deal unsuccessfully with the removal crisis in Florida, the western Seminoles worried about the consequences of their unproductive trip to Florida. They maintained their desire to gain their tribal independence from the Creeks; they wanted nothing to interfere with that goal. Accordingly, in mid-1853, the western Seminoles wrote the new president, Franklin Pierce, and asked that he make them a separate nation. At removal, the "Great Father," through his officers, had informed them that things would "be right" in the West. Yet disadvantages enveloped them. They insisted that they be allowed to remain a tribe separate from the Creeks, regardless of their recent failure to get other Florida Seminoles to migrate west. The western Seminoles pledged to continue their efforts to encourage the peninsula Indians to emigrate.[7]

But avoiding a complete merger with such a powerful tribe as the Creeks remained an arduous task. The Creeks numbered about twenty-five thousand, and some of them, unlike the Seminoles, were long-time allies of the United States. The Creeks had made remarkable progress toward white civilization and achieved considerable influence with the hostile prairie tribes of the West and Southwest. The Creek agent, Philip Raiford, cautioned that efforts should continue to retain their friendship.

Fortunately, Raiford favored giving the Seminoles a country of their own, where they could be independent of other tribes. He claimed that the situation between the tribes was an unnatural one and unsatisfactory to both. Except in pecuniary affairs, the Seminoles fell under the Creeks' jurisdiction. According to Raiford, this embarrassed the Seminoles and would inevitably lead to further difficulties. The tribe needed its own land, and the agent believed the Creeks would surrender a portion of their allotment for a "reasonable consideration."[8]

In the midst of all this concern over securing an independent status, the western Seminoles also found themselves experiencing a change of subagents. Marcellus Duval, subagent since July 1845, was discharged in late 1852. Charged with irregularities relating to his long absences from the subagency and with mistreatment of the blacks, Duval did not receive the commissioner's official notification concerning his dismissal until 3 February 1853. During the intervening months, Duval visited Superintendent John Drennen at Van Buren in an effort to learn more of the rumors about his removal. Drennen was uncooperative and refused to discuss Duval's dismissal, because he claimed that the subagent was no longer in the Indian Bureau.

Duval learned from other sources that Major John C. Henshaw, commander at Fort Arbuckle in the Chickasaw nation, had charged that he mistreated blacks. One specific charge related to a black named Dennis. After Dennis had violated a law, Duval arrested him and placed him in irons for a week. The Seminole chiefs subsequently tried him and ordered that he be given fifty lashes. Duval then told Dennis to go home and conduct himself properly. According to Henshaw, Dennis came to him seeking protection. The black claimed that his Seminole owner, Harriet Bowlegs, had freed him and others but that Duval and Chief Jim Jumper had tried to force them to go to Arkansas, where the Duvals had a farm.

The subagent replied to Henshaw's charges. He asked that the commander appear formally to present his evidence and declared that a court in his own regiment would refuse to believe him. Furthermore, the subagent replied that Henshaw might have been less inclined to believe Dennis if Duval had helped the major, as he had requested by letter, in buying a black girl from the Seminoles. Duval further accused army officers of supporting the blacks after their release to the Indians in 1849.

Duval claimed that his long absences from the subagency were necessary. In the fall of 1852, he made a trip to Texas to recover some blacks who belonged to the Seminoles. He had the Indians' permission to sell the blacks rather than return them. Thus while he worked to recover the Seminoles' property, he was accused of neglecting the Indians. Duval also made business trips to Van Buren for the Creeks at the request of Agent Raiford and Superintendent Drennen.

Duval presented some counter-charges against various federal officials. He claimed that Secretary of War Charles M. Conrad violently opposed him after he informed the government about "the gross injustice" inflicted upon some Seminoles through the loss of their slaves. The subagent further claimed that Conrad "meddled" in his affairs, had a "taste of defamation," and violated the ninth commandment. Duval also cited the failures of Commissioner Lea. When Congress reorganized the Indian Bureau, he received no official authority to continue his duties as subagent. He proceeded to close his subagency, but Drennen asked him to remain at his post until the Indian Bureau decided the matter.

Duval thought political reasons led Drennen to recommend his dismissal. Duval had helped establish the Democratic paper, the *Fort Smith Herald,* a competitor of the *Arkansas Intelligencer.* Duval had used the *Herald* to attack a friend of Drennen's in a previous political campaign in Arkansas. Moreover, according to the subagent, Drennen could cite no specific wrongs that Duval had committed. Instead, Drennen made general charges of Duval's alleged misconduct as subagent.

Duval had no regrets or remorse about his tenure with the Seminoles. He concluded that "although I have been dismissed for neglect of duty, the Department cannot show one instance where the interests of the Government have been intentionally or willfully neglected. . . . The position which I occupy in the nation is the best refutation to the charge."[9]

Regardless of Duval's defense, some of his actions as Seminole subagent appeared questionable. The welfare of the Indians remained secondary to interests of the government. The subagent held some of the Indians in disdain. Duval once complained about having dirty, filthy Indians sitting or leaning on his bed when they came to the agency.

The slave issue was the greatest problem for Duval. During his years as subagent, the three Duval brothers, Marcellus, Gabriel, and William J., were heavily involved in several questionable activities regarding the Seminole blacks. Gabriel participated in slave raids and stayed at the subagency while Marcellus was away. At one time, the brothers claimed a third of the blacks for their services in restoring them to the Indians. The Duval brothers' interest in slaves cast a dark shadow over the years of Duval's service to the Seminoles.[10] Furthermore, after almost seven years of service, the subagent, as his predecessors, left the Seminoles in much the same state as they had been when he arrived.

The new Indian commissioner, George W. Manypenny, a lawyer and Democrat from Ohio who took office in March 1853, thought most of the Department's Indian agents in the West were incompetent. Manypenny was sincerely interested in the welfare of the Indians. He made a tour of the Indian Territory in 1853 and was sadly disappointed by the state of many of the Indians. Later that year, he declared that some agents thought they had fulfilled their duties when they paid the Indians their annuities. Others had worked to benefit the traders and speculators rather than to protect the Indians' rights. Manypenny declared, "From my observation and information deemed reliable, I am satisfied that abuses of the most glaring character have existed in the Indian country, and that a radical reform is necessary there in every department connected with the Indian service."[11]

Without doubt, the abuses of the officials had affected the Seminoles, and the removal of Duval as subagent left their subagency in disarray for several months in late 1852 and early 1853. Duval's replacement, David W. Elkins of Fort Gibson, served only a few days. He accepted the position on 15 December 1852 and resigned the next week to become chaplain at an army post in Texas. The Seminoles had no subagent until 1 June 1853, when Bryant Smithson, who was appointed on 26 April, arrived to take control.

Since the Seminoles had been without a subagent for about six months, Smithson found a multitude of problems in Seminole country. The agency buildings—three log cabins used for an office, warehouse, and dwelling—were dilapidated and unfit for occupancy. In July, the public blacksmith shop had to be closed because of insufficient funds. Smithson reported that for some unknown reason, the annuities for 1852 had failed to arrive. Moreover, the poor crops in 1853 permitted the Indians to subsist only by strict economy.

Their poverty was aggravated by the continuous trafficking in liquor. Some Seminoles, Kickapoos, Caddoes, and Creeks brought whiskey into Indian Territory from the small towns on the Red River in Texas. In previous months, a few Seminoles had also brought in a lot of whiskey from Fort Smith. They had transported it in flat boats or large canoes up the Arkansas River to the Canadian River and to North Fork Town. From there, they had distributed it overland throughout the Creek country to Seminoles and Creeks alike and had created quite a disturbance. These problems, combined with the tribe's dissatisfaction in Creek country, required the subagent's immediate attention.

Smithson, as his predecessor Duval, decried the injustice forced on the Seminoles while they remained subordinate to the Creeks. The subagent declared that the separation of the two tribes was imperative because the Seminoles needed to enforce their own laws, especially those pertaining to blacks.[12]

The number of blacks among the Seminoles had declined rapidly between 1849, when they were returned to the Seminoles' control, and 1852, when Duval was removed. The black villages disappeared as several blacks were captured or sold and others simply left the area. With no sympathy from the Seminoles and no government protection, the blacks, too few in number, were unable to protect themselves. Several still faced threats of Creeks and whites to capture them. Speculators from nearby states, including members of the Methodist and Baptist faiths, tried to persuade the Seminoles to sell the blacks. Often slave raiders stopped the blacks on the roads or in fields and took them at gunpoint. Blacks who lived among the Seminoles led a harrowing life. The Seminole black woman who cooked for Presbyterian missionaries John and Mary Ann Lilley lived in constant fear that her owners might be forced to sell her. Most of those who remained belonged to women or children with guardians assigned to them. These blacks eventually had a very close association with their masters and often lived with them.[13]

Subagent Smithson did little to ease the circumstances of the Seminoles or their blacks. He agreed that the Seminoles should have tribal independence from the Creeks in return for their assistance in removing the Florida Seminoles to the West. He also asked permission to make repairs at the agency. But he apparently lacked the administrative ability to push for concrete improvements, and he failed to send vouchers for his expenses to the Indian Bureau. These weaknesses, combined with his "drinking problem," led to his removal as subagent on 15 April 1854.

Five days later, Josiah H. Washbourne, a subagent who understood and respected the Seminoles, took charge of the subagency. The son of the Cephas Washbournes of Vermont, Washbourne had spent his early years with his missionary parents in Indian Territory. Educated in the East, he had worked as a journalist and later as editor of the *Arkansas Intelligencer* in Van Buren and the *Arkansan* in Fayetteville. In 1847, he had married Susan C. Ridge, daughter of Cherokee leader John Ridge. The thirty-five-year-old Washbourne knew the Indian Territory and its people and used his knowledge to benefit the Seminole nation.[14]

Washbourne worked to promote a separation of the Seminoles and Creeks. The Seminoles in 1854 were still much less acculturated than the other four Civilized Tribes. Although some Seminoles were described as industrious, others were classified as ignorant, lazy, and "addicted to dissipation." They thought the Creek council overshadowed the "vital interests of their feeble nation." Few in number and with scarce resources, they saw no hopes for improvement while they were dominated by the Creeks.

The Seminoles' dissatisfaction caught the attention of Thomas Drew, the new southern superintendent of Indian affairs. Drew believed that the subordination of the western Seminoles to the Creeks caused their Florida counterparts to refuse to emigrate. He also thought that most of the problems in the Southern Superintendency resulted from the government's past policy of forcing weak tribes to unite with stronger ones. Drew believed the Seminoles when they claimed to suffer privations and wrongs under the Creeks. He reported to Commissioner Manypenny that the government should adopt a new Seminole policy that would give independence to the Seminoles and make them a separate nation. They should receive, in addition to a yearly allowance, the essentials for entering a new land and establishing a new way of life. Those Seminoles remaining in Florida would then move West, according to Drew.

Washbourne and the Seminole leaders agreed with Drew's recommendations. Because the treaty of 1845 was responsible for much of the Seminole-Creek discord, Washbourne thought a new treaty should be negotiated. Most Seminole chiefs and headmen realized that they had pledged to abide by the 1845 treaty, but they considered it unjust. The Indians simply wanted separation from the Creeks and hoped that the government would hear their pleas.[15]

Although a portion of the Seminoles fought for tribal independence and separate land, some, who had been deprived of their annuities as Seminoles for several years, had quietly settled among the Creeks with the intention of merging with that tribe. Commissioner Manypenny restored their privileges after he learned of their deprivations. Other Seminoles had refused to participate in the Creek council and opposed obeying Creek laws. They had sowed the seeds of discord since 1845 and supported a movement calling for their own land with their nationality secured and increased annuities.

The Seminoles' problems had continued primarily because they lacked an influential spokesman for their tribe. Inadequate agency buildings, the threat of whiskey, limited funds for a blacksmith shop, and the lack of an efficient education system hindered the tribe's progress.[16] According to Subagent Washbourne in 1855, only John Lilley, the Presbyterian missionary, and his denomination's Home Mission Board had taken any interest in the "unfortunate and stigmatized" Seminoles. Originally from Pennsylvania, Lilley and his wife had worked among the tribe at the Oak Ridge Mission since 1848. Although the Lilleys had opened a school for the Seminoles in 1849, Wild Cat had been dismayed about their slow progress before it opened. He had told the Lilleys that they had been there for months, burned up "all the timber in the country," and still had no school. Wild Cat's impatience was understandable. Lilley declared that no one had interceded previously for these Indians or the treaty of 1845 would have included appropriations for their education. The missionary wanted his Mission Board to help secure a school fund for the tribe.[17]

In addition to supporting plans for an educational fund for the Seminoles, Lilley made trips to eastern cities to seek donations for his mission. Churches in Cincinnati and Philadelphia responded, and their funds provided necessities such as a stove, mill, and sewing machine. The little two-hundred-dollar steel mill, equipped with a belt, was especially useful because the Indian women had previously had to pound their corn and buy more flour than usual after the mission's old mill stopped working.

Getting the supplies to the mission was a greater problem at times than raising funds for them. When the Arkansas River was extremely low, Lilley stored goods at Napoleon at the river's mouth. Often the supplies arrived broken or otherwise damaged. In addition, paying the high transportation costs was a hardship.

The supplies were important to the survival of the mission. The Lilleys usually had coffee, hominy, and fried meat for breakfast, boiled meat and any available vegetables for "dinner," and sofkee, which the Indians liked "better than anything else," for "supper." But in 1855, a drought caused a poor corn harvest, and by December they had nothing preserved from their garden. The couple had bought apples and beans; someone had given them sweet potatoes. The prospects of a corn crop in 1856 were dimmed by the threat of grasshoppers, which often destroyed entire fields and forced the Indians to replant crops. Sometimes the insects would almost cover the ground in places.[18]

In addition, the Lilleys found the winters extremely harsh. During extended periods, the temperature plunged to ten degrees below zero, and rain, hail, and snow added to the misery. The inclement weather and uncomfortable circumstances caused much sickness. Several pupils suffered from a variety of illnesses from which they usually recovered slowly. Trachoma, an eye infection, was a recurring problem for the Indians and the Lilleys.[19]

Despite problems with supplies and weather, Lilley thought changes in the Seminoles demonstrated that his teaching and preaching were beneficial. Twenty to twenty-five students usually attended Lilley's school from October to April. One year, nineteen Seminoles, two Creeks, two Cherokees, and three others attended. The majority of the students learned to read, write, and solve simple problems in arithmetic, and some groups studied geography. In addition to receiving classroom instruction, the boys did farm and garden work, chopped wood, and ground meal, whereas the girls cooked, washed, sewed, and knitted. The head chief had used one of the young girls as an interpreter and seemed pleased.

Lilley believed his preaching had led to improvement in the Seminoles' moral character. They spent less time drinking, gambling, fighting, and horse racing. The Indians, who had begun to improve their appearance, attended the worship services with more enthusiasm and seemed to enjoy praising and praying. Lilley often held services in the Indians' homes on Sunday afternoons and on week nights and the Indians packed the houses. He also went to homes of sick Indians who were unable to attend the mission's services. His preaching brought tears to some Indians and converted several to the Christian faith. Twenty-four Seminoles joined the church in one year.

Although Lilley considered his mission beneficial to the Indians, he was displeased with the activities of his competitors, the Baptists, who had recently begun missionary activities among the Seminoles. Joseph Samuel Murrow, a Baptist missionary from Georgia, had begun working in the Seminole district in 1859 after an unsuccessful stint among the Creeks. He established a Baptist church there in 1860. John Bemo, who had worked earlier among the Seminoles as a teacher and preacher, and others united with the Baptists. Lilley accused one Baptist minister of using every device to persuade the Indians to leave the Presbyterians and join the new group.[20]

Regardless of Lilley's success with a few Seminoles, he and Subagent Washbourne knew that the lack of a school fund hampered the tribe's progress. Lilley asked Washbourne for help in making education and religious instruction available. Washbourne thought it unfair that the Seminoles had no facilities for education and improvement other than Lilley's mission, and he concluded that no improvement would come to the tribe until the government furnished "means of culture" and separated them from the Creeks.[21]

Washbourne explained the Seminoles' lack of improvement. With only a small annuity, no education fund, and their being forced to live in a land controlled by others, advancement seemed impossible. Head Chief John Jumper added that the government had deceived the Seminoles when it was trying to induce them to move to the West. Jumper said that in Florida the government promised his people a country of their own where they could make their own laws. In reality, the Seminoles had to live in Creek country and forfeit their own nationality. They were without a blacksmith and were unable to cultivate the land to support their families. He opposed the treaty of 1845 and wanted the separate land promised them. Jumper and others wanted to visit the president and make a new treaty that would improve their circumstances.[22]

Chief Jumper was committed to gaining separation from the Creeks. Jumper, who stood six feet, four inches tall and weighed more than two hundred pounds, had become chief in the early 1850s after his brother, Jim Jumper, died. A nephew of Micanopy, he was a strong-willed, capable, and natural leader.[23]

The chief apparently worked well with Subagent Washbourne in trying to attain complete tribal independence for the Seminoles. Washbourne wrote Commissioner Manypenny in April 1855:

> There have been many slurs cast upon the Seminoles, as being savage, cruel, improvident, and lawless. . . . It is true that they fought for their country, and savagely, too, as was their custom. It is also true that they have made scarcely any improvement since their removal West.
>
> And what have been their inducements? Their nationality swept away, their country under the control of another tribe, their annuity miserably

small, no provision for schools or any other species of improvement; no incentive of any character whatever—how could they improve? Why, then, should they be blamed for not doing what is morally impossible under the circumstances? Why have slurs been hurled upon them for indulgence, to a less extent, in the vices peculiar to Indians, and more especially to those for whom the Government has done the most?

Washbourne rebutted the slurs cast on the Seminoles by stressing that they were much more law abiding than some other tribes. No Seminole had murdered another tribal member for the past seven years. Neither had the tribe participated in the "forays" against the prairie tribes. Washbourne thought these facts refuted the derogatory descriptions used to identify the Seminoles.[24]

In the summer of 1855, Washbourne presented a list of the Seminoles' "grievances, demands, and desires" to the Creek council with his whole-hearted endorsement. Because no workable union of the tribes was possible, the Seminoles prayed for separation. The tribe planned to send a delegation to the next Congress asking for such a separation.[25]

W. H. Garrett, an agent serving the twenty-five thousand Creeks, agreed that the Seminoles should either have a separate country or be forced to observe the treaty of 1845. He declared that the peace and harmony of the entire frontier required the settlement of the Seminole-Creek issue. Garrett charged that the Seminoles totally disregarded the treaty of 1845, refused to obey Creek laws, and continued to bring in whiskey from Fort Smith, Arkansas. Although the Creeks wanted the Seminoles to become a "happy people," they realized they could no longer live with the Seminoles; they wanted to rid themselves of that tribe. If the government failed to enforce the treaty of 1845, the Creeks planned to "remedy" the situation.[26]

Fortunately for the two tribes, Commissioner Manypenny concurred with Indian Bureau officials in the West. In November, he reported to Secretary of the Interior Robert McClelland that under the 1845 treaty, the Seminoles held the same "undesirable and injurious" position with the Creeks as had the Chickasaws with the Choctaws until the summer of 1855. At that time, the Chickasaws received independence and the right of self-government. The Seminoles needed the same consideration. Further, the Seminoles lived in a small district of the Creek nation as a hopeless minority, practically without government or law because they refused to accept Creek law. The commissioner, fearing violence, recommended that the Seminoles be given a "separate country and jurisdiction with right of self-government." Providing such rights would prove beneficial to the Indians and the government. With their own law and government, the Seminoles would lose their existing state of degradation and become better people, less inclined to violate the law. The Florida Seminoles might also migrate west.[27]

Charles W. Dean, southern superintendent of Indian affairs, also compared the twenty-five hundred Seminoles to the estimated five thousand Chickasaws. Dean stressed that the Seminoles had no country and only a small annuity; the Chickasaws had land and a fund of $5 million. The Seminoles had forfeited their Florida homeland, whereas the Chickasaw nation had sold its Mississippi land. The former tribe had faced neglect, poverty, and scorn; the latter one was affluent. The Seminoles had every right to ask why they had no land, money, schools, or hope.[28]

In December, Commissioner Manypenny gave the Seminoles new hope when he informed them that they could send a delegation to negotiate with Washington officials. The tribe in full council selected four members, Head Chief John Jumper, Tustenucochee, chief of the largest band, Pascofar, band chief, and James Factor, United States interpreter, to go to Washington to discuss the Seminole-Creek situation. The tribe was never more united, and the chiefs were in agreement. In the spring of 1856, the delegation of Seminoles and Creeks and their agents, Washbourne and Garrett, departed for Washington seeking a new tripartite treaty for their two tribes with the United States.[29]

While there, the Seminole delegation sent one of its most eloquent communications to Commissioner Manypenny. The delegates complained about the treaties of 1823, 1832, 1833, and 1845 and reiterated that originally the tribe was of the same "race with Creeks" but had a distinct tribal organization when the United States acquired Florida. Moreover, they said, "Florida is a land of summer, game, fish, clear waters, and orange groves. . . . Though we were rude and savage, love for this beautiful land burned within our bosoms." They listed the many treaty provisions that the United States had not honored. Citing parts of Article Four of the treaty of 1823, in which the United States guaranteed to prevent whites from settling or intruding upon their allotted district, they emphasized that whites did trespass and perpetrate outrages. They further pointed out that the Creeks received no additional territory for accepting the Seminoles as provided in the 1832 treaty. Consequently, the Seminoles had to occupy Creek land, and the Creeks had to accept their settlement. The treaty of 1833 allotted Creek lands for the Seminoles' separate territory, but its provisions lacked clarity.

These uncertain conditions regarding land led some Seminoles to approve the treaty of 1845 rather than remain in their existing state—without Florida and without land in the West. The delegates declared this treaty denationalizing, unjust, and of no benefit to their tribe. It evaded the promises made to the Seminoles by the United States and provoked ill feeling. They blamed Wild Cat, an ambitious man who approved the treaty, for promoting its acceptance. He had hoped to "carry out his own ends" and went to Mexico when he was unable to achieve his personal goals. Other chiefs had hoped the treaty would benefit the tribe by giving it a home. But in reality, the Seminoles gained nothing by the treaty except "squatter rights" to settle on Creek land and the privilege of sitting in a Creek council rather than a Seminole council. The small annuities stipulated had been provided for by former treaties. The Indians claimed they "did not understand the impact of this treaty when made, that we did not knowingly consent to the control of the Creek council, and that we did expect a permanent and valuable provision for homes, peace and improvement." Finally, the Seminoles argued that had they understood it they would have refused to sign a treaty that gave them nothing and in which they gave up their nationality. They would have objected also to being referred to as "troublesome neighbors," as the treaty described them.[30]

The western Seminoles declared that when they visited their Florida relatives and told them of the conditions in the West, they laughed in their faces. The Florida Indians wondered how the western Seminoles could be so "foolish" as to invite them to go west to share in their unhappiness. Tribal members in the East preferred to die in Florida rather than live discontented in the West.

In addition to these complaints, the Seminole delegation made numerous requests. These included $340,000 for their land in Florida, $2,400 annually for schools, $2,000 a year for a blacksmith, $52,650 for the earlier detention of their slaves at Fort Gibson, and $800 annually for educating teachers to teach young Seminoles. The Indians also asked for other compensation.

The Seminoles' extended campaign finally resulted in a new tripartite treaty between the United States, the Creeks, and the Seminoles in 1856. (The other fifty-one treaties negotiated while Manypenny was commissioner extinguished Indian claims to a total of 174 million acres.)[31] The officials of the Indian Bureau, including the commissioner, the Seminole and Creek agents, and both tribes, supported separating the two tribes and providing land for the Seminoles. The Creeks had threatened to settle the Seminole issue if the government failed to do so. Missionary Lilley reported the Creeks now wanted to sell part of their land for the Seminoles. Moreover, the new arrangement might encourage the rest of the Seminoles to leave Florida. With the small Seminole tribe causing such a disturbance both west and east of the Mississippi River, a solution to the tribe's complaints was imperative. Moreover, as the United States moved closer to disunion, finding peaceful solutions to the numerous Indian problems was only logical. Other concerns included the need for promoting education, civilization, and civil government for the Seminoles, the necessity of incorporating provisions of past Seminole and Creek treaties into one document, and settlement of the long-standing and continuous claims the Creeks had against the United States.

The Creeks were well paid for ceding land for the Seminoles and for dropping claims against the United States except for those incorporated in the new treaty. The Creeks received $1 million, of which $200,000 was invested in bonds that paid at least 5 percent, the interest to be used for educating the tribe; $400,000 to be distributed on a per capita basis; $120,000 for Creeks who went west prior to 1832 to equal the value of the land kept by eastern Creeks; and another $80,000 for various individual claims. The United States was to hold the remaining $200,000 until the Florida Seminoles moved west. At that time, that sum was to go to the Creeks on a per capita basis or for projects for their welfare.

The Seminoles also received substantial benefits. The United States guaranteed them a certain tract of land. The Seminoles had the right of self-government with full jurisdiction over individuals and property under their control, excluding white nonmembers. The tribe dropped all claims against the United States and agreed to settle on the new land as soon as possible. The boundaries of their new land began

> on the Canadian River, a few miles east of the ninety-seventh parallel of west longitude where Ock-hi-appo, or Pond Creek, empties into the same; thence, due north to the North Fork of the Canadian, thence, up said North Fork of the Canadian to the southern line of the Cherokee country; thence, with that line, west, to the one hundredth parallel of west longitude; thence south along said parallel of longitude to the Canadian River, and thence down and with that river to the place of beginning.[32]

These limits included approximately 2,169,080 acres of the original 13,140,000 acres held by the Creeks.

In addition to the land, the tribe was to receive numerous other benefits. These included $90,000 for their improvements to their present homes and for removal expenses, $3,000 as an educational fund for ten years, $2,000 for agricultural assistance, and $2,200 for blacksmiths and shops. The Indians were to receive a per capita annuity from $250,000 invested at 5 percent and from an additional $250,000 when the Florida Indians joined them. The United States also agreed to build an agency and council house for the Indians.

The western Seminoles agreed to supply paid delegates to go to Florida on occasion to encourage the Seminoles living there to emigrate. Those who emigrated would enjoy generous provisions as well, and were promised rations and subsistence during removal and for a year after their arrival in the West. Warriors aged eighteen or older were to get rifles, blankets, powder and lead, hunting shirts, shoes, stroud, and tobacco, and the women and children were to receive blankets, shoes, and clothing.

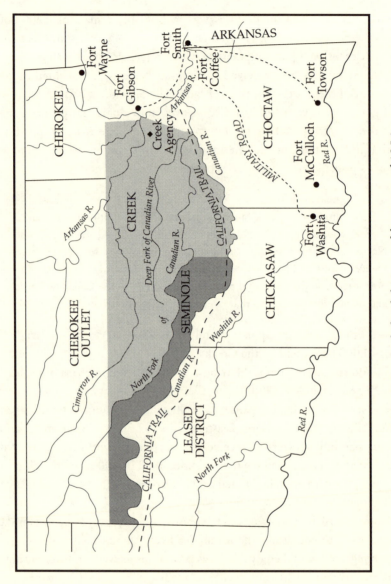

Map 5. Seminole land designated by treaty of 1856.

Twenty thousand dollars for their improvement and three thousand dollars for agricultural equipment would be available when they arrived in the West.

The United States promised the Seminoles protection from aggression by whites or other tribes in their country. Individuals allowed on the land other than the tribal members included government employees and their families, licensed traders, temporary travelers, and those residents who had the government's permission. Officials were to survey the boundary lines established by the treaty.

On 7 August 1856, Commissioner Manypenny and the Seminole and Creek delegations signed the Treaty with the Creeks and Seminoles, which consisted of twenty-three articles. Indians who signed included Seminoles John Jumper, Tustenucochee, Parscofer (Pascofar), and James Factor, and Creeks Tuckabatche Micco, Echo-Harjo, Chilly McIntosh, Benjamin Marshall, George W. Stidham, and Daniel N. McIntosh. Three weeks later, President Pierce signed the document sometimes referred to as the Treaty of Washington.[33]

Finally, the struggle for tribal independence and land that had begun with Chief Micanopy and other Seminoles at Fort Gibson in 1838 had ended successfully. For almost twenty years, Micanopy, Alligator, Wild Cat, John Jumper, other Seminole leaders, the Seminole subagents, and the different Creek agents had either sent or made personal pleas to presidents, secretaries of war and interior, commissioners of Indian affairs, and superintendents of Indian affairs explaining that the Seminoles and Creeks should be separate and independent nations.

The treaty made the Seminoles' protracted efforts worthwhile. The land, separation from the Creeks, and monetary rewards were what the western Seminoles had so desperately sought. Most important, the treaty provided for tribal permanence. Unfortunately, the treaty's provisions were confusing, and the later 1850s found the Seminoles still struggling to adjust in the West. Moreover, the tribe held the new allotment of more than 2 million acres for less than ten years.

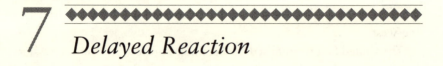

7 Delayed Reaction

The western Seminoles gained their separation from the Creeks in 1856, but the tribe made little progress before the outbreak of the Civil War. Several factors slowed settlement on the new allotted land. The Seminoles were afraid to move westward, so their relocation in the late 1850s was gradual. Moreover, although their problems with land and tribal sovereignty had been resolved satisfactorily, their lack of socioeconomic and political progress persisted. Before the entire tribe had settled in the new district, where it might have become a strong entity, the Civil War erupted and precluded any further opportunities for their advancement.

Subagent Washbourne conveyed the news of the new treaty of 1856 to the Seminole tribe when it gathered to receive its annuities in January 1857. Prior to the meeting, Washbourne had brought in the tribe's annuity goods for 1855 and 1856, the distribution of which had been delayed. He also had visited the Creek agency, from which he sent messages about the treaty to the bands of Seminoles living among that tribe. The subagent talked with some Seminole band chiefs and headmen there and instructed them to visit the Seminole subagency and register to receive the annuity goods. From his subagency, Washbourne also sent runners to inform the bands to appear in council for a census. Some eighteen hundred

Seminoles camped around the agency for ten or twelve days as they waited for the taking of the census and the distribution of goods. "Thinly clad" and with few tents, they were exposed to the extremely cold weather. Still, the Seminoles were patient and did not "murmur." They seemed pleased with the new country provided them, and some Indians had already selected building sites.

The Creeks thought the Seminoles would go to their new land some fifty miles farther west in the spring of 1857. The Creeks expected to take possession of the vacated farms, but the Seminoles failed to remove at that time. It was spring before Congress made appropriations to execute the 1856 treaty.[1] Moreover, the wild Plains tribes presented a major threat to Seminole safety in the new country. In 1857, when a group of Seminoles went to select home sites on the new allotted lands, Comanches stole their horses. The Seminoles had had frequent clashes with the Comanches and other hostile tribes. Now the Comanches and Kiowas had been pushed into the southwestern corner of Indian Territory. The Osages also stole twenty-two horses from one surveying party of Seminoles, forcing them to walk back to their homes during the worst part of winter. Other Osages stole the horse of a young Seminole widow, who with her young child had to walk seventy miles through ice and snow to the subagency to receive the annuity goods.

The Seminoles' fear of moving farther west was justified by other reports as well. A few years earlier Subagent Duval had written Commissioner Medill about hostilities among various western tribes. The Cheyennes and Arapahoes had been at war, and the Delawares and Wichitas located southwest of the agency had recently fought. The massacre of entire villages was common.

Some Bureau of Indian Affairs officials wanted to take steps to make the new district safe for the Seminoles. Elias Rector, an Arkansan who became southern superintendent of Indian affairs in 1857, favored establishing a military post on the tribe's frontier to protect the Seminoles from the "incursions of wandering hostile tribes." Rector also wanted to mark clearly the boundaries between the Creeks and Seminoles established by the 1856 treaty to prevent disputes between the two tribes and to encourage the Seminoles to relocate. When the problem with Plains tribes continued, Commissioner of Indian Affairs Charles E. Mix in August 1858 reported to Secretary of the Interior Jacob Thompson that it was imperative to control the northern Comanches, Kiowas, and other Indians in an area on the Upper Arkansas between the lands of the Seminoles, Choctaws, Chickasaws, and Creeks. Mix called the wild tribes a "lawless horde" who lived by "chase and plunder." The Seminoles' fear of the wild Plains tribes continued throughout the later 1850s. As late as 1860, the Plains tribes still stole ponies and livestock from the Seminoles, who presented the United States a bill for $3,255 as payment for thirty-two horses taken by the Comanches.[2]

While most of the 1,907 Seminoles lingered in their old settlements in Creek country in 1857, they and the Creeks seemed quiet and peaceful. Rector thought the Creek agent could supervise both tribes until the Seminoles moved. They continued to farm and raise livestock. A few of them had relocated, and Subagent Washbourne believed most of the tribe would move in the fall and winter so they could plant crops in the spring.[3]

As the Seminole tribe faced resettlement in the later 1850s, it also seemed to become more aware of the need to improve its cultural and political structures. The Seminoles began an extended and largely unsuccessful search for more educational opportunities. Chief John Jumper and other leaders wanted additional religious and educational instruction made available to the tribe. Jumper specifically favored missionary boarding schools. Two of his nieces spent time at the Presbyterian mission and learned the shorter catechism. Even the aging Chief Alligator sent the children in his band to the mission, and he himself tried to learn the alphabet.

The Seminole council, realizing the importance of schools for the tribe, asked the subagent to present the subject to the Indian Bureau. The Seminoles wanted a missionary board to take charge of their school fund of three thousand dollars for ten years as provided in the recent treaty. The tribe also needed schools in addition to the one operated at Oak Ridge by Presbyterian Missionary John Lilley.

Lilley maintained his ardent interest in educating the Seminoles. In 1856–57, he taught twenty-six students—nineteen Seminoles, two Creeks, three Cherokees, and two others. The missionary described his students as religious and well mannered; some were, he said, intelligent and of fine character. The Indians had respect for Lilley's school and hoped Lilley would move with them to the new country. Although students from other tribes had to pay board and furnish their clothing, there was an overflow of applicants. Chief Jumper wanted the school to accept more students. Lilley continued to support the Seminoles' requests for other schools and reported in the late 1850s that no school other than his (and John Bemo's) had existed in the West for the tribe.[4]

In the end, Lilley, Washbourne, and the Seminoles had little success in expanding the tribe's educational opportunities. As late as 1859, the Indian Bureau had failed to provide any organized education for the Seminoles in the new country, although Congress had appropriated school funds in accordance with the provisions of the 1856 treaty. Both of the Seminole subagents who served in the later 1850s tried to convince Indian Bureau officials that the Seminoles needed education to overcome their ignorance and superstition. The greatest obstacle to the tribe's advancement continued to be its lack of adequate educational facilities, according to one of the subagents.[5]

Meanwhile, the Seminoles were becoming more inclined to accept Christian beliefs. Chief Jumper, who thought Christians were the "best behaved people" in the country, supported Lilley's missionary work and united with the Presbyterians in 1857. He also stressed that no liquor would be brought into the new district.

Lilley continued to face competition from the Baptists. Even Chief Jumper joined the Baptists in 1860 and was baptized by John Bemo. Lilley concluded that the Baptists wanted to "break up" his mission, because they claimed the Presbyterians were wrong in their beliefs. The two denominations differed in regard to observing the Sabbath. According to the Presbyterians, the Baptists allowed the Indian converts to act as they pleased on Sundays. Some of the town chiefs made the Presbyterian converts plant, hoe, and gather corn on Sundays. One Presbyterian missionary, James Ross Ramsey, wanted to excommunicate those who violated the Sabbath, but he hesitated to do so because the Baptist church, "the great receptacle of all trash," would accept those the Presbyterians rejected.[6]

While the denominations argued over their doctrinal beliefs, the Seminoles were concerned about the liquor problems of their tribe and others in the territory. In August 1855, the tribe formulated a law prohibiting the introduction of whiskey into its district. Agent Washbourne reported that this action was the first response of Seminoles to his and the Creek chiefs' requests to give up the use of liquor. The Seminoles previously had maintained their right to buy, sell, and drink whiskey. Most of the tribe tried to obey the new law. No liquor was found when the Seminoles assembled at the agency in 1856 and 1857 to receive the annuity payments.[7]

Nonetheless, problems with the misuse of alcohol continued among the tribes. In the summer of 1857, one traveler in the West described the Indians there as the "most degraded specimens of humanity he ever saw." Although they had good land and could have had the comforts of life, their laziness caused them to suffer even from a lack of food. The largest field of corn that he saw was only three acres, and it was cultivated by the Indian women. While the women worked, the men lounged around the grog shops and drank and fought. The "low class whites" who owned the shops got the Indians drunk and then took their guns and ponies.[8]

Some Seminoles still participated in illegal liquor trafficking. In July 1857, eleven tribal members tried to take whiskey into Choctaw country, and the police of the Choctaw nation had to fight to keep them out.[9] Although Subagent Washbourne reported in 1857 that the Seminoles had introduced little whiskey, two years later his successor reported that liquor still caused problems. Much drunkenness and disorder were reported when annuity payments were made in August 1859. Liquor was available on the grounds and in the neighborhood.[10]

By late 1857, Washbourne was completing his tenure as the Seminoles' subagent. He had served the tribe over three years and had been instrumental in bringing about the Seminoles' separation from the Creeks. Apparently, he had good rapport with the Indians. When he left the subagency, the Seminoles' attitude was perhaps better, but their condition was basically unchanged. As with the other Seminole subagents, Washbourne's supervision of the tribe ended in reproach because of his mishandling of funds and his failure to stay at the agency.

Washbourne's frequent absences from the Seminole agency brought reprimands throughout his years of service. As early as December 1855, the southern superintendent of Indian affairs, Charles Dean, complained to Commissioner Manypenny that Washbourne had been absent one-fourth of the eighteen months that he had been in office. Dean was concerned about the "great destitution" among the dispersed small bands of Seminoles, who suffered probably "more than" they had in several years, and he thought the presence of their subagent among them was indispensable.

Washbourne usually replied to inquiries about his absences by asserting that his wife's poor health required that he stay with her at Fayetteville, Arkansas. He had accepted the agency because he was poor and thought he could be of benefit to the Indians. The subagent claimed that he had performed his duties "conscientiously" and that the Seminoles, pleased with his performance, never complained about his absences. Washbourne used George Aird, "a reliable trader," to oversee the tribe when he was away.

According to Washbourne, serving as the Seminole subagent had definite disadvantages. Whereas other agents in the Southern Superintendency had comfortable quarters and every convenience, he had "two or three relics of rotten log cabins, the best of which is liable to be blown over in a wind, and all are entirely unhabitable." Washbourne, who refused to make his family live in such quarters, stayed with a licensed trader who provided him with board and lodging. Washbourne complained that he was without protection, any means of communication, or anything to show that he represented the United States government. He had "nothing earthly to do but keep the Seminoles 'straight' and pay to them their miserable annuity the goods of which never reach them 'til half rotten."

Washbourne believed that Abraham, the black interpreter, had accused and denounced him to the officers at Fort Arbuckle. Abraham, who had gone to Van Buren to the United States District Court where his sons faced charges for selling whiskey to the Indians, got food at the fort. He claimed he was unsafe in the Seminole country. Washbourne refuted the charge and stressed that Abraham, a heavy drinker, was a bad influence on the Seminoles. Earlier, Washbourne had complained that other free blacks also sold whiskey to the Indians.[11]

Later, more serious accusations involving Washbourne's mishandling of monies appropriated through the treaty of 1856 led to his removal as subagent. He was charged with taking a bribe of thirteen thousand dollars from Seminole chiefs whom he permitted to use tribal funds for their own purposes. Superintendent Rector recommended his removal as subagent in the fall of 1857. The Seminoles were aware of Washbourne's irregularities but still respected him because of his efforts in helping negotiate the treaty of 1856.[12]

Samuel M. Rutherford, a sixty-year-old Virginia native, became Seminole subagent on 5 November 1857. Rutherford probably had the most distinguished record in Indian service of any of his predecessors. In his early years, he had served in the War of 1812 and as a trader and a county sheriff. His experience as a deputy United States marshal for Little Rock, member of the Arkansas territorial legislature, special agent for the removal and subsistence of the Choctaws, Choctaw agent, and acting superintendent of Indian affairs made him well qualified to supervise Seminole affairs.[13]

One of Rutherford's early duties as Seminole subagent was to accompany a delegation of western Seminoles to Florida. The group's efforts were important, because hostilities between the Seminoles and the United States had erupted again into what is termed the Third Seminole War (1855–57). In December 1855, Lieutenant George L. Hartsuff and a party of eleven, while on a surveying trip on the border of the Big Cypress Swamp, had destroyed the prized banana plants of leading Seminole chief Billy Bowlegs. When questioned by the Indians, Hartsuff's party admitted destroying the plants but offered no apologies. Consequently, the Indians attacked the lieutenant's camp and killed several men and wounded Hartsuff. The Indians later attacked other whites, burned their homes, and stole their livestock. Two battles followed; the Indians were defeated but refused to surrender.

Bowlegs, a grandson of Micanopy and a full-blooded Seminole who spoke English and Spanish, had trained under his grandfather during the Second Seminole War and was a perfect marksman. Familiar with the Everglades, he used successfully the usual tactics against United States troops. Colonel Gustavus Loomis and his command failed to overtake Bowlegs and his party.

In 1857, President James Buchanan changed the United States policy toward the Florida Seminoles because of rumors that Bowlegs wanted to surrender. Government officials, including Secretary of War Jefferson Davis, had advocated sending another delegation of western Seminoles to Florida. Davis suggested supplying the officer in charge with fifteen hundred dollars for the delegation's transportation and subsistence. He considered the services of the western Seminoles invaluable in the removal attempt. In accordance with the new policy, the Department of the Interior commissioned Superintendent Rector to take a delegation to Florida to negotiate with Bowlegs.

In the winter of 1857, Rector, Rutherford, and Creek agent William H. Garrett, with forty Seminoles and six Creeks, went to Florida. Rector persuaded the Seminoles to search the Everglades to bring in the Florida Indians. Nevertheless, almost three months of negotiations followed before removal occurred. One Creek chief, Tuckabatche Micco, received special mention for his efforts in getting some Florida Seminoles to agree to removal.

After a council on 14 March 1858, during which Bowlegs heard of the provisions of the treaty of 1856 and other government offers, he and 164 others decided to go west. Some sources indicate that whiskey and money persuaded Bowlegs to emigrate. This party included headmen Assunwha, Nocose Emathla, Foos Hadjo, Nocus Hadjo, and Fuchutchee Emathla. Arpeika (Sam Jones) was too old and feeble to travel, but ten of his Mikasukis migrated. Twelve warriors stayed in Florida with Arpeika, and about one hundred Seminoles remained on the peninsula.

The move from the peninsula was an unusual experience for the Florida Seminoles who went west in 1858. Rector used teams and wagons to gather them. Rector's delegation and 125 Seminoles left Fort Myers aboard the *Grey Cloud*. They stopped at Egmont Key in Tampa Bay to pick up forty other Seminoles brought in by the Florida volunteers. They went west via New Orleans and found their stay in that city an unusual one, according to one secondary source.

Housed in barracks outside the city, only Billy Bowlegs, who was described as a handsome stout man with "flashing black eyes," and about fifty years old, was permitted to go into New Orleans when he pleased.

The prestigious Bowlegs was received as somewhat of a hero and had "much liquor" made available to him. He also had a large amount of money with him, perhaps as much as $100,000. By one account, two wives, a son, five daughters, and a number of blacks were in his group. His prestige plummeted, however, after he was carried out of the city drunk on several occasions. Soon people went to the barracks to see Bowlegs much as they would a caged animal. Nonetheless, the Seminoles still respected Bowlegs because of his leadership in Florida.

At New Orleans, Rector put the Florida Seminoles on the steamer *Quapaw,* and they arrived at Fort Smith in late May 1858. Rutherford, Garrett, and the western Seminole delegates arrived soon after on the *Arkansas.* The new emigrants faced problems similar to those of the emigrants of 1836 as they traveled overland to the Seminole district. Bad roads, inclement weather, high water, and sickness made their journey a difficult one. After they arrived among the western Seminoles on 16 June, a disease similar to typhoid fever attacked them, and the old settlers as well, and caused several deaths.[14]

Because Superintendent Rector had been successful in getting Bowlegs's party to go west at a minimum cost of $70,352.14, he decided to return to Florida to induce the few remaining Seminoles to emigrate. In November 1858, Rector asked Billy Bowlegs to make the trip with him. The following month the superintendent went to Florida with eight Seminoles, including both recent and old settlers and Bowlegs. Again Rector's efforts were successful. Black Warrior and his band of about seventy-five, known for their primitive customs, hatred of whites, and ability to handle boats, agreed to remove in February 1859.[15] The tragic and extended removal of the Seminoles from the East to west of the Mississippi River that had begun in the 1830s was finally at an end. Only a few remained permanently in Florida.

After 1858, the Florida Indians experienced freedom, as the United States Army had no military interest in them. During the next two decades, they remained virtually isolated in the "watery wilderness" of southern Florida, where they escaped the national conflict of the 1860s and other disasters that enveloped their western counterparts. The three bands, two of Mikasuki speakers and one of Creek (Muskogee) speakers, lived in thatched roofed, open-sided "chickees" that were widely scattered throughout the swamp and sawgrass country. They traveled and hunted using their dugout canoes and raised crops such as corn, squash, pumpkins, bananas, and beans. Adhering to their traditional culture, each band had a chief and council of elders. The clan systems and Green Corn dance gave them a common unity.

The recently emigrated Billy Bowlegs had settled near the mouth of Little River, where he soon owned large herds of cattle and ponies and controlled perhaps as many as one hundred blacks. He died in the spring of 1859, when he went to select a home site in the new Seminole district. His followers buried him according to Seminole tradition—with his rifle, money, and other possessions. Some government officials declared that it was fortunate that he had died. Bowlegs had been popular among his people; rumors had stirred that some Seminoles had wanted him to replace John Jumper as head chief.

The old settlers made little progress in 1858 and 1859 as their brethren came from the East. Most of the tribe remained in Creek country and continued to farm, as did other members of the Five Civilized Tribes in the territory. Superintendent Rector was disappointed with the Indians' agricultural habits. The Seminoles and Creeks were small farmers, often having only one acre in five thousand in cultivation. Because there was no individual ownership of land, when they wore out the soil, they moved to another area and left the country filled with abandoned houses. Many Indians had no gardens or orchards, although some produced apples, pears, peaches, and plums and raised cattle, horses, oxen, and hogs. Overall, they seemed to care little for luxuries. The Indians' failure to become prosperous farmers was no fault of the land they held, according to Rector. He reported that the Indian country included rich alluvial valleys with fine rivers and streams, bountiful deposits of coal, limestone, marble, and salt springs.[16]

The Seminoles wrestled with other handicaps in addition to their small-scale farming methods. They had no written laws, organized government, legislative bodies, or court system as did the Cherokees, Choctaws, and Chickasaws. The Seminoles, as did the Creeks, maintained their old political system of principal and town chiefs.

The Seminoles had become more desirous of improving the tribe's general progress. They wanted to build two or three mills for grinding corn and making flour. The subagent knew the mills were essential and asked Superintendent Rector that they be provided. The council agreed also to apply for funds from their annuity to support a government and an efficient police. They had previously been without funds for any organized government or law enforcement. Further, the council approved the use of their remaining installments from the treaty of 1845 for a national fund under supervision of a national committee. Finally, the tribe wanted blacksmith shops and their funds for education as stipulated in the treaty of 1856.[17]

As the Seminoles tried to make tribal improvements, Subagent Samuel M. Rutherford sought to move them to the lands allotted in the treaty of 1856. He thought the construction of agency buildings and a council house would entice them to migrate faster. In 1859, the Seminoles were also told that they would be unable to share in the tribe's annuity if they failed to move during the coming year. Some Seminoles enrolled as Creeks were also expected to move when they gathered their crops. Only about one-third of the 2,253 Seminoles, of whom about one thousand were females, including the recent Florida and Mexican emigrants, had established themselves in the new district, where they lived in comfortable cabins. The men farmed small patches and raised livestock, and the women engaged in "ordinary routines and housewifery."

By 1860, activity in the new Seminole district was increasing. Subagent Rutherford had been able to get an agency building and a council house constructed near the tribe's eastern boundary, where it was safe from wild Indians. The agency was located about sixty miles from the previous one and about one mile west of the eastern boundary of the Seminoles' new lands. Their council house measured thirty-six by twenty feet and was enclosed by a fence. Its two rooms were each furnished with a fireplace, tables, and seats. Rutherford had also helped provide cabins for the Indians who selected home sites. Some Seminoles chose to build their own cabins.[18]

Those Seminoles who moved to the land set aside by the 1856 treaty continued to face difficulties similar to those they had endured in previous years. Several Indians had moved too late to plant crops, and others were expected to produce only enough for seed because of a severe drought. In 1860, the tribe petitioned President Buchanan for relief and asked for ten thousand dollars of the 1861 annuity if no other help was available. A total of five thousand dollars was appropriated under the Indian Appropriations Bill of 1832 to buy corn and other provisions for those Seminoles who were expected to suffer from the effects of the drought.

On the eve of the Civil War, lack of progress and geographical disunity made the Seminoles ready prey for the disasters associated with such a conflict. Only about half the tribe had relocated in the new country; the others remained in Creek country. As the Seminoles pleaded for schools and sought to bring about tribal advancement through an organized tribal government and system of law enforcement, the Civil War struck the Indian Territory and quickly terminated their endeavors.[19]

8 Rendered Asunder

The Civil War brought tribal division, forced emigration, property destruction, untold suffering, and numerous deaths to the Seminoles in Indian Territory. Moved from Florida to the western lands during the twenty-five years prior to 1861, they had barely begun to establish the roots for progress when the dissolution of the Union dealt them havoc. The North-South conflict and the accompanying confusion in federal Indian policy plunged the Seminoles into a difficult situation that undid their prewar efforts for stronger tribal unity and independence.[1]

In early 1861 the less than three thousand Seminoles and the thousands in the other Civilized Tribes, in a total of nearly one hundred thousand Indians in the territory, were confused by the controversies that were developing between the North and South. Some of the tribes, especially the Creeks and Cherokees, were themselves plagued by the old problems of factionalism and conflicts over the slavery issue. With considerable apprehension, in January, the Chickasaws asked the Seminoles, Creeks, Cherokees, and Choctaws to hold council with them to determine those protective actions they might take to preserve tribal and individual rights should the Union dissolve. Only the Seminoles, Creeks, and Cherokees appeared on 17 February, and those present decided to do nothing except to await further developments. At a later meeting in March, the Five

Tribes had different reactions. The Seminoles, Creeks, and Cherokees unanimously opposed joining the southern states, whereas the Choctaws favored making an immediate alliance with the Confederacy. The Chickasaws were divided over the issue.

The Seminoles and other tribes soon split into factions. Indian affairs in the United States by 1860 were in a period of uncertainty. Between July 1850 and March 1861, six commissioners of Indian affairs had served in that office. With this high turnover rate also had come added responsibilities which had required more staff members. The addition of new territories and tribes, especially after the Mexican War, and the creation of new reservations made the understaffed Office of Indian Affairs unable to efficiently meet the needs of the Indian service. Moreover, fraud and inefficiency were rampant in the whole Indian Department, which in the early 1860s was commonly known as the most corrupt division of the government. Politicians, rather than persons experienced in Indian affairs, often received the appointments.

The federal government had made no effort to retain the Indians' loyalty in case war ensued. This inaction stemmed in part from Abraham Lincoln's preoccupation with war policies and politics and from his limited knowledge of Indian affairs. According to one authority, at the Republican presidential convention of 1860, against the wishes of Lincoln, his "convention managers traded the positions of secretary of interior and commissioner of Indian Affairs for Indiana's twenty-six votes." Consequently, Caleb Smith of Indiana and William P. Dole, formerly of Indiana and most recently from Illinois, received those appointments. After Republican campaign officials recommended opening the Indian Territory to whites, some Indians wanted Lincoln defeated.

Other factors, such as bordering the slave states of Arkansas and Texas, having a superintendent and agents in the Indian Territory who were Southern sympathizers, and the removal of federal troops from the forts in the area, caused the Indians to become further confused and divided in their loyalties. Moreover, personal reasons, such as the ties between the mixed bloods and southern whites as well as the uncertainties of emancipation of the blacks, demanded consideration.[2]

Removing federal troops from the territory had disastrous results.

When panic struck Washington after the attack on Fort Sumter in April 1861, the protection of the East seemed imperative. Secretary of War Simon Cameron ordered armed forces withdrawn from the territory to Fort Leavenworth, Kansas, against the wishes of Secretary of Interior Smith. Secretary Smith realized that organized protection of Indian Territory was essential, and he sent "an inquiry" to Secretary Cameron about the removal of the troops. Cameron replied on 10 May that on 17 April his department had issued instructions to remove the troops stationed at Forts Cobb, Arbuckle, Washita, and Smith to Fort Leavenworth. The commanding officer there had the discretion to decide on their replacement by Arkansas Volunteers. Secretary Cameron "closed the door" on other requests for military protection of Indian Territory.

As the Federals left, Texas troops took control of Forts Arbuckle, Cobb, and Washita. Their officers immediately informed the Seminoles that they would sweep the Indian Territory from Texas to the Kansas border and drive out northern men. The Seminoles, Creeks, and Wichitas considered the Texans "mean bad" people. Some of the Wichitas and other Indians near Fort Cobb wanted the Seminoles to help them fight the Texans. Although the Seminoles and Creeks despised the Texans, they were unwilling to oppose them at that time.[3]

After Federal forces departed, most communications between the Indian Office and the tribes ceased. Payment of annuities was suspended, although Smith and Dole wanted Congress to make the appropriations in case a means developed to pay them. When Dole appointed William G. Coffin as southern superintendent on 2 May 1861, Coffin went west with authority to set up his headquarters in Kansas, if necessary, rather than Fort Smith. Coffin located temporarily at Fort Leavenworth, but later in the war, he established his permanent office at Humboldt. After Confederate guerrillas burned parts of Humboldt, including the house in which Coffin had his office, he established his headquarters at LeRoy, Kansas. With the Southern Superintendency moved from Fort Smith to Kansas and with no United States military forces in Indian Territory, by May 1861 the Office of Indian Affairs had lost its two major contacts with the Indians.

Commissioner Dole realized the importance of maintaining the loyalty of the Indians. Although the new federal superintendent and agents who were appointed after March were unable to reach their posts, Dole informed the principal chiefs and heads of leading tribes in the Southern Superintendency that interference with their tribal or domestic institutions would not be tolerated. Moreover, he stated that the United States would appoint competent agents and keep its treaty obligations.

Secretary Smith and Commissioner Dole thought the Indians would renounce the Confederates once the United States reestablished authority in their area. In late 1861, Dole felt "assured that the degree of loyalty amongst them [Indians] is far greater than amongst the whites of most of the rebellious states." He wanted Secretary Smith to have two or three thousand men sent to the territory to secure the Indians' neutrality. But the War Department remained unable to furnish such troops.[4]

While the Federals mishandled their relations with the Indians, the Confederates, hoping to gain control of the territory, proceeded in an organized manner to win their cooperation. Most of the superintendents and agents since the 1830s had been southerners who reflected their sectional biases in supervising the tribes. Southern sympathizers "held or had access to" every governmental position in the Southern Superintendency during the presidency of James Buchanan and influenced the "sources of information." Some postmasters informed the Indians that the "old government had fallen." Such officials as Southern Superintendent Elias Rector of Arkansas, Creek agent William H. Garrett of Alabama, Choctaw and Chickasaw agent Douglas H. Cooper, and Cherokee Agent Pierce M. Butler, as well as the previous Seminole agents, including Samuel Rutherford, advocated secession. In November 1861, Secretary of Interior Smith reported that the earlier southern superintendent and some of his agents had assumed an attitude of revolt against the United States and had "instigated the Indians to acts of hostility." Thus the larger tribes, Cherokee, Chickasaw, and Choctaw, had suspended communications with the newly appointed United States agents.

In February 1861, a bill creating the Confederate War Department placed the Indians under that agency. In the middle of March, a Bureau of Indian Affairs headed by a commissioner was established. David Hubbard became the Confederate commissioner of Indian affairs, and

Albert Pike of Arkansas the commissioner to the Indian nations west of Arkansas and south of Kansas. Pike, with Brigadier General Benjamin McCulloch and Major Douglas H. Cooper, was to negotiate treaties and alliances with the Indians in Indian Territory.[5] In May, McCulloch was given command of the military district, including Indian Territory, and Cooper, who had been United States agent for the Chickasaws and Choctaws, was directed to raise a mounted regiment from those tribes. On 21 May the Confederate states annexed Indian Territory and placed the tribes under their protection.

Consequently, Confederate commissioner Pike was able to negotiate successfully when he went west later that month. At Fort Smith, he consulted with Superintendent Rector, Seminole agent Rutherford, and Cooper, who agreed to continue their duties for the Confederates. Pike then left for Indian Territory, where he met with representatives of the Five Tribes and other Indians and negotiated treaties with them.

Pike negotiated with the other four Civilized Tribes before going to the Seminoles. He met with John Ross, principal chief of the Cherokees, at Tahlequah. Initially Ross cited various reasons for refusing to sign a Confederate alliance. He wanted the Cherokees to maintain friendship with both the Federal and Confederate governments. Moreover, the Cherokee treaties had placed the tribe under the protection of the United States. A strong abolitionist influence also existed among the Cherokees. Without getting a Cherokee treaty, Pike went to North Fork Town in the Creek nation, where he arranged treaties with the representatives of the Creek, Choctaw, and Chickasaw tribes. The Creeks were divided into neutralists and secessionists, but Pike negotiated with a group of southern sympathizers a treaty that was later approved by a general Creek council. The commissioner had no difficulties in persuading the Chickasaws and Choctaws to ally with the South.

The white man's war added to the Seminoles' frustration. These Indians had had enough of war in Florida, and initially they saw no reason to favor either the North or South. The tribe was recovering from the devastating drought of 1860. The Seminoles were also without an official federal subagent, as Rutherford had an unexplained deficit of $46,361 in the last quarter of 1860. Hence, in the middle of the secession crisis and the presidential change from James Buchanan to Abraham Lincoln, William P. Davis was appointed as the new Seminole subagent. Instead of assuming the post, Davis joined the Indiana Volunteers, and it was 7 January 1862 before another federal agent was appointed. Meanwhile Rutherford emphasized to the Seminoles that they were slaveholders and thus should support the South.[6]

In July, Seminole Chief John Jumper and other Seminoles had discussed the conflict between the North and South with E. H. Carruth, United States commissioner for the Creeks and Seminoles, when he was located near Fort Scott. The Seminoles were confused after Pike wrote them asking for an interview at the Creek agency. Jumper sent runners to inform four or five other Seminole chiefs of the Pike request. These Indians carried the letter to Agent Carruth, with whom they spent the day discussing the war. They studied a map of the United States and, eager for information, asked Carruth to read newspaper accounts to them. These Indians understood that if the South lost, seceding tribes would lose their annuities and lands and be liable for punishment. None of the Seminoles favored uniting with the South. Carruth thought they would remain loyal.

Some reports indicate that Jumper and a few others went to the Creek agency when Pike was there. Some Seminoles left after they learned that the Creek chiefs who refused to sign Pike's treaty were sent away. Jumper and the four "self-appointed" delegates remained. The chief heard the Creek treaty interpreted and, planned to advise his people to make a similar treaty.[7]

Pike went from the Creek nation to the Seminole district, where he arrived on 21 July to negotiate with the tribe. Former southern superintendent Rector was present. Seminole chief Pascofar later claimed that the Seminoles were shocked when Pike came to them and that Chief Jumper told the Confederate commissioner that if he had sent word about his visit, he could better have decided how to handle negotiations.

According to Pascofar, Pike told them the other four Civilized Tribes had agreed to fight and insisted that if the Seminoles refused to do so, the "cold people" (northerners) would come and take their country. Chief Jumper asked his lawyers for advice, and they indicated that the tribe must abide by President Lincoln's word. Nonetheless, Pike told the Seminoles who agreed to fight that he would enlist them for sixteen months, in return for which they would receive food, clothing, and pay. Jumper then instructed Pascofar to raise one thousand men for Confederate service, but the latter refused after consulting Billy Bowlegs.

In spite of these disagreements among the Seminoles, at their council ground (in Pottawatomie County) on 1 August 1861, Pike secured a treaty from Jumper and several town chiefs, who represented about half of the tribe. In his report, Pike indicated that he had no difficulty in gaining the Seminoles' loyalty. He made a talk, and "they promptly joined." To satisfy the tribe, Pike provided "an additional compensation" for those delegates who went to Florida in 1857 to get the Seminoles to emigrate.

Pike, with Rector, the agent for the Reserve Indians, twenty-nine Seminoles including Chief Jumper, and thirty-six Creeks and their chief, left the Seminole agency on 3 August to visit the tribes further west. The party met with Comanche bands at the Wichita agency on the sixth. The Seminole and Creek chiefs' assurances that Pike's promises would be honored helped the commissioner obtain a treaty with the Comanches. Pike also notified the Kiowas that he would send one thousand Seminoles and Creeks "to wipe them out" if they warred against the Confederates. Pike and his escort explored the fertile lands in the Wichita Mountains where the commissioner had permission from the Choctaws and Chickasaws to settle Comanches, Shawnees, Delawares, and Kickapoos. On 2 September, Pike left his convoy at Fort Arbuckle. The mission to the Wichita agency had been successful because he made alliances with several small bands and tribes. He also concluded treaties with the Osages, Senecas, Shawnees, and Quapaws after returning to the Cherokee country, where he succeeded in negotiating a treaty with that tribe on October 7.[8]

The Seminoles' Confederate treaty and those of the other Five Civilized Tribes were basically the same. The Confederate government agreed to continue the annuities, pay accrued interest on money invested for the tribes, and obtain the principal and interest of stocks or bonds in both northern and southern states. The Indians could sell their land, except that reserved for agencies, forts, military posts, or roads. Abandoned land was to revert to the Confederacy. The tribes were to have three representatives with the privileges of territorial delegates in the Confederate Congress. One delegate would represent the Seminoles and Creeks, one the Choctaws and Chickasaws, and one the Cherokees. The Seminoles, Creeks, Osages, Quapaws, Senecas, and Shawnees could use the district court of the Cherokees, and the Choctaws and Chickasaws had their own. Moreover, the Choctaw and Chickasaw country could become a state, and the other three of the Five Tribes could join it if they so desired. This provision was later deleted by the Confederate Congress.

The Confederate Seminole treaty had a few special provisions. Pike agreed that the Seminoles would receive five thousand dollars and that there would be an investigation of Seminole claims of payment due them for services of their slaves while they had been detained at Fort Gibson. Their payments for education and blacksmiths as provided by the United States treaty were to continue for a limited number of years, with an extra one thousand dollars provided for "school houses." Pike indicated that he granted these provisions because of the "great bravery and the loyalty of this people, many of whom were so lately in arms against us, and who are now all true to the cause of the South; and because I considered that no object could more command itself to the president than that of educating the yonng [*sic*] among these tribes."

According to Pike, he could have made none of the treaties without the Confederacy's assumption of the monetary provisions in the United States treaties with the various tribes. He wanted the total of $265,927 for arrearages of annuities, annual payments, and interest paid to the Indians in gold or silver as the United States government had paid them. Offering treasury notes for the first payment would have had an "evil effect." Pike was pleased that he did not have to bribe the tribal chiefs, although he gave "moderate compensation" to the Seminole, Creek, Choctaw, and Chickasaw delegates who negotiated the treaties. During his negotiations, which took more than five months, he spent only $18,747. Pike had obtained the necessary supplies with credit or money provided by merchants in Indian Territory.

Pike was ready to defend both his expenses and the treaty provisions. He thought the Indians, with their land rich in coal, limestone, marble, granite, iron, lead, and salt, would be valuable to the South. The Indians promised to accept the Confederates' protection as wards and to abide by their trade laws. They also agreed to furnish troops, with the Seminoles and Osages each providing five hundred men, the Cherokees two regiments, and the Choctaws and Creeks one regiment with the promise of two more. Only twenty-five hundred of these Indians were armed or could provide their own arms. The Confederate government provided only seven hundred small-bore squirrel guns, which were to be used by the Choctaws. Pike added that the Indians were not "a faithless and treacherous people, nor by nature jealous or suspicious, but trusting, frank, and loyal."

Commissioner Pike expressed the opinion that the Indian Bureau had been the most corrupt and incompetent in the federal government. Its agents had been constantly absent from their posts and cared little for the tribes they supervised except as a source of profit. Pike wanted the Confederate agents to be required to stay at their agencies and allowed to leave only by special permission.[9]

Federal Agent Carruth believed Chief Jumper had been bribed to make the alliance of 1 August 1861. Carruth indicated that Jumper initially refused such a compact because it appeared his tribe wanted to remain neutral. According to Carruth, Jumper changed his mind only after the Indians were lied to, threatened, and made promises that the Confederates would not honor. The Confederates told the Indians that they would retain and implement all treaty provisions. Exaggerated tales about Lincoln's excessive drinking caused by the ruin he had brought the nation, the bankruptcy of the United States, and the capture of Washington confused the Seminoles and others.

Carruth blamed the Confederates for Jumper's treason, viewing it more with pity than with anger. He stressed that few Indians had worked harder for their people than Jumper. The agent wanted the northern Indians "let loose" to fight the rebels in Indian country. He thought that three thousand Seminoles and Creeks, with the northern Indians and a few whites to give "nerve to the forces," could clear the territory. When the Union Indians were thoroughly committed, it would be "war to the death." Cruelties would be common, but it was the South that had

The march was undertaken with a short supply of clothing, food, and cooking utensils, and entirely without tents. The Indians were forced to "feed upon their ponies and their dogs, while their scanty clothing was reduced to threads, and in some cases absolute nakedness was their condition." As they moved up the valley of the Verdigris River, there was little time to rest and no shelter to protect them. By the time they reached the Fall River, some sixty miles west of Humboldt, Kansas, they suffered from congested chests, eyes, and throats. Several Indians' toes were frozen and their feet wounded by the sharp ice because they had no shoes. Men, women, and children lay on the frozen ground with only the prairie grass for a bed. The aprons, handkerchiefs, and scraps of cloth that the Indians stretched over saplings for makeshift tents gave no protection against the recurring blizzards.[13]

When the six to eight thousand "famishing and freezing" loyal Indians arrived in Kansas in mid-January, little immediate relief was available. Because the Indian Bureau had made no preparations for the émigrés, they were fed initially from the army stores of General David Hunter, commander of the Department of Kansas, who made every effort to alleviate their suffering. After about three weeks, Hunter informed Commissioner Dole that he could supply the Indians only until 15 February. Dole then directed Special Agent William Kile to buy food and clothing on credit and deliver the supplies to Superintendent Coffin for distribution among the Indians. Later, Congress authorized using the tribe's annuities for the refugees' subsistence.[14]

In the interim, the despair among the Indians continued. One government official wrote that "it would be impossible to give an adequate description of the suffering endured by these people during their flight, and for several weeks after their arrival." About 777 Seminoles under Chiefs Pascofar and Gotza (Cotza) were among those Indians at Fort Roe on the Verdigris River in February 1862. None of the refugees had cooking utensils, axes, or hatchets. They had to eat their provisions of meal and beef uncooked. New arrivals were constantly coming into the camps and often became ill after eating the rations. They also suffered from inflammatory diseases of the chest, throat, and eyes. Clothing was scarce, and some children were completely naked. United States army surgeon

started the Indian warfare. Carruth added that unless the tide was turned against the Confederates, Kansas would be the "scene of the cruelties, northern mothers will be the victims, our children may be slaughtered, our houses burned."[10]

Some Seminoles led by Chief Billy Bowlegs and Long John (John Chupko) denounced the Confederate treaty. Bowlegs believed that those who served the South would be destroyed, and he announced his intention to join Opothleyahola's Creeks, who wanted to maintain neutrality. Long John declared that the Seminoles respected their treaty with the United States. He wanted to abide by it in the hope that the federal government would honor its promises to care for the Seminole women and children. Unfortunately, these loyal Seminoles received no support from the government in Washington. They informed Federal officials that the "wolf has come, men who are strangers tread our soil, our children are frightened and the mothers cannot sleep for fear."[11]

Shortly after Pike's visit to the Seminoles, the loyal Seminole chiefs, including Billy Bowlegs, Long John, Pascofar, Halleck Tustenuggee, and others, gathered their people and went to Creek chief Opothleyahola's camp. Opothleyahola, an elderly and wealthy Upper Creek chief who owned several slaves and controlled two thousand acres of land, opposed those Lower Creeks led by Daniel and Chilly McIntosh who favored the South. Opothleyahola, wanting to remain neutral, had called a general council of the tribes in the territory, and had contacted Federal authorities in Kansas, who promised to send troops to expel the Confederates from Indian Territory. The Creek chief moved his people to an area near Eufaula after learning that the rebels under Douglas Cooper knew they were in contact with Federal authorities in Kansas and planned to attack them. Opothleyahola, however, was unable to avoid combat with the opposing forces.

The rebel Seminoles, with Pike's permission, had proceeded to raise troops for combat in the Confederate service. On 21 September 1861, they organized Companies A and B of what became the First Battalion (later the First Regiment) of Seminole Mounted Volunteers. Enrolled at the Seminole agency and stationed in the Seminole nation, the Indians, with their horses and equipment, were mustered into service for one year after examination by Hu McDonald. These troops went into service immediately with Chief Jumper as major (later honorary lieutenant colonel and colonel) and George Cloud and Foosahatchee Cojokenneys (Fushatchiecochokna) as captains. Companies C through F entered service during the following months, and with Companies A and B and other rebel Indians in the territory, fought against the loyal Indians.

When the Upper Creeks began fleeing, the Lower Creeks under the McIntoshes asked Cooper for help. By early November, Cooper had ready for combat fourteen hundred men and officers, including the First Seminole Cavalry Battalion commanded by Major John Jumper and the First Creek Cavalry Regiment commanded by Lieutenant Colonel Chilly McIntosh, six companies of Choctaw and Chickasaw mounted rifles, and the Ninth Texas Cavalry. These forces left Fort Gibson, forded the Arkansas River, and proceeded west toward the junction of the North Fork and Deep Fork of the Canadian River, where the loyal Seminoles and Creeks were located. Opothleyahola had a force of about two thousand warriors, including the Seminoles under second-in-command Halleck Tustenuggee. Many Seminole and Creek women, children, old men, and about two or three hundred blacks were with them.

On 5 November the loyal Seminoles and Creeks, including "self-respecting and prosperous farmers," broke camp and started northward toward Kansas. They were later joined by some Choctaws, Shawnees, Delawares, Comanches, Kickapoos, and Cherokees. The cavalcade consisted of carriages, ox teams, covered wagons, buggies, droves of livestock, and warriors and scouts. The Confederates pursued and engaged them in the battles of Round Mountain, Chusto Talasah, and Chustenahlah. Cooper's forces followed the trail of the loyal Indians up the Deep Fork of the Canadian River. Late in the afternoon of 19 November, the Confederates attacked the loyal Creeks and Seminoles at Round Mountain near the mouth of the Cimarron River in the first battle of the Civil War in the Indian Territory. The loyals retreated "under cover of the darkness" and left the countryside aflame. Estimates of loyalists' losses at 110 killed or wounded appear exaggerated. Cooper said he had six killed and four wounded, with one reported missing.

During the night, Opothleyahola's group moved along the north bank

of the Arkansas River to Bird Creek, about seven miles northeast of Tulsa. They waited there to obtain supplies and reinforcements from the Cherokees at Camp McDaniel. On 9 December, Cooper's reorganized forces and the loyalists engaged in a four-hour battle at Chusto Talasah. The Confederates returned the next morning to find the loyalists gone. Inaccurate accounts of casualties listed five hundred loyalists killed or wounded and, for the Confederates, fifteen killed and thirty-seven wounded. Instead of following Opothleyahola's forces, Cooper positioned his troops to prevent a large number of Cherokees from joining the loyalists.

On 26 December, the Confederates met the loyalists for the final in the battle of Chustenahlah near Hominy Creek. Loyalist Halleck Tustenuggee and his Seminole warriors were stationed behind trees rocks while others "formed a line" above. The Creeks were mounted reserve. Confederate Colonel James McIntosh's troops charged After brief hand-to-hand combat, the Seminoles withdrew and another "stand at their encampment," but by four o'clock they oughly defeated. The loyalists lost more than two hundred; Mc ported eight killed and thirty-two wounded. The Seminoles l ted that in the battle with McIntosh they lost a great ma warriors, as well as young men and women and children w in "cold blood by the wayside." They also lost their wagons ponies, flour, sugar, salt, and coffee—everything to tak women and children. Nonetheless, in order to keep their "Great Father," they continued toward Kansas. Additiona Cherokees who wanted to escape war with the Confeder

McIntosh's command pursued the Indians the ne about twenty more. Colonel Cooper also followed th the Kansas line, killing six and capturing about 150, children.[12]

As these loyalists moved slowly northward in the ice and snow, they left a trail of three hundred mile from their dead and injured. Families were torn were captured and others, dead or alive, were wolves. A few Indian women gave birth on th

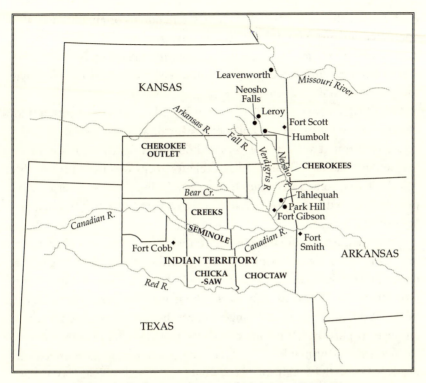

Map 6. *Indian territory and vicinity, 1861–65.*

A. B. Campbell was deeply touched by the hundreds of anxious and dis-appointed Indians who did not receive any provisions. Campbell found it incredible that more was not being done for the refugees and added that "common humanity demands that more should be done . . . to save them from total destruction."

Campbell's report was substantiated by John Turner, a captain and commissary of subsistence at Fort Leavenworth, who had visited the refugees concentrated at Fort Roe. Situated on Indian lands in an area with few settlers, the only other land suitable for them was the valley of the Neosho River, some forty miles to the east. That area was closer to supplies but more densely populated. Turner reported that they needed every necessity of life.[15]

Superintendent Coffin endeavored to divide the tribes and place them under their own agents. Seminole subagent George C. Snow began his duties at Fort Roe on 10 February 1862. That year, Snow supervised more than one thousand Seminoles, about half the tribe. He reported "destitution, misery, and suffering amongst them is beyond the power of any pen to portray." With Indians continually coming into the camps, the five wagons of blankets, clothing, and shoes and boots supplied the needs of less than half of the refugees. Spoiled bacon from Fort Leavenworth made several Indians sick; the subagent described the bacon as unfit for a dog. The harsh conditions caused several cases of consumption and pneumonia among the Seminoles and the five thousand Indians from other tribes who were scattered over the one hundred miles between the Verdigris and Arkansas rivers in southern Kansas. Within a short time, physicians had to amputate one hundred arms and legs while the amputees lay on the ground unable to move. One eight-year-old Creek boy had both feet removed near his ankles. The suffering of the sick, as well as the healthy, was beyond comprehension. By March, one-fifth of the Indians at the Verdigris camp were suffering from mumps, measles, diphtheria, and pneumonia as well as frostbite. Within two months, 240 Creeks alone had died.

The scene was made worse as twelve to fifteen hundred dead ponies lay scattered around the camps and in the rivers. Another two thousand ponies were slowly starving as the Indians watched helplessly. Half of the Seminoles' ponies had starved by early February. As the spring weather warmed, the stench from dead ponies and complaints from whites about the Indians' stealing timber caused some of the Indians to move eastward toward LeRoy on the Neosho River. Early in March, Subagent Snow moved the rest of the Seminoles to LeRoy, and six weeks later he was able to persuade them to move to Neosho Falls.[16]

The loyal Seminoles soon reorganized as a nation in Kansas and voiced several complaints. Under the new head chief, Billy Bowlegs, and with subordinate chiefs, they complained about the unsuitable goods sent them and their failure to receive annuities. The fine delaines and bleached muslins from the government were often traded for goods of much less value, such as corn, chickens, and eggs. The loyalists agreed that the rebelling Seminoles had forfeited their right to money payments but insisted the annuities continue for them.[17]

By late April, George W. Collamore, who was appointed to investigate the conditions in the refugee camps, reported to Dole that it would be best to return the Indians to their homes. It was impossible to care for them properly in Kansas. The Indian Bureau never knew how many Indians required food, because disloyal employees occasionally stole the census records. The high prices for goods in wartime also handicapped efforts to ease the Indians' distress.[18]

Although Confederates had driven Federal forces out of Indian Territory by the end of the first year of war, as early as February, vague plans had been made to return the refugees to Indian Territory. The Seminole and Creek chiefs had agreed with General Hunter to support a Union invasion of the territory to clear it so their people could return. Later, President Lincoln approved having two white regiments escort the Indians to their homes. The tribes organized two regiments of mounted rifles that included 193 Seminoles. Some Union Indian soldiers, outfitted with stiff wool hats and uniforms that were too small or too large, continued to use their traditional war paint and war-whoops. Under the command of Colonel William Weer, they were assigned to the military Department of Kansas, which was commanded by General James Blunt. Special Agents E. H. Carruth and H. W. Martin supervised the Indians and acted as liaisons to the military. Upon entering the territory, the troops were to protect the property of the loyalists, decide if the corn crop would support the refugees, and determine the strength and locations of the Confederates from western Arkansas to Texas.

Weer's command left Humboldt for Indian Territory on 28 June but failed to fulfill its mission. Operating under searing heat and with a lack of potable water, the force managed to get to Tahlequah and Park Hill in the Cherokee nation. But on 18 July Colonel Frederick Salamon of the First Brigade arrested Weer, his superior officer, because he neglected his troops. Salamon claimed that Weer was intemperate, abusive, and violent to the soldiers. He had kept them idle for ten days on the Grand River, about fourteen miles north of Fort Gibson, while their supplies dwindled away. Salamon felt his actions necessary to "save the troops" after Weer had imperiled them.

Salamon then withdrew the white troops to Fort Scott. Some two thousand Cherokees, mostly women and children, who were seeking protection followed them there. The loyalist Indian soldiers stayed behind under Colonel Robert W. Furnas in an attempt to hold the upper part of the territory.

In August, Carruth and Martin informed Dole from Sulphur Springs, which was located between Fort Scott and Fort Gibson, that the Seminoles, Creeks, and others had acted in compliance with their orders. Nevertheless, the territory had not been cleared of rebels, so the refugee Indians remained in Kansas during the winter of 1862–63. A total of 919 Seminoles camped there with the other tribes.[19]

In early 1863, the loyal Indian forces with Colonel William A. Phillips, their new commander, captured Tahlequah and occupied Fort Gibson. From there Seminole chief Bowlegs, captain of Company F of the First Indian Home Guards, asked Commissioner Dole for additional forces to drive the rebels out of the rest of Indian Territory.

With Fort Gibson in loyalist hands, Chief Bowlegs and other leading Seminoles pleaded for permission to return the Seminoles to their homes. They also asked for better treatment for those who remained in Kansas. The latter also wrote Dole, seeking an improvement in their condition. These Indians probably felt it necessary to exert more leadership because Opothleyahola had died at the Sac and Fox reservation in Kansas the previous summer. In August, Pascofar declared that the Seminoles had a good agent, but they failed to get sufficient tents, rations, or clothing. Some members of the tribe had been forced to get money for clothes from the soldiers stationed at Fort Gibson when they came to visit family and friends in Kansas. Pascofar asked especially for coffee, sugar, and heavy material for tents. He stated that they could make their tents if they could get the heavy material. They had been unable to get these necessities from their agent or Coffin. Most of these appeals went unanswered.[20]

Several thousand other loyal Indians faced similar problems at Fort Gibson. In their guerrilla attacks, Confederate Cherokee Stand Watie and his forces destroyed crops, houses, and public buildings in Indian Territory in the summer and fall of 1863. Loyal Indians there fled to Fort Gibson for safety. Among the three thousand soldiers there were about six thousand Indians, mostly half-starved and half-clothed women and children, who huddled around the fort. These refugees suffered from exposure to the hot sun and from dysentery. Although Coffin did send some supplies such as corn, flour, and bacon to Fort Gibson, during the winter of 1863 and 1864, the Cherokees there almost starved.

Those Seminoles who had remained in the Seminole district were supervised by Confederate agent Joseph Samuel Murrow after September 1862. When Murrow arrived to assume his duties, he found a free mulatto man in charge of the agency's buildings and archives. Because the previous agent had been gone about a year, the agency was in disarray, and Murrow found no financial papers indicating the monies received or expended. Although Murrow made repairs while he lived at the old agency, he was forced to leave in 1863.

When the Union took control of Indian Territory in the fall of 1863, after the battles of Honey Springs (17 July) and Perryville (25 August), and the capture of Fort Smith (2 September), those Seminoles allied with the Confederacy became refugees, as had the loyal Seminoles earlier. The Confederate Indians and other Confederate sympathizers fled to the Chickasaw nation and Choctaw country along the Red River and to Texas, where they suffered in much the same manner as did their brethren in Kansas.[21] Getting supplies to these Indian refugees was almost impossible, because the Federals controlled the Mississippi River after the fall of Vicksburg (July 1863).

Confederate Major General Thomas C. Hindman and his successor,

Brigadier General Samuel Maxey, supplied these Indian refugees from their commissariat. This "unauthorized action" kept many of the southern refugees from complete starvation. Later, the Confederate Arkansas and Red River superintendency, headquartered at Fort Towson in the Choctaw nation, supervised the tribes that furnished military units—the Seminoles, Choctaws, Cherokees, Creeks, Chickasaws, Osages, and the mixed group of Reserve Indians. The superintendent was also the military commander of the District of Indian Territory, so the assistant superintendent usually assumed most of the agency's responsibilities. The agency was organized with a superintendent of issues who enrolled the Indians, secured supplies, and supervised subsistence; an inspector who visited the camps at least once a month to determine the Indians' condition and to guard the government's interests; and an issuing agent who distributed provisions. Confederate authorities appointed several physicians and made unsuccessful attempts to establish schools among the refugees. The Cherokees set up workshops with looms and spinning wheels.

The Confederate superintendency was unable, however, to protect the refugees from destitution and suffering. Because the families were so scattered, it proved too inconvenient and involved too much work to supply them from the commissariat. Part of the $238,044 appropriated for the Indians by the Confederate Congress failed to reach them because of poor organization and administration. The widespread sickness, exposure, and starvation led Stand Watie to appeal to Texans to bring surplus goods to Clarksville, Texas, for distribution among the refugees. Elias Boudinot, Cherokee delegate to the Confederate Congress, obtained a $100,000 loan from the Confederacy to help the Cherokees.[22]

The southern Seminole agent Murrow, described as a devoted and caring individual who had been appointed by the Confederates upon the request of Chief Jumper, had a precarious position. Murrow had served as a Baptist missionary to the Seminoles and Creeks since 1857, and had been Chief Jumper's pastor since 1860, when Jumper left the Presbyterian church and associated with the Baptists. After leaving the Seminole district, Murrow in 1863 established his agency at Hatsboro near Fort Washita. That year he also became subsistence agent for the old men, women, and children of the Osage, Comanche, and Creek tribes in addition to serving the Seminoles. The Confederate government provided him money for flour, corn, salt, and beef. According to Murrow, these refugees had been wanderers since shortly after the Federals took control of their country. The bad weather, unsanitary conditions, and presence of Union troops had kept them "moving from place to place" and in constant peril. Further, Indian country was raided and terrorized by Kansas jayhawkers and Texas bushwhackers, who drove off cattle by the thousands, burned houses, destroyed fields, and reduced the Seminole country to a wilderness.

By July 1864, there were 574 Seminoles and 441 Creeks in refugee camps near Oil Springs, about fifty miles west of Fort Washita along the Red, Washita, and Blue rivers. These refugees and the Reserve Indians were provided rations by the same contractors. In 1864, Charles F. Ricketts acted as the issuing agent to the 1,015 Seminoles and Creeks among the total of 14,790 Indians subsisted by the Confederacy. These Creeks were either related to, or had a close affinity with, the Seminoles and always stayed with them. But Agent Murrow complained several times that the contractors failed to comply with the contracts and that more supplies were needed. Murrow directed Chief Jumper to take an application to Fort Towson, requesting permission to export two hundred bales of cotton to raise money for clothing and other necessities for the Seminoles and Creeks. Nonetheless, Assistant Superintendent Roswell Lee criticized Murrow for staying near Fort Washita and concluded that if he lived among the Seminoles and Creeks, he would have had less occasion to complain of problems with the contractors and the late arrival of supplies.[23]

Although Murrow did not live among his charges, he was active in promoting religious endeavors for them. After moving to his new location, he built a brush arbor and held services every Sunday during the war, except once when the Indians had to flee from Federal troops. He served as the official chaplain for Jumper's battalion and officiated at different ceremonies. He also conducted funerals, especially for those who had died from measles and smallpox. Murrow visited other camps, but he did not minister to those on the battlefields because active hostilities were usually in other areas.[24]

The Confederate Seminole troops under John Jumper, Stand Watie's

Cherokees and Choctaws, the Creeks under Daniel N. McIntosh, and Texas troops were sometimes located near the southern refugees. Almost all of the men from these tribes were in active Confederate service. The Indian forces suffered from the same hardships as did the women, children, and old men in the camps. Moreover, discipline was poor because the officers elected often were not strict. The troops were poorly equipped and often served without pay, sufficient clothes, or blankets. Goods sent to them were commandeered en route. On occasion troops at Fort Smith opened boxes intended for the Indians and took what they wanted. Of items shipped to them, the Indians received only nineteen hundred of eight thousand pairs of shoes, seventy-five of one thousand tents, nine hundred of seven thousand suits of clothes, and one thousand of four thousand shirts. When Albert Pike served as commander of the Military Department of Indian Territory, he complained that the Indians only received refuse or crumbs from the "white man's table."

Those Seminole troops commanded by Jumper fared no better than the others. Poorly drilled, armed, and disciplined, with their mediocre ponies, many of the Indians thought it useless to fight. Still, Colonel Cooper recommended them for guerrilla warfare. In mid-1862, Lieutenant Colonel John Jumper's Seminole Battalion, with the Creek and Chickasaw Battalions, operated in the Salt Plains area with instructions to take Fort Larned, the post at Walnut Creek, and Fort Wise. They also had orders to intercept wagon trains going to New Mexico. The Seminole soldiers participated in several other engagements and were ordered to report to Bourland for frontier defense in late 1863. Despite such service, by 1863 some white Confederates wanted to furlough the Indian troops. The Indians, however, wished to remain on active duty because they had forfeited federal annuities and had their property destroyed after aligning with the southerners.[25]

The Confederate Indian troops were also used in areas outside Indian Territory, which was a violation of the terms of their treaties. A few thousand Indians, possibly some Seminoles, under Brigadier General Albert Pike fought at the Battle of Pea Ridge in Arkansas in early March 1862. After this Confederate defeat, the main southern army withdrew to eastern Arkansas as the Indian troops retreated to Indian Territory. Colonel

Stand Watie's Indian forces then received orders to conduct raids in Missouri. Pike stationed the other Indian troops at Fort McCulloch in the Choctaw nation.

Pike, as commander of the Indian Territory since January 1862, opposed using Indian troops outside their territory. The removal of such forces from the Cherokee nation cleared the way for a Federal invasion of the area. By May, Pike had strongly opposed providing a six-gun battery of artillery to accompany white troops to Arkansas as the commander of the Trans-Mississippi Department, Major General Thomas C. Hindman, had ordered. Pike believed the remaining forces were inadequate to protect Indian Territory. Later, he resigned his position as commander of the Indian Territory and was captured on Hindman's orders in November 1862. This disagreement had left Confederate military affairs in Indian Territory in much confusion.[26]

As the southern Indian troops and refugees battled to survive in the white man's war, Union colonel Phillips took the initiative in early 1864 to clear Indian Territory so that the civilian refugees might return from Kansas. A force deployed by Phillips went up the Canadian River to Seminole country and swept north to the Arkansas, where it crossed and went to Fort Gibson. The troops distributed Indian translations of Lincoln's amnesty proclamation and sent messages of goodwill to the tribal chiefs. Phillips planned to leave no subsistence for the Confederate army and wanted to force it to obtain supplies from Red River points about 180 miles away. The colonel considered such action necessary to crush the rebel troops who had stayed in Red River country at Doaksville, Fort Washita, Boggy Depot, Fort McCulloch, and Armstrong Academy during the winter of 1863–64.

Phillips sent a copy of the amnesty proclamation and a letter each to Colonel Jumper, Governor Colbert of the Chickasaws, Una McIntosh (Creek), and the Choctaw council, proclaiming that "their day of grace was over." He asked Jumper to consider the interests of his tribe, because it could in no way overthrow the United States government. Moreover, Lincoln proposed mercy, pardon, and peace—a liberal and honest offer according to Phillips. If the Indians refused to accept the amnesty offer, the Seminoles would be "blotted out in blood."[27]

Although Phillips was largely responsible for the Union taking control of Indian Territory, his record with the Indian troops seemed less praiseworthy. On 10 March 1864, Long John, who had entered the Union army with Chief Bowlegs, wrote President Lincoln and described an Indian soldier's life under Phillips's command. At Fort Gibson, the Indian soldiers had a spade in one hand and a rifle in the other as they tried to build a fort while under rebel fire. They exchanged shots daily with Confederates on the opposite side of the Arkansas River. While Phillips commanded at Fort Gibson, there was little to eat. The Indian soldiers usually had only beef and the little wheat, which they gathered and pounded. The Confederates told the Union Indians that they had plenty to eat and would starve the loyalists out. When General Blunt came to the fort, however, he brought plenty of food.

Long John also reported some questionable orders he received from Phillips. The colonel ordered Long John to take one hundred Indians on a scouting trip with six days rations, fully cognizant that no rations were available. They made the journey without food and returned to find nothing to eat. Phillips had also ordered Long John to take six men and cross the river in the bitterly cold, waist-deep water and go to the old agency, still without rations. When Long John refused, Phillips tried to put him in the guard house. The Indian regiments then held council with the captains and lieutenants and asked if the federal government knew that the Indians were starving, naked, and barefoot. The officers replied in the affirmative, but stated that the government had no wagons to haul provisions to the Indians.

Concluding that they might as well be killed as starve, the Indians decided to go to their own country. They wanted to find food and rebels to fight. The white officers informed Phillips that he had caused the Indians' dissatisfaction. Phillips asked the Indians to wait for a large company of friends coming to the fort. Believing that Phillips was lying to them, Long John and his party left Fort Gibson, although they had no food for the campaign. The few Confederates they encountered were driven off, and their food and other possessions were taken. The Indians proceeded across Creek country, down through the Chickasaw district, and back through the Creek country without finding any rebels. Nor were there any Confederates in Seminole country. But Long John's party did meet Colonel Jumper's Seminoles in the Chickasaw district. A battle ensued in which several were killed, with the loyalists defeating the rebels.

Long John simply wanted Lincoln to keep the promise made to Billy Bowlegs in the fall of 1863. The president had assured the chief that his people could return home when the territory was cleared. Now Long John asked that Lincoln allow them to go back.[28]

Pascofar, the second chief of the Union Seminoles, wrote the president on the same day as Long John and asked that his tribe be allowed to return home as the country was now cleared of Confederates. He also felt the Indian soldiers had been unfairly used by the North. According to their agreements with General Hunter when the Indians enlisted in 1861, they were to serve for three years and only in Indian Territory. Yet Indian troops had fought in Missouri, Arkansas, and other places. The Union Seminole chief Bowlegs had died in service. Thus Pascofar, as Long John, felt they had earned the privilege of returning home.[29]

With Indian Territory in Union hands, several federal officials began promoting the return of the loyal Indian refugees. As early as January 1864, Senator James R. Doolittle of Wisconsin, chairman of the Senate Committee on Indian Affairs, suggested that the Indians should return to their homeland to raise crops. Although the government had to pay sixty thousand dollars a month to maintain the thousands of refugee Indians, most congressmen hesitated to send the Indians back to the territory until it was safe.

In February, Commissioner Dole declared that the United States forces held Forts Smith and Gibson and had control of the Indian country in a limited sense. However, he thought that rebel guerrillas might operate in the area and that it was entirely unsafe for persons outside the military posts. The country was infested with guerrillas, bushwhackers, thieves, robbers, and murderers. The military could not protect Indians on farms, and so he concluded that the country should be made more secure before the loyal Indians returned.[30]

Three months later, the United States Congress appropriated $223,000 of the requested $491,720 to remove the Union Indian refugees from

Kansas. On 16 May, most of these Indians, including a few Seminoles with some Creeks, Cherokees, Uchees, and Chickasaws, began their march homeward. A cavalcade six miles long of some five thousand Indians, three hundred wagons, and several hundred dogs was escorted to the southern border of Kansas by Major General Samuel R. Curtis, commander of the Department of Kansas. Brigadier General Frederick Steele of the Department of Arkansas provided protection from the Kansas border. After traveling about ten miles a day in searing heat and heavy rain, the procession reached Fort Gibson by 15 June. Along the way there were sixteen births and six deaths, including four caused by lightning.

Those Indians who arrived joined another nine or ten thousand, mostly women, children, and old men. About fifteen thousand Indians, dependent on the government's subsistence, were now at Fort Gibson or Fort Smith. These Indians suffered because of a shortage of supplies because getting supply trains to Fort Gibson proved difficult. Rain, snow, and disloyal escorts kept some supplies from reaching the Indians.

Quarrels between the civil and military authorities added to the chaos. Phillips accused Coffin of paying contractors for beef that was stolen from the Indians. On the other hand, Phillips was said to have wanted to eliminate competition for his own gain. Blunt had indicated that corruption existed in the Southern Superintendency and reported that "unscrupulous spectators" victimized the refugees. Thousands of cattle from Indian herds were rustled as the Indians starved.[31]

Those 470 (they had lost 80) Union Seminoles who had to remain at Neosho Falls, Kansas, under Agent Snow and those Seminoles who returned to Indian Territory in mid-1864 had been in poor condition in the previous months. A recent smallpox epidemic had caused Superintendent Coffin to refuse to integrate them with the other tribes. Pascofar, as directed by Billy Bowlegs, had assisted Agent Snow in caring for the Seminole women and children. Over the months Pascofar had appealed to Dole for clothing to dress the tribe, stressing that most of the time the Indians had enough to eat, but that their clothes were thin and inadequate. The Seminole women earlier had wanted two dresses each, one of good calico and one of a heavy coarse fabric.[32] Their old clothing had worn out before new garments arrived in January 1864. They had been without educational and agricultural opportunities, and the extreme cold weather in the winter of 1863–64 caught the Indians without sufficient blankets, clothing, or shelter.

Because of their extreme deprivations, suffering and death frequented the Seminoles. Several died from "fatal organic lesions. . . . Others dragged out a miserable existence for a few weeks or months and expired." Moreover, smallpox hit the tribe in September 1863, ran its course, and then reappeared. The Seminoles were vaccinated, but the first virus was inert; another was only partially successful, leaving the sufferers with a mild varioloid. The catarrhal diseases with their frequent complications similar to typhoid were usually prevalent in the winter and spring. The gastroenteric diseases affected the Indian refugees in the summer and fall. One of the physicians who treated the refugees declared that the Indians required twice as much medication as whites. By September 1864, the smallpox had subsided, and the Seminoles remaining in Kansas wanted and intended to return to Indian Territory in the spring of 1865.[33]

While some loyal Seminoles stayed at Fort Gibson and the others were in Kansas making plans to return to Indian Territory, those Southern Seminoles under Colonel Jumper were reenlisting for Confederate service. The commander of the District of Indian Territory, Samuel B. Maxey, had asked Jumper to reorganize his troops for more combat. On 6 July 1864, at Camp Limestone Prairie, headquarters of the First Seminole Regiment, Jumper discussed the matter with the Seminole and Creek soldiers. Jumper vigorously supported the South because the Seminoles' homes, families, and interests were in the South, and he still believed the Confederates could win. He added, "Fellow-citizens, we are but a small people it is true, yet our fathers in Florida were the same, and they for a long time kept a large and powerful nation at bay. Let us emulate their glorious example, and live or if need be die 'freemen.' We gained a name in that war, and what was of more value, a place as a separate and independent people in this country, living upon our own lands and making our own laws. It is in defense of these inestimable rights we are now fighting."

Jumper pointed out that the Federals had invaded the territory and destroyed property, and now the Confederates had to drive them out. The colonel noted the men had served faithfully, but now reorganization and reenlistment were the only alternatives, and he hoped they would remain loyal to the Confederacy. After Jumper's impressive speech, a group representing the First Seminole Regiment, including its president, William Roberson, Major James Factor, Lieutenant George Cloud, Captain Fus-Hutche-Cochokenee, and Chief So-War-Nak Yar-Har-La, agreed to reenlist for the duration of the war.[34]

As the closing months of the war came, the dismal condition of the southern Seminoles and their northern counterparts continued. The Confederates still endured the shortages of clothing and equipment in their camps at Oil Springs. The needs of the Indian refugees remained secondary when the Trans-Mississippi Department depended on trade from across the Mexican border and blockade runners for supplies. Moreover, the guerrilla attacks on wagon trains and the limited transportation and industry in the area kept Indian supplies at a minimum.

Those Seminoles in Kansas continued in their destitute state. In late March 1865, George Reynolds, a native of New York who was living in Kansas, became Seminole agent replacing George C. Snow, who became the Neosho agent. Reynolds immediately pleaded for a few plows, hoes, and other utensils to enable his tribe to farm to survive.[35]

A few days later, the white man's war was over, but the punishment for the Seminoles' actions was yet to come. Although General Robert E. Lee surrendered on 9 April, the southern Seminoles held out for two more months. General Stand Watie yielded for the Seminoles, Cherokees, Creeks, and Osages to Lieutenant Colonel C. A. Matthews and W. H. Vance at Doaksville in Choctaw country on 23 June 1865.[36]

For the Seminoles and the other tribes in the territory, no opportunity existed for them to emerge victorious from the war that had snared them at its beginning. Those who had remained loyal, while hoping the United States would protect them and uphold their treaties, had to leave their homes and migrate to Union territory, where many suffered and died from experiences beyond belief. Moreover, they had to furnish soldiers who had to fight fellow Indians while trying to regain their own land. On the other hand, Confederate Indians, who depended on the Confederates' treaty promises, also had to leave their homes and become refugees, facing sickness, starvation, and death. Their soldiers too had to battle against other Indians to regain control of a homeland that in reality belonged to both Indian factions. In the end, the casualties and destruction in the territory were probably proportionately greater than anywhere else in the United States. At least forty-five to fifty thousand Indians had to become refugees or soldiers, and thousands lost their lives. Of the more than thirty-five hundred loyal Indian soldiers, more than one-fourth died either in battle or from wounds or disease. Their Confederate counterparts suffered heavy losses as well. Both factions had to return to a homeland that had been burned, pillaged, and ravaged by guerrillas, outlaws, profiteers, and murderers.

Still, for the Seminoles and the other tribes, another disaster would be added to the high casualties and territorial destruction. They had to face punishment for those who had rebelled and succumbed to the promises and threats of the Confederates. Nearly a year passed before they received the final verdict for their offense.

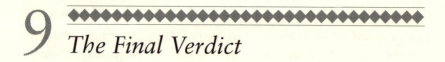

The Final Verdict

The penalty for the disloyalty of the Seminoles and other Indians who had united with the South was decided long before 1865. Several Indian tribes from the East had settled in Kansas prior to 1854, when it was the upper part of Indian Territory. Commissioner William P. Dole had stated categorically that Kansans would never "shut up" until the Indians left their state. In 1864, Dole was unwilling to renew treaties with rebel tribes until the government obtained part of their land for these eastern Indians in Kansas. After the Civil War, the Kansans still wanted to rid their state of its Indian population. Kansas senators James Lane and Samuel Pomeroy worked to structure the reconstruction program for Indian Territory. As early as February 1863 they won passage of legislation permitting the president to "suspend treaties with the Five Civilized Tribes, to appropriate certain portions of their domains, and to direct the removal of the tribes from Kansas to the Indian Territory."

Thus Dennis N. Cooley, the new commissioner of Indian affairs, with Elijah Sells, the southern superintendent, and other commissioners, Thomas Wistar, W. S. Harney, and Ely S. Parker, presented grim information when they met with representatives of the Seminoles, the other Four Tribes, and the Osages, Senecas, Shawnees, and Quapaws at the peace council called at Fort Smith in September 1865.[1] The Seminoles and the others were informed that they must sign a treaty of permanent peace with the United States in which they would relinquish a portion of their land to loyal tribes from Kansas and elsewhere. They must also abolish slavery, incorporate freedmen into their tribe giving them full rights, and help to control the Plains tribes.[2]

The loyal Seminole delegates, Long John, Pascofar, Fo-hutshe, Fos Harjo, and Chocote Harjo, along with black interpreters Robert Johnson and Caesar Bruner, had gone to Fort Smith with Agent George Reynolds. They were hesitant to make the required commitments. After they heard the demands of the United States government as presented by the commissioners, the Seminole delegates claimed that they thought the purpose of the meeting was to reunite them with the rebel Seminoles. Moreover, they argued that they needed time to discuss such a treaty with their people. Later, the loyal Seminole delegates told the commissioners they could accept those blacks who had been associated with their tribe, but they could not provide for other blacks. The commissioners finally drew up a preliminary treaty, which the Seminoles signed. It renounced the Confederate treaty and reaffirmed allegiance to and peace with the United States.

The Southern Seminole delegates, who had been meeting at Chahta Tamaha in the Choctaw nation, arrived on the eighth day of the conference. They also claimed to be confused by the commissioners' demands. The following day the two factions issued a joint statement in which they stated that they had settled their differences and would accept the terms written in any treaties with the United States. At the same time, however, the united representatives announced that they wanted to return to the tribe for a treaty council to determine the wishes of their nation. A few days later, southern Seminole delegates John Jumper, George Cloud, and James Factor changed their minds and stated that they would not accept the treaty as it had been presented to them. They complained that they had not fully understood the terms of the agreement, and they opposed especially the provisions relating to the forfeiture of land and the inclusion of the freedmen in the tribe as full tribal members.[3]

Jumper pleaded for his people in a paper presented to the commissioners at the council. He declared that they were just emerging from the

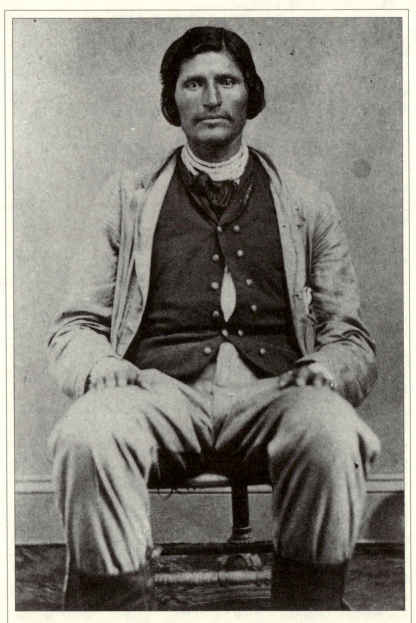

John Chupco, or Long John. A band chief who refused to sign the Confederate Seminole treaty of 1861, John Chupco emigrated to Kansas with the loyal Seminoles, Creeks, and others. He became a leader of the loyal Seminoles and fought to help regain Indian Territory. At the signing of the treaty of 1866, government agents considered him the principal chief of the Seminole nation. After the war, he served as head chief with John Jumper. He died in 1881. Courtesy, National Anthropological Archives, Smithsonian Institution.

"darkness and poverty of barbarism" when the whites drew them into their war. The conflict had left them a feeble and suppliant tribe with no fields in the Washita River lowlands, where they had been since 1864. They planned to return soon to their own land and needed immediate relief. Jumper indicated that they were anxious to reestablish themselves with their loyalist Seminole brethren and to maintain good relations with the United States. Commissioner Cooley said Jumper's communication, although not properly a part of the council's proceedings, would be placed on file.[4] The council ended after thirteen days with the understanding that Indian delegations would later go to Washington to formalize treaties with the United States.[5]

In the interim, the Seminoles remained scattered in Indian Territory and Kansas. In October 1865, about half of the loyal Seminole refugees were living on Creek and Cherokee lands near Fort Gibson. An additional five hundred still remained in Kansas near Neosho Falls. A month later, most of the former rebel Seminoles with a few blacks had returned to Seminole country, where they found destruction and rubble created by foraging armies and guerrilla bands. Reynolds visited these Seminoles and concluded that about 987 lived in the old homes. Although they were energetically repairing their houses and fences and had sowed wheat, their condition was poor. They lacked clothing, shoes, and means of subsistence and therefore needed calico and other cloth, flour, and beef. The southern superintendent instructed Reynolds to make no distinction between the loyal and rebel Seminoles. Reynolds told the former Confederate Seminoles to go to Fort Gibson to get supplies.

Reynolds informed Commissioner Cooley of the Seminoles' plight. Their condition was now worse than before the war. They were a stricken, divided, and beggared people scattered over hundreds of miles, situated far from their agent, and with almost no means of transportation.[6]

With the tribe so scattered, it was impossible to choose at one time the delegates to represent the nation at the treaty negotiations in Washington. Therefore, three Seminoles representing the loyalists, Long John, Chocote Harjo, and Fos Harjo, and one representative of the rebel Seminoles, John F. Brown, with black interpreter Robert Johnson and Agent

John Jumper. John Jumper succeeded his brother Jim as principal Seminole chief in the early 1850s. Under his leadership, the Seminoles gained separation from the Creeks through the treaty of 1856. Jumper signed the Confederate treaty of 1861 and headed the rebel Seminole faction. He also served as a major and an honorary lieutenant colonel and colonel for the Confederates. After the war, he and John Chupco served as head chiefs. He resigned in 1877 to devote full time to the Baptist ministry. Courtesy, National Anthropological Archives, Smithsonian Institution.

Reynolds negotiated for the tribe. Reynolds had earlier favored setting aside part of the Seminoles' land for the Osages. He also had recommended in October that the Seminoles be placed on "small tracts of land or head-rights," and that most of their annuities be used to improve their farms.

Although the "treaty of perpetual peace and friendship" signed on 21 March 1866 granted general amnesty, its real objective was clearly stated: the United States "in view of its urgent necessities for lands in the Indian Territory, requires a cession by said Seminole nation of a part of its reservation" for a "reasonable price." The Seminoles were to cede their entire domain of 2,169,080 acres and were promised adequate land where the United States would protect them from other tribes. They received $325,362, or fifteen cents an acre, for their land. They then paid fifty cents an acre, or $100,000, for 200,000 acres of the western portion of Creek land.[7]

Commissioner Cooley contended that the Seminole treaty was beneficial to the Indians and the government. The discrepancy in the price of the land resulted from the fact that a large portion of the Seminole land was worthless, unproductive gypsum lands. By contrast, the land sold to the Seminoles was the best portion of the real estate recently acquired from the Creeks. Cooley recounted that the "commissioners preferred to let the Seminoles keep part of the best portion of their old reservation and purchase the remainder at 15 cents per acre, rather than cede the 200,000 [2 million] acres as provided by the terms of this treaty, but the Seminoles preferred the new reduced reservation as the better bargain and the most desirable future home."[8]

The treaty, which constituted a full settlement of all claims of Seminoles from damages and losses of the war, provided for the dispersal of the remainder of the $325,362. The Seminoles were to receive $30,000 to reestablish their farms; $20,000 for agricultural implements, seed, and stock; $15,000 for a mill; $40,362 for subsistence; and interest at 5 percent on a fund of $50,000 for the support of education and on $20,000 for the support of tribal government.

A total of fifty thousand dollars went only to loyal Seminoles who had suffered losses in the war. A board of commissioners was to determine legal recipients, both Indians and blacks, from a list submitted by their agent. The commissioner of Indian affairs and the secretary of the interior had to study the evidence and make awards from the amount stipulated in the treaty.

Under other minor treaty provisions, the federal government agreed to build new Seminole agency buildings costing no more than ten thousand dollars, and religious denominations that agreed to educate and teach their doctrines to the Seminoles could receive 640 acres of land. This acreage would revert to the Indians when not in use.

On 21 March 1866, Commissioners Cooley, Sells, and Parker and the representatives of the loyal Seminoles, John Chupko (Long John), Chocote Harjo, and Fos Harjo signed the Treaty with the Seminole Indians. Robert Johnson, the Seminoles' black interpreter, also signed. Agent Reynolds was a witness.

On the same day, the southern Seminole delegate, John F. Brown, son-in-law of Chief Jumper and former lieutenant in the Confederate army, put his objections to the treaty on paper. He objected to the price the government gave the Seminoles for their land and to the tribe's small allotment of 200,000 acres. The Seminoles were a weak tribe, but if the Creeks, Choctaws, and Cherokees were entitled to 160 acres per capita, the Seminoles should get the same, Brown contended. He further requested that his protest be filed with the treaty, and he waited until 30 June to sign that document. The Senate ratified the treaty on 19 July, and President Andrew Johnson added his signature on 16 August.[9]

The Civil War was costly for the Seminoles. They faced the problems of tribal division, property destruction, and social and emotional upheaval, starvation, diseases, and deaths, and then were forced to accept a greatly reduced land area. As late as April 1866, some fifteen hundred Seminoles near Fort Gibson subsisted on flour alone. Agent Reynolds asked that the Indian Department provide beef to prevent starvation. The next month Commissioner Cooley informed Secretary of the Interior James Harlan that $343,103 was needed for the subsistence of several thousand loyal Seminoles, Creeks, and Wichitas for March to July. Hoping that Congress, which had made earlier appropriations for the Indians, would appropriate this money promptly, Cooley said that "when

human creatures are starving, I can not hear their complaints with indif-
ference."[10]

By 1866, after thirty years in the West, the Seminoles found themselves with little property, no schools, no unified government, a meager
subsistence, and in much the same physical state as when they had migrated from Florida. A variety of factors had contributed to this small
tribe's misfortunes in the West. Their wars with the United States in
Florida and their refusal to merge with the Creeks in the West caused
some federal officials to regard them with contempt. Moreover, governmental neglect, irresponsible Indian agents, delayed annuities, and the
adverse effects of the Civil War plagued them during the thirty years after their arrival. These difficulties resulted in part from the poor implementation of United States Indian policies and the ineffectiveness of the
infant Office of Indian Affairs. This agency struggled during the first half
of the nineteenth century with the overwhelming responsibility of developing and enforcing the nation's Indian removal policy. Consequently,
the various agents who served the Seminoles were often corrupt or incompetent or both. Some of them were removed for intemperance or misconduct in handling tribal funds or for being absent from their posts too
frequently. The lack of strong tribal organization and unity, the lack of
education, and the necessity of using black interpreters impeded both the
tribe's progress and its relationship with government officials.

The first two decades found the Seminoles objecting to their settlement among the Creeks as their treaties seemingly required. While the
Florida emigrants relocated several times as they pleaded for their own
land, they also had to make countless adjustments in a different environment among various other tribes. Smallpox and measles epidemics,
threatening wild Plains tribes, and troublesome migrants bound for California aggravated the Seminoles. They found few opportunities for advancement.

But the Seminoles had survived in a different land with a different climate. They overcame threats of tribal subjugation and their fear of the
wild Plains tribes. The poor implementation of the Indian Bureau's policies, the delays in receiving annuities, and the corruption of some of their
agents failed to break their spirit. Limited educational and cultural op-

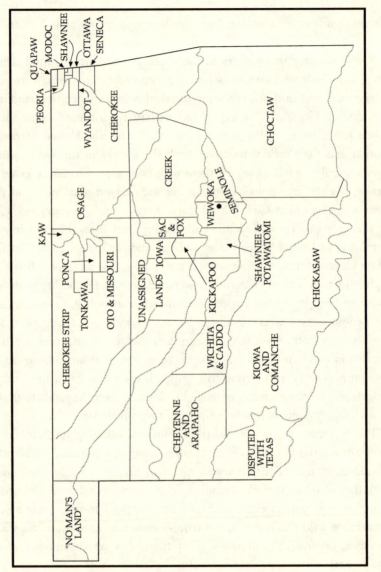

Map 7. Western Seminole land after treaty of 1866.

portunities and problems with alcoholism limited their progress but not their courage. Lack of a strong tribal organization and the dispersal of the tribe's members added to the chaos in the West but could not destroy the Seminoles' tribal identity. To these difficulties the Civil War added property destruction, forced emigration, suffering, death, and, at the end, a great reduction in the tribe's land. But by 1866, the Seminoles had secured both a small allotment of land, 200,000 acres, and their tribal independence—the two rights for which they had long sought. They clung now to their determination to survive as they began the period of the Second Seminole nation in the West.[11]

Appendix

Confederate Officers of the First Seminole Battalion
(Later Regiment)

John Jumper, major, lieutenant colonel, and colonel
George Cloud, major
Charles C. Dyer, A.Q.M.
Shadrack B. Hagan, adjutant
W. W. Burnes, assistant surgeon
D. R. Patterson, adjutant
H. McDonald, A.Q.M.
George Patterson, adjutant

Company A—Enrolled 21 September 1861

George Cloud, captain, later major
Thomas Cloud, captain
Nocus or Nocose Harjo, second lieutenant
Frazier McLish or McClish, second lieutenant
Waxi Imathla or Waxie Emathla, second lieutenant

William Aird, first lieutenant
Cho Fixico, second lieutenant

Company B—Enrolled 21 September 1861

Fushatchiecochokna, captain
William Robinson, first lieutenant to captain, Company D
Echo Yohola, second lieutenant
Micco Muchasse, second lieutenant
H. E. A. Washbourne, first lieutenant
Thlalo Fixico, second lieutenant

Company C—Enrolled 5 November 1861

James Factor, captain
Chitto Tustenuggee, first lieutenant to captain
Mathu lokee or Matoloke, second lieutenant
Itse Yohola or Yahola, second lieutenant to first lieutenant, Company D
Tustenucochee, first lieutenant
Passuchee Yohola, second lieutenant
Nokfah Harjo, second lieutenant

Company D—Enrolled 12 December 1861

Tustanucogee or Tustenuk Ochee, captain to first lieutenant, Company C
John Reid or Reed, first to second lieutenant
Compiere Starpes, second lieutenant to Company F
Eufala Tustanuggee, second lieutenant
William Robinson, captain
Itsin Yohola, first lieutenant
D. R. Patterson, second lieutenant

Company E—Enrolled 2 January 1862

Sam Hill, captain
Charles C. Dyer, first lieutenant to A.Q.M.

D. R. Patterson, adjutant to second lieutenant, Company D

Alex Johnston, or Johnson, second lieutenant

John White, second lieutenant

Tulsee Yohola, captain

Daniel McGirt, first lieutenant

A. M. Taylor, second lieutenant

Klehomata Fixico, second lieutenant

Shadrack B. Hagan, second lieutenant to adjutant

Company F—Enrolled 21 November 1862

Osuchee Harjo, captain

Nocose Yoholah, first lieutenant

Compere Starpes, second lieutenant

John Reed, Sr., second lieutenant

SOURCE: Records Relating to Military Service, RG 109, Microcopy 861, Roll 74 (Washington, D.C.: National Archives Microfilm Publications, 1971). Names appear as spelled in the records.

Notes

1. From the East to the West

1. U.S. Office of Indian Affairs, *Annual Reports of the Commissioner of Indian Affairs to the Secretary of the Department of the Interior, for the Fiscal Years Ended 30 June 1832–30 June 1866* (rpt. Washington, D.C.: Microcard Editions, 1968) (hereafter cited as C.I.A., *Annual Report,* with year). For information on the background of removal and the arrival of the Seminoles in the West, see Edwin C. McReynolds, *The Seminoles* (Norman: Univ. of Oklahoma Press, 1957), 63–242; Charles Coe, *Red Patriots: The Story of the Seminoles* (Cincinnati: Editor Publishing, 1898); Joshua R. Giddings, *The Exiles of Florida* (Columbus: Follett, Foster and Company, 1858).

2. *Tribes under the Administrative Jurisdiction of the Muskogee Area Office* (Muskogee, Okla.: Area Tribal Operations Office); Robert V. Remini, *Andrew Jackson and the Course of American Empire, 1767–1821* (New York: Harper and Row, 1977), 344; Wilton Marion Krogman, "The Racial Composition of the Seminole Indians of Florida and Oklahoma," *Journal of Negro History* 19 (Jan. 1934): 427–28; Dale Van Every, *Disinherited: The Lost Birthright of the American Indian* (New York: William Morrow, 1966), 175–76.

3. George Walton, *Fearless and Free: The Seminole Indian War, 1835–1842* (New York: Bobbs-Merrill, 1977), 28–30; Daniel F. Littlefield, Jr., *Africans and Seminoles: From Removal to Emancipation* (Westport, Conn.: Greenwood Press, 1977), 8–11.

4.   Laurence Foster, *Negro-Indian Relationships in the Southeast* (Philadelphia: By the author, 1935; rpt. New York: AMS Press, 1978), 19–20.

5.   For emergence of the Seminoles, see Jose A. Zuni, Memorandum on Results of Research Report on Seminole Judgment in Dockets 73 and 151 before the Indian Claims Commission, 26 November 1976. Office of Tribal Operations, Muskogee Area Agency, Muskogee, Oklahoma, 2–3; Jerry L. Burk, "Oklahoma Seminole Indians: Origin, History, and Pan-Indianism," *Chronicles of Oklahoma* 51 (Summer 1973): 211–12; Krogman, "Racial Composition," 412–29; Angie Debo, *The Road to Disappearance,* 2d ed. (Norman: Univ. of Oklahoma Press, 1967), 5; *Tribes under the Administrative Jurisdiction;* Van Every, *Disinherited,* 176; John Swanton, *The Indian Tribes of North America* (Washington, D.C.: Govt. Printing Office, 1952), 107, 115–16, 119, 127, 132, 133, 139–43, 152, 166, 253, 301–2; Muriel Wright, "Seal of the Seminole Nation," *Chronicles of Oklahoma* 34 (Autumn 1956): 262–71; Alvin M. Josephy, Jr., *Now that the Buffalo's Gone: A Study of Today's American Indian* (Norman: Univ. of Oklahoma Press, 1984), 5–15; J. Leitch Wright, Jr., *The Only Land They Knew: The Tragic Story of the American Indians in the Old South* (New York: Free Press, 1981), 47, 217–18, 230–37; William L. Williams, ed., *Southeastern Indians since the Removal Era* (Athens: Univ. of Georgia Press, 1979), 9; Harry A. Kersey, Jr., *The Seminole and Miccosukee Tribes: A Critical Bibliography* (Bloomington: Indiana Univ. Press, 1987), 13–15; Merwyn S. Garbarino, *Big Cypress: A Changing Seminole Community* (New York: Holt, Rinehart, and Winston, 1972), 7. See also Robert S. Cotterill, *The Southern Indians: The Story of the Five Civilized Tribes Before Removal* (Norman: Univ. of Oklahoma Press, 1954); Michael D. Green, *The Politics of Indian Removal: Creek Government and Society in Crisis* (Lincoln: Univ. of Nebraska Press, 1982); David L. Corkran, *The Creek Frontier, 1540–1782* (Norman: Univ. of Oklahoma Press, 1967); James F. Doster, *The Creek Indians and Their Florida Lands, 1740–1823* (New York: Garland Publishing, 1974); and J. Leitch Wright, Jr., *Creeks and Seminoles: Destruction and Regeneration of the Muscogulge People* (Lincoln: Univ. of Nebraska Press, 1986). According to an 1823 census by the War Department, there were 4,833 Seminoles in Florida. They were governed by a hereditary head chief chosen for life and several band chiefs. The Seminoles apparently had no strong tribal chief in Florida. The United States for its "own purposes" appointed the Hitchiti Chief Nea Mathla as chief of the Seminole nation in order to conclude the treaty of 1823. Later Nea Mathla and his followers moved into southern Alabama and the Americans made the Mikasuki John Hicks (Tokose Emathla) head chief. By 1832 some considered John Blount principal chief of the Florida Indians.

6. Foster, *Negro-Indian Relationships*, 21.

7. Krogman, "Racial Composition," 428; John K. Mahon, *History of the Second Seminole War, 1835–1842*, rev. ed. (Gainesville: Univ. of Florida Press, 1991), 21–30.

8. Van Every, *Disinherited*, 176; Zuni, Memorandum, 4.

9. Remini, *Andrew Jackson*, 344–45; *Narrative of a Voyage to the Spanish Main in the Ship "Two Friends,"* with an introduction and index by John W. Griffin (Gainesville: Univ. Presses of Florida, 1978), 290–91; Foster, *Negro-Indian Relationships*, 23–24. The fort near the mouth of the Apalachicola River, built by the British officer Edward Nicholls, had been left to blacks in the spring of 1815. Called the Negro Fort, cannon fire from a United States vessel passing up the Apalachicola destroyed it on 27 July 1816; Mahon, *Second Seminole War*, 21–30.

10. McReynolds, *The Seminoles*, 81–82.

11. Harold C. Syrett, *Andrew Jackson: His Contribution to the American Tradition* (New York: Bobbs-Merrill, 1953), 69–70.

12. McReynolds, *The Seminoles*, 86–87; Zuni, Memorandum, 5.

13. *Tribes under the Administrative Jurisdiction;* Zuni, Memorandum, 5.

14. Mahon, *Second Seminole War*, 31. See Edward Brett Randolph, Diary, Southern Historical Collection, Univ. of North Carolina Library, Chapel Hill (hereafter cited as Southern Historical Collection).

15. Remini, *Andrew Jackson*, 366.

16. *Narrative of a Voyage*, 286, 307; Samuel Flagg Bemis, *John Quincy Adams and the Foundations of American Foreign Policy* (New York: Knopf, 1949), 325–26.

17. U.S. Dept. of State, *Treaties and Other International Agreements of the United States of America, 1776–1949* (Washington, D.C.: Govt. Printing Office, 1974), vol. 11: 528–36; U.S. Bureau of Indian Affairs, Report to the Department of the Interior 1968, by Charles E. Grounds. Tribal Operations Office, Muskogee Area Agency, Muskogee, Oklahoma, 3. Spain ratified the treaty in October 1820. The president of the United States signed on 22 February 1821, the date it entered into force.

18. Remini, *Andrew Jackson*, 420–21. Remini says that Jackson was willing to establish a reservation for the Seminoles on the banks of the Apalachicola even though he thought removing them to Creek country was more desirable.

19. Grounds, Report, 3. Grounds, a Seminole attorney, reported that some Seminoles left for either Mexico or the Bahamas.

20. Remini, *Andrew Jackson*, 422.

21. Foster, *Negro-Indian Relationships,* 28–29.

22. *U.S. Statutes at Large* 7: 224–28. Article Ten raises questions about this treaty, because the agent, Colonel Gad Humphreys, and the interpreter, Stephen Richards, were each to receive a square mile of land at Tallahassee and Ochesee Bluffs, respectively. Charles Grounds stated in his 1968 Report that the United States commissioners offered the Seminoles $106 million for their lands if they moved to the interior. Military force made them move, and the money was never paid. Georgians had also demanded the Seminoles move, according to Muriel Wright in "Seal of the Seminole Nation," 264. Yet several Indians refused to move, according to Zuni in his Memorandum, 5. For additional information on the treaty of 1823 and Nea Mathla as head of the Seminole delegation, see J. L. Wright, *Creeks and Seminoles,* 232–35.

23. Zuni, Memorandum, 2, 5. The Seminole nation used and occupied this area prior to the 1823 treaty, according to the Indian Claims Commission (1964).

24. Burk, "Oklahoma Seminole Indians," 214–15.

25. Zuni, Memorandum, 2, 5.

26. C.I.A., *Annual Report,* 1829, 164.

27. Vince Lovett and Larry Rummel, with Dick Hardwick, Glen Robertson, and Vince Monico. *American Indians* (Washington, D.C.: Govt. Printing Office, 1984), 8–9. For detailed information on the problems faced by the Bureau of Indian Affairs in its early years, see Alban W. Hoopes, *Indian Affairs and Their Administration with Special Reference to the Far West, 1849–1860* (Philadelphia: Univ. of Pennsylvania, 1932; rpt. New York: Kraus Reprint, 1972) and Francis Paul Prucha, *The Great Father: The United States Government and the American Indians* (Lincoln: Univ. of Nebraska Press, 1986).

28. C.I.A., *Annual Report,* 1832, 160; Ronald Satz in *American Indian Policy in the Jacksonian Era* (Lincoln: Univ. of Nebraska Press, 1975), explains in a comprehensive manner the removal period. Francis Paul Prucha, ed., *The Indian in American History* (Hinsdale, Ill.: Dryden Press, 1971), 67–74.

29. Wayne Lollar, "Seminole–United States Financial Relations, 1823–1866," *Chronicles of Oklahoma* 50 (Summer 1972): 198.

30. Grounds, Report, 4; Zuni, Memorandum, 6.

31. *U.S. Statutes at Large* 7: 368–70; John Robert Irelan, *History of the Life, Administration, and Times of Martin Van Buren* (Chicago: Fairbanks and Palmer Publishing, 1887), 483. Seminole chiefs and headmen who signed this 1832 treaty were Holati Emarthla, Jumper, Fuck-ta-lus-ta Hadjo, Charley Emarthla, Coa Hadjo, Ar-pi-uck-i or Sam Jones, Ya-ha Hadjo, Meco Noha, Tokose-Emarthla or John Hicks, Cat-sha-Tusta-nuck-i, Hola-at-a-Meco, Hitch-

it-i-Meco, E-ne-hah, Ya-ha-emarthla Chup-ko, Moke-his-she-lar-ni. Florida residents had also agitated for this treaty. Indian names are always listed as they appear on the different treaties.

32. C.I.A., *Annual Report,* 1832, 161.

33. *U.S. Statutes at Large* 7: 377–78; C.I.A., *Annual Report,* 1832, 161; 1833, 184–85. Treaties were reportedly signed with other bands.

34. F. W. Armstrong to R. N. McCabe, 31 Mar. 1835, Grant Foreman Collection, Thomas Gilcrease Museum Library, Tulsa, Oklahoma (hereafter cited as Grant Foreman Collection).

35. Grounds, Report, 4; Carolyn Foreman, "The Jumper Family of the Seminole Nation," *Chronicles of Oklahoma* 34 (Autumn 1956): 273. Shortly thereafter, Phagan was removed from office because of numerous charges, including "defrauding the Indians," neglect of duty, and favoritism in office. See also George Center to James M. White, 29 Nov. 1831, Letters Received by the Office of Indian Affairs, 1824–81, Seminole Agency, microcopy 234, roll 800 (Washington, D.C.: National Archives Microfilm Publications, 1956) (hereafter cited as Letters Received).

36. *U.S. Statutes at Large* 7: 417–20.

37. *U.S. Statutes at Large* 7: 423–24. The names of the signers, as spelled on the treaties, were John Hicks (representing Sam Jones), Holata Emarthla, Jumper, Coi Hadgo, Charley Emarthla, Ya-ha-hadgo, and Ne-ha-tho-clo (representing Fuck-a-lusti-hadgo).

38. C. Foreman, "Jumper Family," 273–75; Tuskoma Brown Miller, *Este-Cate (Red Man),* Seminole Nation Historical Society, 1982. Additional information on the trip west and the 1833 treaty is found in Irelan, *Martin Van Buren,* 483; Margaret A. Chaney, "A Tribal History of the Seminole Indians" (Master's thesis, Univ. of Oklahoma, 1928), 18–20; Zuni, Memorandum, 6; Grounds, Report, 4; Bruce Gilbert Carter, "A History of Seminole County, Oklahoma" (Master's thesis, Univ. of Oklahoma, 1932), 6–7. Grounds in his Report, 4, states that the Seminoles were imprisoned in Fort Gibson and required to state that they approved the land.

39. Miller, *Este-Cate (Red Man).*

40. McReynolds, *The Seminoles,* 140–41.

41. C. Foreman, "Jumper Family," 274.

42. C.I.A., *Annual Report,* 1834, 237–39.

43. Louise Welsh, "Seminole Colonization in Oklahoma," *Chronicles of Oklahoma* 54 (Spring 1976): 86; McReynolds, *The Seminoles,* 129–30, 134. Welsh states that Blount's uncle had settled in the Trinity River area years earlier.

44. Irelan, *Martin Van Buren,* 500–501.

45. Ibid.; McReynolds, *The Seminoles,* 145; C. Foreman, "Jumper Family," 275–76.

46. McReynolds, *The Seminoles,* 152–55; For detailed information regarding the Second Seminole War, consult Mahon, *Second Seminole War;* Walton, *Fearless and Free;* George E. Buker, *Swamp Sailors: Riverine Warfare in the Everglades, 1835–1842* (Gainesville: Univ. Presses of Florida, 1975); George Cassel Bittle, "In the Defense of Florida: The Organized Florida Militia from 1821 to 1920" (Ph.D. diss., Florida State Univ., 1965), 151–70; and Sara Alice Woodward, "The Second Seminole War with Especial Reference to the Attitude of Congress" (Master's thesis, Columbia Univ., 1929). For information regarding Osceola, see W. Alva Wells, "Osceola and the Second Seminole War" (Master's thesis, Univ. of Oklahoma, 1936) and William Hartley and Ellen Hartley, *Osceola: The Unconquered Indian* (New York: Hawthorn Books, 1973).

47. Burk, "Oklahoma Seminole Indians," 216; L. Welsh, "Seminole Colonization in Oklahoma," 98.

48. L. Welsh, "Seminole Colonization in Oklahoma," 98; Irelan, *Martin Van Buren,* 530; James F. Sunderman, ed., *Journey into Wilderness: An Army Surgeon's Account of Life in Camp and Field during the Creek and Seminole Wars, 1836–1838,* by Jacob Rhett Motte (Gainesville: Univ. of Florida Press, 1963), 312.

49. William T. Sherman, *Memoirs of General W. T. Sherman,* 2d ed. (New York: D. Appleton, 1904), 17–28; Rachel Sherman Thorndike, ed., *The Sherman Letters: Correspondence between General Sherman and Senator Sherman from 1837 to 1891,* with a foreword by John Y. Simon (New York: Da Capo Press, 1969), 13–22; William Tecumseh Sherman to P. Ewing, 24 Oct. 1840, P. Ewing Collection, Archives-Library, Ohio Historical Society, Columbus (hereafter cited as P. Ewing Collection).

50. Woodward, "Second Seminole War," 11–12; U.S. House, *Seminole War—Slaves Captured,* Doc. 55, 27th Cong., 2d sess., 1842, 1–3.

51. Krogman, "Racial Composition," 421; Littlefield, *Africans and Seminoles,* 12, 19.

52. R. K. Call to the President, 22 Mar. 1835, The Seminole Papers, Thomas Gilcrease Museum Library, Tulsa, Oklahoma (hereafter cited as Seminole Papers).

53. C. A. Harris to General Wiley Thompson, 22 May 1835, Seminole Papers.

54. Littlefield, *Africans and Seminoles,* 16.

55. Irelan, *Martin Van Buren,* 530.

56. James Erwin and Erwin and Greathouse—Claims for Losses under Contracts Made in 1834–35 for subsisting and transporting Creek and Seminole Indians 1847–55, Special Files of the Office of Indian Affairs, 1807–1904, microcopy M574, roll 7, file 62 (Washington, D.C.: National Archives Microfilm Publications, 1965) (hereafter cited as Special Files).

57. Joseph W. Harris to Lewis Cass, 25 July 1836, and J. Van Horne to George Gibson, 23 May 1835, Grant Foreman Collection; Captain Jacob Brown to General George Gibson, 7 May 1836 and 10 Sept. 1836, RG 75, Commissary General of Subsistence-Seminole, National Archives; J. Van Horne, Journal, Grant Foreman Collection.

58. J. Van Horne, Journal, Grant Foreman Collection; J. Van Horne to General George Gibson, 5 May [June] 1836, 23 May 1836, and 21 June 1836, Grant Foreman Collection. According to D. M. Sheffield in a letter to General George Gibson, 4 June 1836, RG 75, Commissary General of Subsistence-Seminole, National Archives and Jacob Brown to General George Gibson, 1 June 1836, in same location, Sheffield arrived at Little Rock on 1 June 1836, with a party of eight (or nine) Florida Indians; Harris to Cass, 25 July 1836, Grant Foreman Collection.

59. Harris to Cass, 25 July 1836, Grant Foreman Collection. Harris hoped that treaty stipulations would provide agricultural tools, household utensils, and livestock, because the Seminoles were interested in agriculture.

2. Among the Creeks and Cherokees

1. C.I.A., *Annual Report,* 1832–42; Report Books of the Office of Indian Affairs, microcopy 348, rolls 1–4 (Washington, D.C.: National Archives Microfilm Publications, 1963) (hereafter cited as Report Books).

2. M. Wright, "Seal of the Seminole Nation," 265; C. Foreman, "Jumper Family," 274a; *U.S. Statutes at Large* 11: 175; C.I.A., *Annual Report,* 1836, 3, 14–15; 1837, 25; J. Van Horne, Muster Roll, Seminole Agency Emigration, Oklahoma Indian Archives, Oklahoma City.

3. C.I.A., *Annual Report,* 1834, 95; 1836, 3, 14–15.

4. C.I.A., *Annual Report,* 1836, 14–15; 1837, 56–57, 127–29. Thomas Elton Brown, "Seminole Indian Agents, 1842–1874," *Chronicles of Oklahoma* 51 (Spring 1973): 60.

5. C.I.A., *Annual Report*, 1837, 3. The primary responsibilities of the commissioner of Indian affairs in 1837 included:

> negotiations with the tribes east of the Mississippi for extinguishing their titles; those of western prairie, for the establishment of friendly relations between them and the United States and with the indigenous and emigrated tribes beyond the Mississippi and Missouri rivers for the adjustment of difficulties and the preservation of peace. They include[d] the removal of the Indians in New York, Ohio, Indiana, Illinois, Michigan, and Wisconsin, in the north, the west, and the northwest, and in Georgia, North Carolina, Tennessee, Alabama, Mississippi, Florida in the south and southwest, to new homes southwest of the Missouri River—the location and sale of reservations, the investment or payment of the proceeds, and of the proceeds of lands ceded, with the collection and disbursement of the interest thereon. They involved[d] a supervision of the execution of treaty stipulations, for the subsistence of emigrants, the examination and payment of debts and claims, the education of the young, the supply of agricultural implements, and assistance, the employment of interpreters, farmers, mechanics, and laborers. They demand[ed] a constant attention to the conduct of the numerous agents and officers necessarily employed; commissioners to hold treaties, or to investigate claims, superintendents of emigration, and of the four divisions of the department; agents and sub-agents. They call[ed] for an exact adherence to the laws, and for the adoption, from time to time, of the regulations requisite to give them full effect. They involve[d] the superintendence of the investment of nearly two million. The annual disbursement of appropriations not less, in the last three years than $5 million, and the disposition of interest of about $200,000. And the welfare of a population estimated at 330,000 scattered over [the] country.

6. Articles of Capitulation and Micanopy Agreement, Seminole Papers; Zuni, Memorandum, 6; Littlefield, *Africans and Seminoles,* 18; C. Foreman, "Jumper Family," 278.

7. John G. Reynolds to C. A. Harris, 26 May 1838, Grant Foreman Collection; Littlefield, *Africans and Seminoles,* 41; Miscellaneous Muster Rolls of Apalachicola and Seminole of Florida, entry 301, RG 75, National Archives; Chaney, "Tribal History," 20. Estimates of these groups vary. Although records indicate Reynolds disbursed 1,221 Indians, Negroes, and Spaniards, the number diminished when seven Spaniards stayed in New Orleans, civil authorities took thirty-two blacks, and several died. The party that apparently began with more than 1,200 decreased to 1,069.

8. Van Every, *Disinherited,* 251; Grant Foreman, *The Five Civilized Tribes* (Norman: Univ. of Oklahoma Press, 1934), 224; C.I.A., *Annual Report,* 1838, 470–74. On 8 July 1838, Congress approved temporary subsistence for western

Indian emigrants unable to support themselves, and the Seminoles were included. Numbers in the annual reports vary, and the figure of 1,651 is the best estimate.

9. C.I.A., *Annual Report, 1837,* 18, 78; 1839, 472; M. Wright, "Seal of the Seminole Nation," 265; Krogman, "Racial Composition," 428; Mahon, *Second Seminole War,* 127; C.I.A., *Annual Report,* 1837, 18, 78; 1839, 472; John Bartlett Meserve, "Chief Opothleyahola," *Chronicles of Oklahoma* 9 (Dec. 1931): 444–52. For information about Opothleyahola's leadership in the East, see Green, *Politics of Indian Removal* and Brad Agnew, *Fort Gibson: Terminal on the Trail of Tears* (Norman: Univ. of Oklahoma Press, 1980), 150–200.

10. T. Hartley Crawford to J. R. Poinsett, 14 Jan. 1839, Report Books, roll 1, vol. 1: 64; C.I.A., *Annual Report,* 1847, 166–67.

11. See also W. W. Newcomb, Jr., *The Indians of Texas: From Prehistoric to Modern Times* (Austin: Univ. of Texas Press, 1961), 347; William L. Mann, "James O. Rice: Hero of the Battle on the San Gabriels [*sic*]," *Southwestern Historical Quarterly* 55 (July 1951): 39; Gerald S. Pierce, *Texas Under Arms* (Austin: Encino Press, 1969), 106–7.

12. T. Hartley Crawford to J. R. Poinsett, 14 Dec. 1838, 33 and 14 Jan. 1839, 63–64, Report Books, roll 1, vol. 1; J. R. Poinsett to John Bell and J. R. Poinsett to H. L. White, 18 Dec. 1838, Report Books, roll 1, vol. 1: 39; G. Foreman, *The Five Civilized Tribes,* 155; Ronald N. Satz, "Thomas Hartley Crawford, 1838–45," in *The Commissioners of Indian Affairs, 1824–1977,* eds. Robert M. Kvasnicka and Herman J. Viola (Lincoln: Univ. of Nebraska Press, 1979), 23–27.

13. Crawford to Poinsett, 14 Jan. 1839, Report Books, roll 1, vol. 1: 63–65; Poinsett to Bell and White, 18 Dec. 1838, Report Books, roll 1, vol. 1: 39; U.S. Senate, *Message from the President of the United States in Relation to the Condition of the Seminole Indians Who Have Emigrated,* S. Doc. 88, 25th Cong., 3d sess., 1839, 1–3.

14. U.S. Senate, *Message from the President . . . Seminole Indians Who Have Emigrated,* 1; T. Hartley Crawford to Cave Johnson, 21 Mar. 1840, Report Books, roll 1, vol. 1: 492–93.

15. *U.S. Statutes at Large* 5: 316.

16. C.I.A., *Annual Report,* 1839, 329, 334, 472.

17. Ibid., 329, 346–47, 423, 472. A total of 1,735 Seminoles were subsisted for four months at $14,204, according to the Appropriations Act, 7 July 1838.

18. Crawford to Johnson, 21 Mar. 1840, Report Books, roll 1, vol. 1: 491–93; T. Hartley Crawford to William Wilkins, 7 May 1844, Report Books, roll 4, vol. 4: 183. The actions of the Seminoles in the West and East had a far-reaching

impact on federal policies and politicians. Van Buren's biographer, John Irelan, in *Martin Van Buren,* 521, wrote that although Van Buren detested the "slave-hunting war in Florida," he refused to oppose Southern politicians. Still unable to gain the confidence of the South, the "disreputable war, the secret history of which it seemed to be his interest to conceal aided in his defeat" in the election of 1840 and at the convention in 1844.

19. T. Hartley Crawford to John Bell, 3 July 1841, Report Books, roll 2, vol. 2: 437–39; Michael E. Welsh, "The Road to Assimilation: The Seminoles in Oklahoma, 1839–1936" (Ph.D. diss., Univ. of New Mexico, 1983), 3–4.

20. T. Hartley Crawford to John Bell, 28 Apr. 1841, Report Books, roll 2, vol. 2: 401–2; interview with Thomas Palmer Band Chief Dwayne Miller, Oklahoma City, Oklahoma, 17 May 1985; G. Foreman, *The Five Civilized Tribes,* 226–27; McReynolds, *The Seminoles,* 227–28; Arrell Morgan Gibson in *The American Indian: Prehistory to the Present* (Lexington, Mass.: D. C. Heath, 1980), 328–29, describes Osceola's capture.

21. C.I.A., *Annual Report,* 1839, 423–25; Miller interview. In 1842, the Cherokee agent told Zachary Taylor, the commander at Fort Smith, about the Seminoles. Taylor informed them to move to their own lands but postponed forcing them after they had planted crops. Moreover, he hesitated to drive women and children from their homes. See Brainerd Dyer, *Zachary Taylor* (Baton Rouge: Louisiana State Univ. Press, 1946), 135, 142–43. For information about Fort Gibson, see Grant Foreman, *Advancing The Frontier, 1830–1860* (1933; rpt. Norman: Univ. of Oklahoma, 1968), 51–58.

22. C.I.A., *Annual Report,* 1840, 245, 314; T. Hartley Crawford to J. R. Poinsett, 28 Nov. 1840, Report Books, roll 2, vol. 2: 240, 260.

23. *Niles National Register,* 21 Nov. 1840; 30 Jan. 1841; C.I.A., *Annual Report,* 1840, 245.

24. *U.S. Statutes at Large* 5: 414–15. J. R. Poinsett to John Bell, 18 Jan. 1841, Report Books, roll 2, vol. 2: 295–96. Poinsett also hoped to use influential citizens near St. Augustine to effect removal of the remaining Seminoles.

25. U.S. House, *Expenditure in 1841—Florida Indians, etc.* H. Ex. Doc. 247, 27th Cong., 2d sess., 1842, 2–3, 12. W. B. Lewis of the Treasury Department made this report to the Secretary of War in 1842. Of the fifteen thousand dollars, William Armstrong requisitioned nine thousand, which left six thousand dollars in the treasury.

26. Ibid., 4–12.

27. T. Hartley Crawford to John C. Spencer, 12 May 1842, Report Books, roll 3, vol. 3: 171. Figures listed in the following years are somewhat lower. By

1842, views regarding the war against the Florida Indians changed. In February, Colonel William Jenkins Worth wrote Commanding General of the United States Army Winfield Scott that hostilities should cease against the Indians in Florida. It was impractical to search for the few remaining Seminoles. A few months later Congress passed an act that provided for the armed occupation of eastern Florida by white settlers. They were to receive a quarter of a section of land after they lived on it five years, cultivated five acres, and built a house. Settlers rushed onto the 200,000 acres set aside for such purpose. This settlement, it was hoped, would eliminate a need for the use of the military against Indians. Also in August, President John Tyler told Congress that further pursuit of the Seminoles was injudicious. Subsequently, on 14 August 1842, Colonel Worth declared the Second Seminole War at an end. Those three hundred Indians who remained were permitted to stay in a certain area of southwest Florida. A peace treaty never officially ended the war. See also Mahon, *Second Seminole War,* 316–18; Clarence Edwin Carter, *The Territory of Florida, 1839–1845* (Washington, D.C.: Govt. Printing Office, 1962), 520–21; Francis Paul Prucha, *The Sword of the Republic: The United States Army on the Frontier, 1783–1846* (London: Macmillan, 1969), 300; Carolyn Osburn Wilson, "The Development of the Florida Territory, 1821-1845," (Master's thesis, Vanderbilt Univ., 1932), 128–41.

28.   McReynolds, *The Seminoles,* 226.

29.   As quoted in Irelan, *Martin Van Buren,* 537.

30.   C.I.A., *Annual Report,* 1838, 512; 1840, 314; 1842, 444; Foster, *Negro-Indian Relationships,* 41; Littlefield, *Africans and Seminoles,* 4–6; Krogman, "Racial Composition," 423; L. Edward Carter, "The Seminole Nation after Leaving Florida, 1855–1860," *Chronicles of Oklahoma* 55 (Winter 1977–78): 436–37; Mahon, *Second Seminole War,* 251–52; McReynolds, *The Seminoles,* 210–14; *Arkansas Intelligencer,* 2 Dec. 1843.

31.   C.I.A., *Annual Report,* 1842, 444.

32.   T. Hartley Crawford to J. R. Poinsett, 27 Feb. 1841, Report Books, roll 2, vol. 2: 372–73; T. Hartley Crawford to John Bell, 10 Aug. 1841, Report Books, roll 2, vol. 2: 476–78.

33.   to John Bell, 7 June 1841, Report Books, roll 2, vol. 2: 421–22; T. Hartley Crawford to J. R. Poinsett, 27 Feb. 1841, Report Books, roll 2, vol. 2: 372–73; T. Hartley Crawford to John Bell, 10 Aug. 1841, Report Books, roll 2, vol. 2: 476–78.

34.   Zuni, Memorandum, 7; G. Foreman, *The Five Civilized Tribes,* 224–25. Because of a tremendous variance in statistics reported, these numbers are estimates at best. C.I.A., *Annual Report,* 1842, 443.

35. Brown, "Seminole Indian Agents," 59–62; McReynolds, *The Seminoles,* 237–38, 254–55; M. E. Welsh, "Road to Assimilation," 4–5; William Armstrong to John McKee, 2 Apr. 1842, Letters Received, roll 800. G. Foreman, *Advancing the Frontier,* 201–4; J. L. Wright, *Creeks and Seminoles,* 226–27, 236.

36. Brown, "Seminole Indian Agents," 59–62; M. E. Welsh, "Road to Assimilation," 4–5; McReynolds, *The Seminoles,* 237–38, 254–55; Robert M. Utley, *The Indian Frontier of the American West, 1846–1890* (Albuquerque: Univ. of New Mexico Press, 1984), 41–42.

3. Divided We Stand

1. Brown, "Seminole Indian Agents," 59–63; M. E. Welsh, "Road to Assimilation," 4–5; McReynolds, *The Seminoles,* 237–38, 251.

2. C.I.A., *Annual Report,* 1841, 241, 316, 320; 1842, 443–44; 1843, 408, 418, 419; 1844, 176; Carolyn Thomas Foreman, ed., "Journal of a Tour in the Indian Territory," by N. Sayre Harris, *Chronicles of Oklahoma* 10 (June 1932): 235.

3. C.I.A., *Annual Report,* 1843, 419; 1844, 174–76. In 1844, a total of 3,316 Seminoles, excluding slaves, lived in the West; E-con-chattimicco had four hundred in his Apalachicola band, whereas Chief Co-ah-thlack-co presided over 114, formerly under Blount and Davy.

4. Debo, *The Road to Disappearance,* 135–38; *Arkansas Intelligencer,* 15 July 1843; G. Foreman, *Advancing the Frontier,* 205–14.

5. C.I.A., *Annual Report,* 1843, 372–73; 1844, 77, 175; C. Foreman, "Journal of a Tour," 235; M. Wright, "Seal of the Seminole Nation," 270.

6. G. Foreman, *Advancing the Frontier,* 25–33, 59; Gibson, *American Indian,* 273; Mahon, *Second Seminole War,* 28; McReynolds, *The Seminoles,* 239.

7. Mahon, *Second Seminole War,* 28; C. Foreman, "Journal of a Tour," 234–37; C.I.A., *Annual Report,* 1844, 176; G. Foreman, *Advancing the Frontier,* 63–64, 171; McReynolds, *The Seminoles,* 197–98, 254. Fields's daughters were educated in New Hampshire. One daughter married Delos B. Sackett, a West Point graduate and later inspector general of the United States Army. Fort Gibson was a center of society and gaiety in Indian Territory, and many Indian girls married soldiers stationed at Fort Gibson.

8. C.I.A., *Annual Report,* 1843, 418; 1844, 174–75; Brown, "Seminole Indian Agents," 63; Littlefield, *Africans and Seminoles,* 81–84.

9. C.I.A., *Annual Report,* 1844, 174; 1845, 506; Brown, "Seminole Indian Agents," 63; C. Foreman, "Journal of a Tour," 235.

10. C.I.A., *Annual Report,* 1844, 4, 27–29; Littlefield, *Africans and Seminoles,* 86.

11. Littlefield, *Africans and Seminoles,* 86.

12. *Arkansas Intelligencer,* 30 Mar. 1844. Wild Cat wrote:

I have been at war with the United States. I defended the soil of my birthplace with my blood. It was dear to me, and to my people as our homes, and as our country of our fathers. But, that war is now ended. My people were overcome by a stronger party. What the sword did not destroy, your money bought. Like the rain that falls upon the earth from the Heavens, the memory of that war is absorbed and forgotten. We emmigrated [*sic*] to this country upon the faith of your people—promises were made us of another home, a separate and distinct soil, where we could gather again the fragments of a distracted and unhappy people. The hand that could conquer, should possess the heart to fulfill promises made to a subdued people. None knows our condition better than you do. Look at us! A distracted people, alone, without a home, without annuities—destitute of provisions, and without a shelter for our women and children—strangers in a foreign land, dependent upon the mercy and tolerance of our Red Brothers, the Cherokees, transported to a cold climate, naked, without game to hunt or fields to plant, or huts to cover our poor little children—they are crying like wolves, hungry, cold and destitute!

13. *Arkansas Intelligencer,* 2 Mar. 1844; T. Hartley Crawford to William Wilkins, 7 May 1844, Report Books, roll 4, vol. 4: 182–83; C.I.A., *Annual Report,* 1844, 31.

14. C.I.A., *Annual Report,* 1844, 174–75.

15. Ibid., 4, 25–26; *Arkansas Intelligencer,* 3 Feb. 1844.

16. G. Foreman, *The Five Civilized Tribes,* 236–37; *Arkansas Intelligencer,* 8 June 1844; Brown, "Seminole Indian Agents," 62–65; C.I.A., *Annual Report,* 1844, 174; Littlefield, *Africans and Seminoles,* 88–89.

17. *Arkansas Intelligencer,* 30 Mar., 8 June 1844; McReynolds, *The Seminoles,* 251–52.

18. *Arkansas Intelligencer,* 8 June 1844.

19. McReynolds, *The Seminoles,* 253–54.

20. Brown, "Seminole Indian Agents," 62–65.

21. C.I.A., *Annual Report,* 1844, 174; Brown, "Seminole Indian Agents," 63; C. Foreman, "Journal of a Tour," 235; G. Foreman, *The Five Civilized Tribes,* 237.

22. T. Hartley Crawford to William Wilkins, 20 May 1844, Report Books, roll 4, vol. 4: 193–94; C.I.A., *Annual Report,* 1844, 29–31.

23. C.I.A., *Annual Report,* 1844, 4, 29–32. The number of Seminoles in the West in 1844 was listed as 3,136, with 3,824 the total number removed. T. Hartley Crawford to ———, 1 July 1842 [1844], Report Books, roll 4, vol. 4: 194–95.

24. Arrell Morgan Gibson, "An Indian Territory United Nations: The Creek Council of 1845," *Chronicles of Oklahoma* 39 (Winter 1961): 402–3, 407; Littlefield, *Africans and Seminoles,* 77–78, 91; *Arkansas Intelligencer,* 11 Jan. 1845.

25. *U.S. Statutes at Large* 9: 821, 823; C.I.A., *Annual Report,* 1845, 449.

26. *U.S. Statutes at Large* 9: 821–25. Comments on the treaty of 1845 are found in M. Wright, "Seal of the Seminole Nation," 266; Coe, *Red Patriots,* 166; Chaney, "Tribal History," 24; C.I.A., *Annual Report,* 1845, 449, 506; Brown, "Seminole Indian Agents," 63–64; *Arkansas Intelligencer,* 11 Jan. 1845; 13 Sept. 1845. Those Seminoles who signed in January were: Miccanope (Micanopy), Co-ah-coo-che or Wild Cat, Alligator, Nocose Yoholo, Halleck Tustunnuggee, Emah-thloo-chee, Octi-ar-chee, Pas-cof-far, Tus-se-kiah, E-con-chat-te-micco, Black Dirt, Itch-hos-se Yo-ho-lo, Kap-pe-chum-e-choo-che, O-tul-ga Harjo, Yo-ho-lo Harjo, O-switchee Emarthla, Kub-bit-che, An-lo-ne, Yah-hah Fixico, Fus-hat-chee Micco, O-chee-see Micco, and Tus-tun-nug-goo-chee. The fifteen Seminoles who signed the two amendments in May were: Mic-can-o-pe, Co-ah-coo-che or Wild Cat, Alligator, Ho-la-tah, Mic-coo-che, Tus-se-kiah, Halleck Tustunnuggee, Oc-ti-ar-che, Black Dirt, George Cloud, Cho-co-tee, Pas-co-far, Yo-ho-lo Harjo, Kap-pe-Chum-e-coo-che, E-cho Emah-thlor-chee, and Jim Jumper. The Seminoles, because of their inability to speak English, as usual had a black interpreter.

27. *U.S. Statutes at Large* 9: 32–33; *Arkansas Intelligencer,* 22 Feb., 29 Mar. 1845; McReynolds, *The Seminoles,* 259.

28. Alexander Spoehr, "Oklahoma Seminole Towns," *Chronicles of Oklahoma* 19 (Sept. 1941): 372–80; C.I.A., *Annual Report,* 1845, 530; 1846, 66; McReynolds, *The Seminoles,* 260–61; *Osceola Times* (Wewoka, Oklahoma), 11 Jan. 1985; Miller interview. Years later the towns consolidated into twelve: Hitchiti, Mikasuki, Chiaha, Eufaula No. 1, Eufaula No. 2, Eufaula No. 3, Thliwahili, Ocisi, Okfuski, Talahasuci, Fus Huci, and Newcomers. In the 1980s, twelve bands of Indians and two bands of freedmen (blacks) formed the Seminole nation. Of the ten clans, the Wind Clan ranked first and produced the tribal leaders. Most of the Seminoles were Muskogee speakers.

29. *Osceola Times* (Wewoka, Oklahoma), 11 Jan. 1985; J. L. Wright,

Creeks and Seminoles, 18–32; James H. Howard, with Willie Lena, *Oklahoma Seminoles: Medicine, Magic, and Religion* (Norman: Univ. of Oklahoma Press, 1984), 23–29, 104, 123–53, 181–82, 223–34.

30. Gibson, "An Indian Territory," 398–413.

31. Brown, "Seminole Indian Agents," 64–65.

32. *Arkansas Intelligencer,* Oct. 1844.

33. Brown, "Seminole Indian Agents," 65; McReynolds, *The Seminoles,* 249.

4. A Subagent's Dilemma

1. C.I.A., *Annual Report,* 1845, 506, 529–31; 1846, 69; Miller interview; Brown, "Seminole Indian Agents," 59, 64–65.

2. C.I.A., *Annual Report,* 1846, 66–69; 1847, 169; Marcellus Duval to William Medill, 20 Mar. 1846, Letters Received, roll 801.

3. C.I.A., *Annual Report,* 1846, 68–69, 151; J. L. Wright, *Creeks and Seminoles,* 227; Josephy, *Now that the Buffalo's Gone,* 16–24.

4. Robert A. Trennert, "William A. Medill, 1845–49," *Commissioners of Indian Affairs,* 29–37; C.I.A., *Annual Report,* 1849, 188.

5. McReynolds, *The Seminoles,* 123, 163, 167, 257; Littlefield, *Africans and Seminoles,* 91, 101; C.I.A., *Annual Report,* 1849, 188.

6. C.I.A., *Annual Report,* 1846, 66; 1847, 168; 1848, 521.

7. Littlefield, *Africans and Seminoles,* 98–105; Giddings, *The Exiles of Florida,* 329–33.

8. McReynolds, *The Seminoles,* 165, 205–6.

9. Giddings, *The Exiles of Florida,* 325–27; Littlefield, *Africans and Seminoles,* 105–7, 121–22; G. Foreman, *Advancing the Frontier,* 106.

10. Brown, "Seminole Indian Agents," 67; Littlefield, *Africans and Seminoles,* 105–11, 121–22.

11. Giddings, *The Exiles of Florida,* 326–28; Littlefield, *Africans and Seminoles,* 124. Mason declared that according to Jesup's proclamation, only those slaves brought in by Alligator during the Second Seminole War were free.

12. U.S. House, *Message from the President of the United States Transmitting Information in Regard to the Difficulties between the Creek and Seminole Indians,* Ex. Doc. 15, 33d Cong., 2d sess., 18 Dec. 1854, 10–11, 21–22; Marcellus Duval to the Commissioner of Indian Affairs, 8 Apr. 1853, Gilcrease Collection of Imprints, Gilcrease Museum Library, Tulsa, Oklahoma (hereafter

cited as Gilcrease Collection of Imprints); Brown, "Seminole Indian Agents," 68; Giddings, *The Exiles of Florida,* 329; Littlefield, *African and Seminoles,* 132.

13. U.S. House, *Message from the President . . . between the Creek and Seminole Indians,* 19–25; Marcellus Duval to the Commissioner of Indian Affairs, Gilcrease Collection of Imprints.

14. U.S. House, *Message from the President . . . between the Creek and Seminole Indians,* 25–27.

15. C.I.A., *Annual Report,* 1849, 188; Marcellus Duval to William Medill, 4 June 1849, Grant Foreman Collection; G. Foreman, *Advancing the Frontier,* 247.

16. Hoopes, *Indian Affairs,* 16–20. Trennert, "William Medill, 1845–49," and "Orlando Brown, 1849–50," *Commissioners of Indian Affairs,* 36–45.

17. Holman Hamilton, *Zachary Taylor: Soldier in the White House* (New York: Bobbs-Merrill, 1951), 184.

18. U.S. Senate, *Message from the President of the United States Communicating Information, in Answer to a Resolution of the Senate, Relative to Hostilities Committed by the Seminole Indians in Florida during the Past Year, Their Removal etc.,* S. Ex. Doc. 49, 31st Cong., 1st sess., 21 May 1850, 3, 71.

19. Hamilton, *Zachary Taylor,* 183–85; Mahon, *Second Seminole War,* 183, 240, 251, 274; Dyer, *Zachary Taylor,* 135, 142–43. McReynolds in *The Seminoles,* 264, does, however, refer to this crisis as the Third Seminole War.

20. U.S. Senate, *Message from the President of the United States . . . Relative to Hostilities Committed by the Seminole Indians in Florida,* 105–6.

21. U.S. House, *Message from the President . . . between the Creek and Seminole Indians,* 10–11, 28–30.

22. U.S. Senate, *Message from the President of the United States . . . Relative to Hostilities Committed by the Seminole Indians in Florida,* 116, 137–43.

23. Ibid.; Mahon, *Second Seminole War,* 281, 294, 315; Irelan, *Martin Van Buren,* 537–38; McReynolds, *The Seminoles,* 287. The Seminole chiefs did not expect Duval to be away for such an extended period. Neither the Creek agent nor the superintendent claimed authority to distribute their annuities. Without needed funds, they had sold clothing to buy food. The Agency Office had also been robbed in late December. See Seminole chiefs to Marcellus Duval, 10 Feb. 1850, Letters Received, roll 801.

24. U.S. Senate, *Message from the President of the United States . . . Relative to Hostilities Committed by the Seminole Indians in Florida,* 141–46; *Arkansas Intelligencer,* 27 Oct. 1849.

25. U.S. Senate, *Message from the President of the United States . . . Rela-*

tive to Hostilities Committed by the Seminole Indians in Florida, 82–87, 147–72. McReynolds, *The Seminoles,* 265–68. One of the delegates (and probably both) was left behind after leaving the group to buy whiskey. He returned later on a different boat.

26. U.S. House, *Message from the President . . . between the Creek and Seminole Indians,* 16–18; *Fort Smith Herald,* 14 Sept. 1850; Littlefield, *Africans and Seminoles,* 146–48. M. Duval to Commissioner of Indian Affairs, 30 May 1850. Letters Received, roll 801.

5. Give Us Liberty

1. Kenneth W. Porter, "Seminole in Mexico, 1850–1861," *Chronicles of Oklahoma* 29 (Summer 1951): 154; U.S. Senate, *Message from the President of the United States . . . Relative to Hostilities Committed by the Seminole Indians in Florida,* 145; Giddings, *The Exiles of Florida,* 333; McReynolds, *The Seminoles,* 175, 256–57; C.I.A., *Annual Report,* 1848, 582; W. T. Sherman to P. Ewing, 8 May 1841, P. Ewing Collection; Mahon, *Second Seminole War,* 302; William Armstrong to T. Hartley Crawford, 4 June 1843, Letters Received, roll 800; Grounds, Report, 3; J. L. Wright, *Creeks and Seminoles,* 306.

2. *Fort Smith Herald,* 2 Mar. 1850.

3. U.S. House, *Message from the President . . . between the Creek and Seminole Indians,* 3, 11–12; Irelan, *Martin Van Buren,* 531; Giddings, *The Exiles of Florida,* 331–35; Porter, "Seminole in Mexico," *Chronicles,* 154; Littlefield, *Africans and Seminoles,* 143, 146–47, 156–57, 169; Brown, "Seminole Indian Agents," 68.

4. Littlefield, *Africans and Seminoles,* 103, 120–21, 127–28; Porter, "Seminole in Mexico," *Chronicles,* 163; Mahon, *Second Seminole War,* 224; McReynolds, *The Seminoles,* 259.

5. U.S. House, *Message from the President . . . between the Creek and Seminole Indians,* 3, 11–12; Irelan, *Martin Van Buren,* 531; Giddings, *The Exiles of Florida,* 331–35; Porter, "Seminole in Mexico," *Chronicles,* 154.

6. Walter Prescott Webb, *The Texas Rangers: A Century of Frontier Defense,* with a foreword by Lyndon B. Johnson (Austin: Univ. of Texas Press, 1935, 1965), 7, 133; C.I.A., *Annual Report,* 1849, 30–33; *Fort Smith Herald,* 20 July 1850; Hoopes, *Indian Affairs,* 3.

7. Webb, *Texas Rangers,* 133.

8. *Fort Smith Herald,* 20 July 1850; U.S. House, *Message from the Presi-*

dent . . . between the Creek and Seminole Indians, 31–32; Kenneth W. Porter, "The Seminole in Mexico, 1850–1861," *Hispanic American Historical Review* (hereafter abbreviated as *HAHR*), vol. 31 (Feb. 1951): 4.

9. Porter, "The Seminole in Mexico," *HAHR,* 13–14, 31, 5; Marcellus Duval to Luke Lea, 21 and 30 Sept. 1850, Letters Received, roll 801.

10. U.S. House, *Message from the President . . . between the Creek and Seminole Indians,* 13–14, 31–32; Webb, *Texas Rangers,* 133–35; *Fort Smith Herald,* 4 Oct. 1850; Porter, "The Seminole in Mexico," *HAHR,* 5; McReynolds, *The Seminoles,* 280.

11. Brown, "Seminole Indian Agents," 67–68; Dorman H. Winfrey and James M. Day, *The Indian Papers of Texas and the Southwest, 1825–1916,* 5 vols. (Austin: Pemberton Press, 1959–66), vol. 4: 92–93.

12. Winfrey and Day, *Indian Papers* 3: 127–29. According to Webb in *Texas Rangers,* 136, no record exists of the capture of any of Wild Cat's blacks by federal troops, Texas Rangers, or Comanches.

13. Ralph A. Smith, "Indians in American-Mexican Relations before the War of 1846," *Hispanic American Historical Review* 43 (Feb. 1963): 34, 59–60.

14. U.S. Senate, *Message from the President of the United States Communicating a Translation of a Note from the Mexican Minister in Relation to the Wild Indians of the United States on the Frontier of Mexico,* S. Ex. Doc. 44, 31st Cong., 1st sess., 3 Apr. 1850, 1–2; C.I.A., *Annual Report,* 1848, 408.

15. U.S. House, *Message from the President of the United States Transmitting a Communication from the Mexican Minister Relative to Indian Incursions upon the Mexican Frontier,* H. Ex. Doc. 4, 31st Cong., 2d sess., 10 Dec. 1850, 1.

16. Porter, "The Seminole in Mexico," *HAHR,* 1–4.

17. Ibid., 6–9, 11–13; Coe, *Red Patriots,* 168.

18. J. Fred Rippy, "The Indians of the United States in the Diplomacy of the United States and Mexico, 1848–1853," *Hispanic American Historical Review* 2 (Aug. 1919): 363–65, 383, 386, 395.

19. Porter, "The Seminole in Mexico," *HAHR,* 6–9, 11–13. Coe, *Red Patriots,* 168.

20. Ernest C. Shearer, "The Callahan Expedition, 1855," *Southwestern Historical Quarterly,* 54 (Apr. 1951): 433–34.

21. C.I.A., *Annual Report,* 1851, 43.

22. George T. Howard and Horace Capron, Special Agents, Claims for Expenses Incurred Removing Intruding Indians from Texas, 1853–1854, Special Files, roll 6, file 55. Probably few, if any, of these Seminoles had been associated with Wild Cat.

23. U.S. House, *Message from the President . . . between the Creek and Seminole Indians,* 3–9. Mexico had been quiet only about a year following the withdrawal of United States forces after the Mexican War. Santa Anna had been recalled and made dictator in February 1853. After he drove out or imprisoned his opposition, he later fled from Mexico in 1855. In the later 1850s, the struggle between the conservatives and liberals led to several changes in government leadership. See R. J. MacHugh, *Modern Mexico* (New York: Dodd, Mead, 1914), 44–50; Robert Ryal Miller, *Mexico: A History* (Norman: Univ. of Oklahoma Press, 1985), 229–39; Porter, "The Seminole in Mexico," *HAHR,* 7.

24. J. Fred Rippy, "Border Troubles along the Rio Grande, 1848–1860," *Southwestern Historical Quarterly* 23 (Oct. 1919): 99–100; Winfrey and Day, *Indian Papers* 3: 243–45.

25. Ronnie C. Tyler, "The Callahan Expedition of 1855: Indians or Negroes?" *Southwestern Historical Quarterly* 70 (Apr. 1967): 575–76; Rippy, "Border Troubles," 100; Porter, "Seminole in Mexico," *Chronicles,* 166–67. Mexico had considered using the blacks at the border to stop the entry of American filibusters.

26. Tyler, "Callahan Expedition," 579–83; Rippy, "Border Troubles," 100–103. Many destitute Mexicans who sought food in Texas were treated harshly in certain areas. Rippy says that several Mexicans were ordered to leave in September 1856 after a slave plot was discovered in Columbus, Colorado County.

27. Winfrey and Day, *Indian Papers* 3: 255. Dumas Malone, ed., *Dictionary of American Biography,* 22 vols. (New York: Charles Scribner's Sons, 1935), vol. 17: 331.

28. Shearer, "The Callahan Expedition, 1855," 446–47.

29. Kenneth W. Porter, "Wild Cat's Death and Burial," *Chronicles of Oklahoma* 21 (Mar. 1943): 43; Porter, "Seminole in Mexico," *Chronicles,* 154–57, 159–64; Coe, *Red Patriots,* 169–70; Mary Ann Lilley, "The Autobiography of Mary Ann Lilley," unpublished, n.d., Western History Collections, Univ. Libraries, Univ. of Oklahoma, Norman, 37.

30. Winfrey and Day, *Indian Papers* 5: 320.

31. Coe, *Red Patriots,* 170; Porter, "Seminole in Mexico," *Chronicles,* 153–60. It is believed that Wild Cat's son probably returned to the territory in 1861.

32. Although the Seminoles left their Mexican land between 1858 and 1861, the tribe maintained an interest in the area. According to information in the Grant Foreman Collection, in 1897 the Seminoles thought of leaving Indian Territory for the "land of promise" in Mexico. Also, in the early twentieth century, Seminole John Morgan and others met for several years and discussed plans

to take several families to Mexico. In the 1930s, Morgan chaired a delegation that met with Mexico's Indian commissioner. The Mexicans wanted the Seminoles to exchange the Musquiz property for another larger, but poorer, location about sixteen miles from Musquiz—land reached only by wagon trails and where the Seminoles found Kickapoos living in tents. The commissioner arranged for the delegation to travel by train to Mexico City to meet with officials of the Interior Department. The agreements were not made public, and Morgan called no other meetings regarding the Mexican land. By 1985, Floyd Harjo, former Seminole nation chief, who accompanied the 1930s delegation as its chauffeur had learned nothing of the negotiations between the officials.

6. Free at Last

1. C.I.A., *Annual Report,* 1851, 143–48; C. Foreman, "Jumper Family," 284–85. In 1851, the Southern Superintendency was created. It included the Seminole subagency and the Cherokee, Creek, Choctaw, Chickasaw, and Neosho agencies. The headquarters was moved in 1853 from Van Buren to Fort Smith in Arkansas. See Tom Holman, "William G. Coffin, Lincoln's Superintendent of Indian Affairs for the Southern Superintendency," *Kansas Historical Quarterly* 39 (Winter 1973): 491.

2. C.I.A., *Annual Report,* 1851, 144–48; Brown, "Seminole Indian Agents," 66.

3. Luke Lea to A. H. H. Stuart, 14 Feb. 1852, Report Books, roll 7, vol. 7: 67–68; Robert A. Trennert, "Luke Lea, 1850–53," *Commissioners of Indian Affairs,* 49.

4. Coe, *Red Patriots,* 171; Carolyn Thomas Foreman, "Billy Bowlegs," *Chronicles of Oklahoma* 32 (Winter 1955): 523; U.S. Senate, *Message from the President of the United States to the Two Houses of Congress at the Commencement of the Second Session,* S. Ex. Doc. 1, 32d Cong., 2d sess., 6 Dec. 1852, 11; Luke Lea to A. H. H. Stuart, 30 Nov. 1852, 182, and 10 Jan. 1853, Report Books, roll 7, vol. 7: 198; U.S. House, *Seminole Indians: Message from the President of the United States in Reference to the Indians Remaining in Florida,* H. Ex. Doc. 19, 32d Cong., 2d sess., 19 Jan. 1853, 1–7.

5. U.S. House, *Seminole Indians: Message . . . Indians remaining in Florida,* 1–3.

6. Thomas Brown to Captain William B. , 1853, Thomas Brown Collection, Manuscript Collections, Robert Strozier Library, Florida State Univ., Tallahassee.

7. Coe, *Red Patriots,* 172. According to Carolyn Foreman in "John Jumper," *Chronicles of Oklahoma* 29 (Summer 1951), 138, another delegation went to Florida in December 1853.

8. Survey of the Creek Boundary Line, 1848–1856, Special Files, roll 8, file 77. The Creek agent had other concerns about his tribe. Several Creeks had entered the Second Seminole War as allies of the United States. The families of the soldiers who were killed or who died in service were to receive pensions. None had received them, and the Creek agent wanted the promises kept. The Creeks also wanted their eastern boundary marked, the western boundary completed, and a patent issued for their land. Their eastern boundary was later marked with iron columns at an expense of eleven hundred dollars. These columns, painted white, stood five feet above the ground. The Creeks also received their land patent. C.I.A., *Annual Report,* 1855, 255.

9. Marcellus Duval to Commissioner of Indian Affairs, 8 Apr. 1853, Gilcrease Collection of Imprints; Brown, "Seminole Indian Agents," 66–68.

10. Brown, "Seminole Indian Agents," 65–68. See also chapter 4 of the present volume.

11. George W. Manypenny to Robert McClelland, 9 Nov. 1853, Report Books, roll 7, vol. 7; Robert M. Kvasnicka, "George W. Manypenny, 1853–57," *Commissioners of Indian Affairs, 1824–1977,* 57–65. The Indian Bureau was housed in seven shabby rooms in the War Department Building when Manypenny took control.

12. C.I.A., *Annual Report,* 1852, 103; 1853, 159–62; Brown, "Seminole Indian Agents," 66–69.

13. Littlefield, *Africans and Seminoles,* 162, 173; M. E. Welsh, "The Missionary Spirit: Protestantism Among the Oklahoma Seminoles, 1842–1885," *Chronicles of Oklahoma* 61 (Spring 1983): 33.

14. Brown, "Seminole Indian Agents," 69–71.

15. C.I.A., *Annual Report,* 1854, 12–13, 111–12, 128–29; 1855, 171.

16. Ibid., 1854, 128; 1855, 120–21.

17. Ibid., 1855, 171; John Lilley to I. L. Wilson, 25 Mar. 1856, American Indian Correspondence, box 6, reel 1, Oklahoma Indian Archives, Oklahoma City, Oklahoma (hereafter cited as American Indian Correspondence); McReynolds, *The Seminoles,* 282–85; Welsh, "Missionary Spirit," *Chronicles,* 32.

18. John Lilley to I. L. Wilson, 26 June, 4 Aug., 31 Dec. 1855; 30 Jan., 1 June 1856; American Indian Correspondence, box 6, reel 1; Lilley, "Autobiography," 47.

19.   John Lilley to I. L. Wilson, 30 Jan. 1856, American Indian Correspondence, box 6, reel 1.

20.   C.I.A., *Annual Report,* 1854, 129; 1855, 173; John Lilley to Mr. Washbourne, 20 Aug. 1855 and John Lilley to I. L. Wilson, 23 Apr. 1855, 30 Jan., 25 Mar., and 1 June 1856, American Indian Correspondence, box 6, reel 1; Welsh, "Missionary Spirit," 35–37.

21.   C.I.A., *Annual Report,* 1855, 171, 173; John Lilley to I. L. Wilson, 4 Aug. 1855 and John Lilley to Mr. Washbourne, 20 Aug. 1855, American Indian Correspondence, box 6, reel 1.

22.   C.I.A., *Annual Report,* 1855, 136–37; Coe, *Red Patriots,* 173; L. E. Carter, "Seminole Nation," 439.

23.   C. Foreman, "John Jumper," 146–51; C. Foreman, "Jumper Family," 285.

24.   As quoted in Coe, *Red Patriots,* 173.

25.   L. E. Carter, "Seminole Nation," 440–41; McReynolds, *The Seminoles,* 275.

26.   C.I.A., *Annual Report,* 1855, 136–37, 172, 255; L. E. Carter, "Seminole Nation," 440.

27.   C.I.A., *Annual Report,* 1855, 9–10; L. E. Carter, "Seminole Nation," 440.

28.   C. W. Dean to George Manypenny, 28 Dec. 1855, Letters Received, roll 802.

29.   J. W. Washbourne to C. W. Dean, 24 Jan. 1856, Letters Received, roll 802; John Lilley to I. L. Wilson, 25 Mar. 1856, American Indian Correspondence, box 6, reel 1; U.S. House, *Creek and Seminole Indians: Message from the President of the United States, Transmitting a Report as to the Cause of the Difficulties between the Creek and Seminole Indians,* H. Ex. Doc. 58, 34th Cong., 1st sess., 17 Mar. 1856, 2.

30.   Seminoles Delegates to George Manypenny, 3 May 1856, Letters Received, roll 802.

31.   Ibid.; Kvasnicka, "George W. Manypenny, 1853–57," 60, 62; Brown, "Seminole Agents," 71.

32.   *U.S. Statutes at Large* 11: 699–702, M. Wright, "Seal of the Seminole Nation," 266; John Lilley to Walter Lourie, 17 Dec. 1855, American Indian Correspondence, box 6, reel 1.

33.   *U.S. Statutes at Large* 11: 699–707.

7. Delayed Reaction

1. George Manypenny to Robert McClelland, 22 Nov. 1856, Report Books, roll 10, vol. 10: 3–14; J. R. Ramsey to I. L. Wilson, 24 Nov. 1856, American Indian Correspondence, box 6, reel 1; C.I.A., *Annual Report,* 1857, 226; *Arkansas Intelligencer,* 17 Apr. 1857; J. W. Washbourne to C. W. Dean, 27 Jan. 1857, Letters Received, roll 802.

2. Charles E. Mix to Jacob Thompson, 18 Aug. 1858, Report Books, roll 11, vol. 11: 45; L. E. Carter, "Seminole Nation," 444–45; C.I.A., *Annual Report,* 1857, 192; 1860, 127; McReynolds, *The Seminoles,* 290. Charles Mix, a Connecticut native, worked for years as clerk or chief clerk in the Office of Indian Affairs. He also served as commissioner between 14 June 1858 and 8 November 1858, and as acting commissioner at various times in the 1850s. He was a proponent of Indian assimilation and provided continuity in basic Indian policy. See Harry Kelsey, "Charles E. Mix, 1858," *Commissioners of Indian Affairs,* 77–78; M. Duval to William Medill, 4 June 1849, Grant Foreman Collection.

3. Coe, *Red Patriots,* 175; C.I.A., *Annual Report,* 1857, 201–5, 227–29.

4. John Lilley to I. L. Wilson, 15 Aug. 1856 and 7 (month unknown) 1857, American Indian Correspondence, box 6, reel 1; Coe, *Red Patriots,* 174–75; C.I.A., *Annual Report,* 1857, 227–30; 1858, 154–55.

5. C.I.A., *Annual Report,* 1859, 184, 186–87; 1860, 127; *U.S. Statutes at Large* 11: 282; Brown, "Seminole Indian Agents," 74.

6. John Lilley to I. L. Wilson, 15 Aug. 1856 and J. R. Ramsey to I. L. Wilson, 28 Oct. 1856 and 8 Jan. 1857, American Indian Correspondence, box 6, reel 1; C. Foreman, "John Jumper," 139–40.

7. J. W. Washbourne to Charles W. Dean, 24 Jan. 1856 and 27 Jan. 1857, Letters Received, roll 802.

8. Margaret Ann Ulmer, Letter, 24 July 1857, Southern Historical Collection.

9. *Fort Smith Herald,* 25 July 1857.

10. C.I.A., *Annual Report,* 1857, 229; 1859, 185.

11. J. W. Washbourne to Thomas Drew, 16 July 1854, 30 Jan. 1855, 1 Mar. 1855; J. W. Washbourne to C. W. Dean, 20 Dec. 1855; C. W. Dean to George Manypenny, 31 Dec. 1855; and J. W. Washbourne to George Manypenny, 8 May 1856, Letters Received, roll 802.

12. L. E. Carter, "Seminole Nation," 445–46; Brown, "Seminole Indian Agents," 72.

13. Brown, "Seminole Indian Agents," 73.

14. C. Foreman, "Billy Bowlegs," 516–28; *Arkansas Intelligencer,* 28 May 1858; McReynolds, *The Seminoles,* 287; Littlefield, *Africans and Seminoles,* 175–76; Zuni, Memorandum, 7; Burk, "Oklahoma Seminole Indians," 220; Jefferson Davis to Robert McClelland, 3 and 22 Nov. 1856, Letters Received, roll 802; C.I.A., *Annual Report,* 1858, 152–53; Records of United States Army Continental Commands, 1821–1920, microcopy 1084, roll 1, RG 393 (Washington, D.C.: National Archives Microfilm Publications); and Records of the United States Army Continental Commands, 1821–1920, microcopy 1090, roll 1, RG 393 (Washington, D.C.: National Archives Microfilm Publications).

15. Charles E. Mix to Jacob Thompson, 6 Nov. 1858, Report Books, roll 11, vol. 11: 92; C. Foreman, "Billy Bowlegs," 529–30; Zuni, Memorandum, 8; McReynolds, *The Seminoles,* 287; L. E. Carter, "Seminole Nation," 448; M. E. Welsh, "Road to Assimilation," 14–15.

16. C.I.A., *Annual Report,* 1858, 126–28, 151–54; 1859, 160–61; L. E. Carter, "Seminole Nation," 449; Harry A. Kersey, Jr., "Those Left Behind: The Seminole Indians of Florida," in *Southeastern Indians since the Removal Era,* ed. Williams, 174–75; C. Foreman, "Billy Bowlegs," 529–30.

17. C.I.A., *Annual Report,* 1858, 151–54; 1859, 159–65, 185; L. E. Carter, "Seminole Nation," 451.

18. C.I.A., *Annual Report,* 1859, 159–65, 183–87; 1860, 17, 26, 126–27; A. B. Greenwood to Jacob Thompson, 30 Nov. 1860, Report Books, roll 12, vol. 12: 50.

19. C.I.A., *Annual Report,* 1860, 17, 26, 126–27; L. E. Carter, "Seminole Nation," 452; G. Foreman, *The Five Civilized Tribes,* 278.

8. Rendered Asunder

1. McReynolds, *The Seminoles,* 243–45, 289–312; Annie Heloise Abel, *The Slaveholding Indian,* 3 vols. (Cleveland: Arthur H. Clark, 1925; rpt. New York: Johnson Reprint, 1970), *The American Indian under Reconstruction,* vol. 3: 23, 319–21; C.I.A., *Annual Reports,* 1861–1866.

2. Harry Kelsey, "William Dole and Mr. Lincoln's Indian Policy," *Journal of the West* 10 (July 1971): 484; Edwin C. McReynolds, *Oklahoma: A History of the Sooner State* (Norman: Univ. of Oklahoma Press, 1954), 202; McReynolds, *The Seminoles,* 289; Gibson, *American Indian,* 366–67; David Nichols, *Lincoln and the Indians: Civil War Policy and Politics* (Columbia: Univ. of Missouri Press, 1978), 5–7; C.I.A., *Annual Report,* 1861, 46; 1923, iv; Harry Kelsey, "William

Dole, 1861–65," in *Commissioners of Indian Affairs,* 89–96; Sammy David Buice, "The Civil War and the Five Civilized Tribes—A study in Federal-Indian Relations" (Ph.D. diss., Univ. of Oklahoma, 1970), 40–42; Edmund J. Danziger, Jr., "The Office of Indian Affairs and the Problem of Civil War Indian Refugees in Kansas," *Kansas Historical Quarterly* 5 (Autumn 1969): 257–59.

3. C.I.A., *Annual Report,* 1861, 46–47; Buice, "Civil War," 40–42; Danziger, "Office of Indian Affairs," 258–59; McReynolds, *The Seminoles,* 291; Prucha, *The Great Father,* 136–40.

4. C.I.A., *Annual Report,* 1861, 3, 9, 11, 35; T. Holman, "William G. Coffin," 491–96; Gary E. Moulton, "John Ross and W. P. Dole: A Case Study of Lincoln's Indian Policy," *Journal of the West* 12 (July 1973): 414–16.

5. Buice, "Civil War," 16–17, 26; O. O. Howard, *My Life and Experiences among Our Hostile Indians* (Hartford, Conn.: A. D. Worthington, 1907), 99; Kenny A. Franks, "The Implementation of the Confederate Treaties with the Five Civilized Tribes," *Chronicles of Oklahoma* 51 (Spring 1973): 24–26; Kinneth McNeil, "Confederate Treaties with the Tribes of Indian Territory," *Chronicles of Oklahoma* 42 (Winter 1964–65): 408–10; Littlefield, *Africans and Seminoles,* 182; McReynolds, *The Seminoles,* 290; Brown, "Seminole Indian Agents," 72; C.I.A., *Annual Report,* 1861, 3.

6. Albert Pike, *Report of Albert Pike on Mission to the Indian Nations* (Richmond: Enquirer Book and Job Press, Tyler, Wise, Allegre, and Smith, 1861; rpt. Washington, D.C., 1968), 19–26; C. Foreman, "John Jumper," 140–41; Pascofar to Abraham Lincoln, 10 Mar. 1864, Letters Received, roll 803; Buice, "Civil War," 27–30; C.I.A., *Annual Report,* 1861, 46–47; Alice Mackay, "Father Murrow: Civil War Period," *Chronicles of Oklahoma* 12 (Mar. 1934): 59–60; Brown, "Seminole Indian Agents," 74–75; McNeil, "Confederate Treaties," 409–15.

7. Buice, "Civil War," 27–30; C.I.A., *Annual Report,* 1861, 46–47; McNeil, "Confederate Treaties," 410–15; Pike, *Report,* 19–26; C. Foreman, "John Jumper," 140–41; Wiley Britton, *The Union Indian Brigade in the Civil War* (Kansas City: Franklin Hudson Publishing, 1922), 34.

8. Pike, *Report,* 19–26; George H. Shirk, "Civil War in Indian Territory: One Hundred Years Ago in Indian Territory," unpublished, n.d, Oklahoma Historical Society Library, Oklahoma City, Oklahoma, 8–14; McNeil, "Confederate Treaties," 410–15; Pascofar to Abraham Lincoln, 10 Mar. 1864, Letters Received, roll 803.

9. Pike, *Report,* 28–39. Pike's expenses included: $6,914.86 for provisions supplied at Indian councils; $2,992.57 for the Seminole and Creek escort;

$2,397.02 to Indian delegates and interpreters; $1,550.00 for a secretary and an assistant; and $677.39 for presents for Comanches, Reserve Indians, and others. The Indian delegates to the Confederate Congress had to be twenty-one years of age and were elected to serve two-year terms. Samuel Benton Callahan, the only delegate of the Seminoles and Creeks to serve in the Confederate Congress, was elected on 30 May 1864 and served until two or three weeks before the war ended. Callahan, with no known Indian lineage, had a Scottish-Irish background. Born in Mobile, Alabama, in 1833, he attended school in Texas. Callahan moved to Indian Territory in 1858, where he raised cattle. Prior to his election as the Seminole-Creek delegate, he was a member of the First Creek Mounted Volunteers. During the last months of the war, Callahan and Elias Boudinot, the Cherokee delegate, worked vigorously to bring relief to their tribes. See T. Paul Wilson, "Delegates of the Five Civilized Tribes to the Confederate Congress," *Chronicles of Oklahoma* 53 (Fall 1975): 353–65.

10. C.I.A., *Annual Report,* 1861, 47–48; C. Foreman, "John Jumper," 140–41; Buice, "Civil War," 51–52.

11. Mackay, "Father Murrow," 60; Burk, "Oklahoma Seminole Indians," 218; Shirk, "Civil War," 14; C. Foreman, "John Jumper," 143. Pascofar to Abraham Lincoln, 10 Mar. 1864, Letters Received, roll 803.

12. Meserve, "Chief Opothleyahola," 444–47; Edwin C. Bearss, "The Civil War Comes to Indian Territory, 1861: The Flight of Opothleyoholo," *Journal of the West* 11 (Jan. 1972): 9–12, 15–16, 27–38; Danziger, "Office of Indian Affairs," 260–61. About 1 November 1861, a delegation of Seminoles, Creeks, and Cherokees went to Kansas with federal agent George Cutler. After talking with General David Hunter and other officers, they went to Washington, D.C., where their belief in the federal government was strengthened. When they returned to Indian Territory, however, Opothleyahola's party had already fled. See C.I.A., *Annual Report,* 1862, 138; 1865, 332; Dean Trickett, "The Civil War in the Indian Territory," *Chronicles of Oklahoma* 18 (Sept. 1940): 266–80; Records Relating to Military Service, microcopy 861, roll 74, RG 109 (Washington, D.C.: National Archives Microfilm Publications, 1971).

13. Edmund Jefferson Danziger, Jr., *Indians and Bureaucrats: Administering the Reservation Policy during the Civil War* (Chicago: Univ. of Illinois Press, 1974), 131–32; McReynolds, *The Seminoles,* 293–303; Coe, *Red Patriots,* 179; Wilcomb E. Washburn, *The American Indian and the United States: A Documentary History,* 4 vols. (New York: Random House, 1973), vol. 1: 96; Danziger, "Office of Indian Affairs," 261; C.I.A., *Annual Report,* 1862, 139, 156; Debo, *The Road to Disappearance,* 152.

14. C.I.A., *Annual Report,* 1862, 26–27.

15. C.I.A., *Annual Report,* 26, 147–53.

16. C.I.A., *Annual Report,* 1862, 142, 145–46, 156–57; Buice, "Civil War," 83–85; Danziger, "Office of Indian Affairs," 262–65.

17. Seminole chiefs to W. Dole, 14 Apr. 1862, Letters Received, roll 803; C.I.A., *Annual Report,* 1862, 142. There were more than 150 blacks, who claimed to be free, with the loyalists. Most of them spoke English. They also knew how to farm.

18. Danziger, "Office of Indian Affairs," 262–65; Buice, "Civil War," 83–85.

19. Danziger, "Office of Indian Affairs," 266–68; Danziger, *Indians and Bureaucrats,* 170–71; C.I.A., *Annual Report,* 1862, 137, 160, 163; Buice, "Civil War," 92; Edward Everett Dale and Morris L. Wardell, *History of Oklahoma* (New York: Prentice-Hall, 1948), 168–69; Abel, *The Slaveholding Indian* 2: 139–41.

20. Billy Bowlegs to Commissioner of Indian Affairs, 2 Mar. 1863, 13 May 1863 and Pascofar to Commissioner of Indian Affairs Dole, 29 Aug. 1863, Letters Received, roll 803; Kenny Franks, "Confederate States," 439–43. Bowlegs had lost his horse, two revolvers, and a saddle and bridle in a fight with a bushwhacker. This Billy Bowlegs was apparently not Halpuda Mikko, who emigrated from Florida in 1858. See C. Foreman, "Billy Bowlegs," 514, 529–30; Pascofar to William Dole, 29 July 1863. Pascofar indicated that he always encouraged the soldiers to return to their company when they came to the camps. Meserve, "Chief Opothleyahola," 451.

21. Danziger, "Office of Indian Affairs," 269–70; Annie Heloise Abel, "The Indians in the Civil War," *American Historical Review* 15 (Jan. 1910): 294; Dale and Wardell, *History of Oklahoma,* 168–69; Danziger, *Indians and Bureaucrats,* 136, 170–73; C.I.A., *Annual Report,* 1865, 256.

22. Franks, "Confederate States," 439–52; Mackay, "Father Murrow," 64; Allan C. Ashcraft, "Confederate Indian Department Conditions in August 1864," *Chronicles of Oklahoma* 41 (Winter 1963): 270–85.

23. Chaney, "Tribal History," 36–37, 42–43; Ashcraft, "Confederate Indian Department," 270–84; Franks, "Confederate States," 444–52; Mackay, "Father Murrow," 62; Burk, "Oklahoma Seminole Indians," 219.

24. Mackay, "Father Murrow," 64.

25. Ibid., 63–64; Abel, "Indians in the Civil War," 294; *The War of the Rebellion: A Compilation of the Official Records of the Union and Confederate Armies,* 128 vols. (Washington, D.C.: Govt. Printing Office, 1880–1901), ser. 1,

vol. 22, pt. 2, 1052–53; Abel, *American Indian as Participant,* 122, 152, 312; Franks, "Confederate States," 448–51; according to Records Relating to Military Service, microcopy 861, roll 74, as late as 21 November 1862, the noncommissioned rebel Seminoles had received no pay since enlisting.

26. Franks, "Confederate States," 439–53.

27. *War of the Rebellion,* ser. 1, vol. 34, pt. 1, 106–12; Abel, *American Indian as Participant,* 322–23.

28. Long John to Abraham Lincoln, 10 Mar. 1864, Letters Received, roll 803. Long John was not alone in complaining about troops at Fort Gibson. Cherokee agent Justice Harlan wrote in December 1863 that federal troops there spent most of their time drinking, dancing, and recovering from diseases "not brought on by any particular piety." See Buice, "Civil War," 184.

29. Pascofar to Abraham Lincoln, 10 Mar. 1864, Letters Received, roll 803.

30. Danziger, *Indians and Bureaucrats,* 175–76; U.S. Congress, Joint Resolution, *Senator Lane Speaking on the Removal of Indians from Kansas,* S. Doc. 32, 38th Cong., 1st sess., 1863–64, 921; William Dole to John Usher, 9 Feb. 1864, Report Books, roll 13, vol. 13: 303–4.

31. Buice, "Civil War," 204–5; T. Holman, "William G. Coffin," 508–14; C.I.A., *Annual Report,* 1864, 31–32, 303; Danziger, "Office of Indian Affairs," 268–74.

32. Buice, "Civil War," 205; Pascofar to William Dole, 29 July 1863, Letters Received, roll 803.

33. C.I.A., *Annual Report,* 1863, 185–86; 1864, 304, 307–8.

34. Speech of Colonel Jumper to Creeks and Seminoles of 1st Seminole Regiment, 6 July 1864, Gilcrease Collection of Imprints.

35. Franks, "Confederate States," 446–52; Brown, "Seminole Indian Agents," 76–77; George Reynolds to W. Dole, 25 Mar. 1865, Letters Received, roll 803.

36. Chaney, "Tribal History," 46–47; Franks, "Confederate States," 452–53. See also Kenny A. Franks, *Stand Watie and the Agony of the Cherokee Nation* (Memphis: Memphis State Univ. Press, 1979).

9. The Final Verdict

1. *U.S. Statutes at Large* 14: 755; *New York Times,* 16 Sept. 1865; Gibson, *American Indian,* 384; McReynolds, *The Seminoles,* 313–16; Chaney, "Tribal History," 51; May Trees, "Socioeconomic Reconstruction in the Seminole Na-

tion, 1865–1870," *Journal of the West* 12 (July 1973): 491; C. Foreman, "John Jumper," 143; Littlefield, *Africans and Seminoles,* 184–87. Commissioner Cooley became Indian commissioner in July 1865, five days after William Dole resigned. Cooley, a native of New Hampshire and a lawyer from Iowa, strove to reduce the corruption among the agents and to promote efficiency in Indian affairs. Nonetheless, Indian policy fell under the control of President Andrew Johnson, Secretary of War Edwin M. Stanton, Secretary of the Interior James Harlan, and General John Pope. See Gary L. Roberts, "Dennis Nelson Cooley, 1865–1866," *Commissioners of Indian Affairs,* 99–106.

2. M. E. Welsh, "Road to Assimilation," 26; Gibson, *American Indian,* 384–95.

3. Littlefield, *Africans and Seminoles,* 185–87; C.I.A., *Annual Report,* 1865, 283.

4. C. Foreman, "John Jumper," 141–44; Trees, "Socioeconomic Reconstruction," 492.

5. Littlefield, *Africans and Seminoles,* 187.

6. Ibid., 188–93; Gibson, *American Indian,* 398; George A. Reynolds to D. N. Cooley, 13 and 20 Jan. 1866, Letters Received, roll 803.

7. U.S., *Statutes at Large* 14: 755–61; C.I.A., *Annual Report,* 1865, 283. The area was described as

> beginning on the Canadian river where the line dividing the Creek lands according to the terms of their sale to the United States by their treaty of 6 February 1866, following said line due north to where said line crosses the north fork of the Canadian river; thence up said north fork of the Canadian river a distance sufficient to make two hundred thousand acres by running due south to the Canadian river; thence down said Canadian river to the place of beginning.

The other Civilized Tribes ceded land to the United States as well. On 28 April, the Choctaws and Chickasaws relinquished the "Leased District" of 6.8 million acres for $300,000. If they did not give full rights to their freedmen, that amount was to become a fund for the blacks. The Choctaw-Chickasaw cession was to provide land for Indians from Texas. The Creeks ceded 3,250,560 acres for $975,168. On 19 July, the Cherokees ceded 800,000 acres in Kansas to be sold for their benefit. See C.I.A., *Annual Report,* 1866, 9–11.

8. D. N. Cooley to James Harlan, 2 Apr. 1866, Report Books, roll 15, vol. 15: 175.

9. D. N. Cooley to James Harlan, 2 Apr. 1866, Report Books, roll 15, vol. 15: 175–76; *U.S. Statutes at Large* 14: 755–61; John Brown's Protest, 21 Mar.

1866, Letters Received, roll 803; M. Wright, "Seal of the Seminole Nation," 266–68. Brown served as principal chief from 1877 until 1919 except for a two-year period. In September 1865, when the council convened at Fort Smith, Seminole chiefs Long John, Pascofar, and Chocote Harjo appointed Perry Fuller of Kansas as "true agent and attorney" for the tribe. Fuller had authority to sign the Indians' names and to receive money due the Seminoles from losses sustained during the Civil War. Fuller witnessed the ratification of the treaty in Washington, D.C., and perhaps participated in other ways. See, Indians Power of Attorney to Perry Fuller, Letters Received, roll 803.

10. D. N. Cooley to James Harlan, 7, 10, 11 May 1866, Report Books, roll 15, vol. 15: 258–72. An estimated, and no doubt inaccurate, statistical report of the Seminoles was made by Agent George Reynolds in September 1866 in compliance with a July 1865 requirement of the commissioner of Indian affairs. His report listed a population of 2,950, including 1,425 males and 1,525 females, probably Seminoles, blacks, and some Creeks. Total individual wealth was fifty-four thousand dollars. Other property included two hundred horses and fifteen hundred cattle, ten frame houses, and two hundred log cabins. See C.I.A., *Annual Report*, 1866, 322.

11. In Miller's *Este-Cate (Red Man)*, the western Seminoles refer to the years between the beginning of Reconstruction in 1866 and the allotment of their lands in 1907 as the Second Seminole nation. According to Muriel Wright in "Seal of the Seminole Nation," 271, the first Seminole constitution that provided for the first Seminole nation in the West was adopted after the 1856 treaty; this document was lost.

Bibliography

Primary Sources

Manuscripts and Collections

American Indian Correspondence. Box 6. Reel 1. Oklahoma Indian Archives, Oklahoma City.

Commissary General of Subsistence—Seminole. RG 75. National Archives.

Edward Brett Randolph. Diary. Southern Historical Collection. Univ. of North Carolina Library, Chapel Hill.

Gilcrease Collection of Imprints. Thomas Gilcrease Museum Library, Tulsa, Oklahoma.

Grant Foreman Collection. Thomas Gilcrease Museum Library, Tulsa, Oklahoma.

J. Van Horne. Muster Roll. Seminole Agency Emigration. Oklahoma Indian Archives, Oklahoma City.

Letters Received by the Office of Indian Affairs, 1824–81. Seminole Agency. Microcopy 234. Rolls 800–806. Record Group 75. Washington, D.C.: National Archives Microfilm Publications, 1956.

Lilley, Mary Ann. "The Autobiography of Mary Ann Lilley." Unpublished MS. Western History Collections. Univ. Libraries, Univ. of Oklahoma, Norman, n.d.

Margaret Ann Ulmer Collection. Letter. Southern Historical Collection. Univ. of North Carolina Library, Chapel Hill.

Miscellaneous Muster Rolls. Entry 301. RG 75. National Archives.

Records of United States Army Continental Commands, 1821–1920. Microcopy 1084. Roll 1. RG 393. Washington, D.C.: National Archives Microfilm Publications.

Records of United States Army Continental Commands, 1821–1920. Microcopy 1090. Roll 1. RG 393. Washington, D.C.: National Archives Microfilm Publications.

Records Relating to Military Service. Microcopy 594. Roll 225. RG 94. Washington, D.C.: National Archives Microfilm Publications, 1964.

Records Relating to Military Service. Microcopy 861. Roll 74. RG 109. Washington, D.C.: National Archives Microfilm Publications, 1971.

Register of Letters Received, 1831–1836. Entry 198. RG 75. National Archives.

Report Books of the Office of Indian Affairs. Microcopy 348. Rolls 1–15. Record Group 75. Washington, D.C.: National Archives Microfilm Publications, 1963.

Seminole Papers. Thomas Gilcrease Museum Library, Tulsa, Oklahoma.

Shirk, George H. "Civil War in Indian Territory: One Hundred Years Ago in Indian Territory." Unpublished MS. Oklahoma Historical Society Library, Oklahoma City, n.d.

Special Files of the Office of Indian Affairs, 1807–1904. Microcopy M574. Rolls 6, 7, 8. Record Group 75. Washington, D.C.: National Archives Microfilm Publications, 1965.

Thomas Brown Collection. Manuscript Collections. Robert Strozier Library, Florida State Univ., Tallahassee.

U.S. Bureau of Indian Affairs. Report to the Department of the Interior 1968. By Charles E. Grounds. Tribal Operations Office. Muskogee Area Agency, Muskogee, Oklahoma.

U.S. Department of Interior. Bureau of Indian Affairs. Memorandum on Results of Research Report in Oklahoma Seminole Award in Docket 247. 19 Mar. 1981. By Acting Deputy Commissioner of Indian Affairs. Tribal Operations Office, Muskogee, Oklahoma.

William Tecumseh Sherman Letters. P. B. Ewing Collection. Ohio Historical Society Library, Columbus.

Zuni, Jose A. Memorandum on Results of Research Report on Seminole Judgment in Dockets 73 and 151 before the Indians Claims Commission. 26 Nov. 1976. Office of Tribal Operations. Muskogee Area Agency, Muskogee, Oklahoma.

Government Documents and Other Publications

Carter, Clarence Edwin. *The Territory of Florida 1839–1845*. Washington, D.C.: Govt. Printing Office, 1962.

Lovett, Vince, and Larry Rummel, with Dick Hardwick, Glen Robertson, and Vince Monico. *American Indians*. Washington, D.C.: Govt. Printing Office, 1984.

Statutes at Large of the United States, 1821–1980. 90 vols. Washington, D.C.: Govt. Printing Office, 1821–1980.

Swanton, John. *The Indian Tribes of North America*. Washington, D.C.: Govt. Printing Office, 1952.

Tribes under the Administrative Jurisdiction of the Muskogee Area Office. Muskogee, Okla.: Area Tribal Operations Office.

U.S. Congress. Joint Resolution. *Senator Lane Speaking on the Removal of Indians from Kansas*. 38th Cong., 1st sess., 1863–64. S. Res. 32.

U.S. Department of Interior. Bureau of Indian Affairs. *Constitution of the Seminole Nation of Oklahoma*. Muskogee, Okla.: Tribal Operations Office, 1969.

U.S. Department of Interior. Office of Indian Affairs. *Annual Report of the Commissioner of Indian Affairs to the Secretary of the Department of the Interior, for the Fiscal Years Ended June 30, 1832–1866*. Rpt. Washington, D.C.: Microcard Editions, Industrial Products Division of the National Cash Register Company, 1968.

U.S. Department of State. *Treaties and Other International Agreements of the United States of America, 1776–1949*. 13 vols. Washington, D.C.: Govt. Printing Office, 1968–1976.

U.S. House. *Creek and Seminole Indians: Message from the President of the United States, Transmitting a Report as to the Cause of the Difficulties between the Creek and Seminole Indians*. 34th Cong., 1st sess., 1856. H. Ex. Doc. 58.

U.S. House. *Expenditure in 1841-Florida Indians, etc.* 27th Cong., 2d sess., 1842. H. Ex. Doc. 247.

U.S. House. *Message from the President of the United States Transmitting a Communication from the Mexican Minister Relative to Indian Incursions upon the Mexican Frontier*. 31st Cong., 2d sess., 1850. H. Ex. Doc. 4.

U.S. House. *Message from the President of the United States Transmitting Information in Regard to the Difficulties between the Creek and Seminole Indians*. 33d Cong., 2d sess., 1854. H. Ex. Doc. 15.

U.S. House. *Seminole Indians: Message from the President of the United States in Reference to the Indians Remaining in Florida.* 32d Cong., 2d sess., 1853. H. Ex. Doc. 19.

U.S. House. *Seminole War—Slaves Captured.* 27th Cong., 2d sess., 1842. Doc. 55.

U.S. Senate. *Message from the President of the United States Communicating Information, in Answer to a Resolution of the Senate, Relative to Hostilities Committed by the Seminole Indians in Florida during the Past Year, Their Removal, Etc.* 31st Cong., 1st sess., 1850. S. Ex. Doc. 49.

U.S. Senate. *Message from the President of the United States Communicating a Translation of a Note from the Mexican Minister in Relation to the Wild Indians of the United States on the Frontier of Mexico.* 31st Cong., 1st sess., 1850. S. Ex. Doc. 44.

U.S. Senate. *Message from the President of the United States in Relation to the Condition of the Seminole Indians Who Have Emigrated.* 25th Cong., 3d sess., 1839. S. Doc. 88.

U.S. Senate. *Message from the President of the United States to the Two Houses of Congress at the Commencement of the Second Session.* 32d Cong., 2d sess., 1852. S. Ex. Doc. 1.

The War of the Rebellion: A Compilation of the Official Records of the Union and Confederate Armies. 128 vols. Washington, D.C.: Govt. Printing Office, 1880–1901.

Books and Articles

Adams, Ephraim Douglass, ed. "British Correspondence Concerning Texas—Elliott to Aberdeen." *Southwestern Historical Quarterly* 19 (Apr. 1916): 405–439.

Britton, Wiley. *The Civil War on the Border.* New York: G. P. Putnam's Sons, 1899.

———. *The Union Indian Brigade in the Civil War.* Kansas City, Miss.: Franklin Hudson Publishing, 1922.

Foreman, Carolyn Thomas, ed. "Journal of a Tour in Indian Territory." By N. Sayre Harris. *Chronicles of Oklahoma* 10 (June 1932): 219–256.

Giddings, Joshua R. *The Exiles of Florida.* Columbus: Follett, Foster and Company, 1858.

Howard, O. O. *My Life and Experiences among Our Hostile Indians.* Hartford, Conn.: A. D. Worthington, 1907.

Irelan, John Robert. *History of the Life, Administration, and Times of Martin Van Buren.* Chicago: Fairbanks and Palmer Publishing, 1887.

McCall, George A. *Letters from the Frontiers.* With an introduction and index by John K. Mahon. Gainesville: Univ. Presses of Florida, 1974.

Miller, Tuskoma Brown. *Este-Cate: "Red Man".* Seminole Nation Historical Society, 1982.

Narrative of a Voyage to the Spanish Main, in the Ship, "Two Friends." With an introduction and index by John W. Griffin. Gainesville: Univ. Presses of Florida, 1978.

Pike, Albert. *Report of Albert Pike on Mission to the Indian Nations.* Richmond: Enquirer Book and Job Press, Tyler, Wise, Allegre, and Smith, 1861; Washington, D.C., 1968.

Sherman, William T. *Memoirs of General W. T. Sherman.* 2d ed. New York: D. Appleton, 1904.

Sunderman, James F., ed. *Journey into Wilderness: An Army Surgeon's Account of Life in Camp and Field during the Creek and Seminole Wars, 1836–1838,* by Jacob Rhett Motte. Gainesville: Univ. of Florida, 1963.

Thorndike, Rachel Sherman, ed. *The Sherman Letters: Correspondence between General Sherman and Senator Sherman from 1837 to 1891.* With a foreword by John Y. Simon. New York: Da Capo Press, 1969.

Winfrey, Dorman H., and James M. Day. *The Indian Papers of Texas and the Southwest 1825–1916.* 5 vols. Austin: Texas State Library and The Pemberton Press, 1959–1966.

Newspapers

Arkansas Intelligencer (Van Buren)
Fort Smith (Arkansas) Herald
New York Times
Niles National Register
Osceola Times (Wewoka, Okla.)

Interviews by Author

Ardenna Dodd. Seminole. 21 May 1985.

George Goodner. Superintendent of Wewoka (Seminole) Agency. Bureau of Indian Affairs. 21 May 1985.

Floyd Harjo. Former Seminole Nation Chief. 21 May 1985.

Dwayne Miller. Seminole Band Chief. 17 May 1985.

Dennis Springwater. Area Tribal Operations Officer. Muskogee, Oklahoma. 22 May 1985.

Secondary Materials

Abel, Annie Heloise. "The Indians in the Civil War." *American Historical Review* 15 (Jan. 1910): 281–96.

———. *The Slaveholding Indians*. 3 vols. Cleveland: Arthur H. Clark, 1915–25; New York: Johnson Reprint, 1970.

Agnew, Brad. *Fort Gibson: Terminal on the Trail of Tears*. Norman: Univ. of Oklahoma Press, 1980.

Andrews, Thomas F. "Freedmen in Indian Territory: A Post–Civil War Dilemma." *Journal of the West* 4 (July 1965): 367–76.

Ashcraft, Allan C. "Confederate Indian Department Conditions in August, 1864." *Chronicles of Oklahoma* 41 (Winter 1963): 270–85.

Balman, Gail. "The Creek Treaty of 1866." *Chronicles of Oklahoma* 48 (Summer 1970): 184–96.

Bearss, Edwin C. "The Civil War Comes to Indian Territory, 1861: The Flight of Opothleyoholo." *Journal of the West* 11 (Jan. 1972): 9–42.

Bemis, Samuel Flagg. *John Quincy Adams and the Foundations of American Foreign Policy*. New York: Knopf, 1949.

Brown, Thomas Elton. "Seminole Indian Agents, 1842–1874." *Chronicles of Oklahoma* 51 (Spring 1973): 59–83.

Buker, George E. *Swamp Sailors: Riverine Warfare in the Everglades, 1835–1842*. Gainesville: Univ. Presses of Florida, 1975.

Burk, Jerry L. "Oklahoma Seminole Indians: Origin, History, and Pan-Indianism." *Chronicles of Oklahoma* 51 (Summer 1973): 211–23.

Carter, L. Edward. "The Seminole Nation after Leaving Florida, 1855–1860." *Chronicles of Oklahoma* 55 (Winter 1977–78): 433–53.

Coe, Charles H. *Red Patriots: The Story of the Seminoles*. Cincinnati: Editor Publishing, 1898.

Covington, James W. "Migration of the Seminoles into Florida 1700–1820." *Florida Historical Quarterly* 46 (Apr. 1968): 340–57.

———. *The Billy Bowlegs War, 1855–1858: The Final Stand of the Seminoles Against the Whites.* Chuluota, Fla.: Mickler House Publishers, 1981.

———. *The Seminoles of Florida.* Gainesville: Univ. Press of Florida, 1993.

Dale, Edward Everett, and Morris L. Wardell. *History of Oklahoma.* New York: Prentice-Hall, 1948.

Danziger, Edmund J., Jr. *Indians and Bureaucrats: Administering the Reservation Policy during the Civil War.* Chicago: Univ. of Illinois Press, 1974.

———. "The Office of Indian Affairs and the Problem of Civil War Indian Refugees in Kansas." *Kansas Historical Quarterly* 35 (Autumn 1969): 257–75.

Debo, Angie. *A History of the Indians of the United States.* Norman: Univ. of Oklahoma Press, 1970.

———. *And Still the Waters Run.* Princeton, N.J.: Princeton Univ. Press, 1940.

———. *The Road to Disappearance.* 2d ed. Norman: Univ. of Oklahoma Press, 1967.

Denham, James M. "Some Prefer the Seminoles": Violence and Disorder Among Soldiers and Settlers in the Second Seminole War, 1835–1842." *Florida Historical Quarterly* 70 (July 1991): 38–54.

Doran, Michael F. "Population Statistics of Nineteenth Century Indian Territory." *Chronicles of Oklahoma* 53 (Winter 1975–76): 492–515.

Dyer, Brainerd, *Zachary Taylor.* Baton Rouge: Louisiana State Univ. Press, 1946.

Fairbanks, Charles H. *The Florida Seminole People.* Phoenix: Indian Tribal Series, 1973.

Fischer, LeRoy H. "The Civil War Era in Indian Territory." *Journal of the West* 12 (July 1973): 345–55.

Ford, John Salmon. *Rip Ford's Texas.* Edited and with an introduction and commentary by Stephen B. Oates. Austin: Univ. of Texas Press, 1963.

Foreman, Carolyn T. "Billy Bowlegs." *Chronicles of Oklahoma* 32 (Winter 1955): 512–32.

———. "John Jumper." *Chronicles of Oklahoma* 29 (Summer 1951): 137–52.

———. "The Jumper Family of the Seminole Nation." *Chronicles of Oklahoma* 34 (Autumn 1956): 272–85.

Foreman, Grant. *Advancing the Frontier, 1830–1860.* 1933. Rpt. Norman: Univ. of Oklahoma Press, 1968.

———. *Indian Removal: The Emigration of the Five Civilized Tribes of Indians.* Norman: Univ. of Oklahoma Press, 1932.

————. *The Five Civilized Tribes*. Norman: Univ. of Oklahoma, 1934.

Foster, Laurence, *Negro-Indian Relationships in the Southeast*. Philadelphia: By the author, 1935; New York: AMS Press, 1978.

Franks, Kenny A. "The Confederate States and the Five Civilized Tribes." *Journal of the West* 12 (July 1973): 439–61.

————. "The Implementation of the Confederate Treaties with the Five Civilized Tribes." *Chronicles of Oklahoma* 51 (Spring 1973): 21–33.

————. *Stand Watie and the Agony of the Cherokee Nation*. Memphis: Memphis State Univ. Press, 1979.

Gaines, W. Craig. *The Confederate Cherokees: John Drew's Regiment of Mounted Rifles*. Baton Rouge: Louisiana State Univ. Press, 1989.

Garbarino, Merwyn, S. *Big Cypress: A Changing Seminole Community*. New York: Holt, Rinehart, and Winston, 1972.

Gibson, Arrell Morgan. "An Indian Territory United Nations: The Creek Council of 1845." *Chronicles of Oklahoma* 39 (Winter 1961): 398–413.

————. *The American Indian: Prehistory to the Present*. Lexington, Mass.: D. C. Heath, 1980.

Gifford, John C., ed. *Billy Bowlegs and the Seminole War*. Coconut Grove, Fla.: Triangle, 1925.

Green, Michael D. *The Politics of Indian Removal: Creek Government and Society in Crisis*. Lincoln: Univ. of Nebraska Press, 1982.

Hamilton, Holman. *Zachary Taylor: Soldier in the White House*. New York: Bobbs-Merrill, 1951.

Hartley, William, and Ellen Hartley. *Osceola: The Unconquered Indian*. New York: Hawthorn Books, 1973.

Hill, Edward E. *The Office of Indian Affairs, 1824–1880: Historical Sketches*. New York: Clearwater Publishing, 1974.

Holman, Tom. "William G. Coffin, Lincoln's Superintendent of Indian Affairs for the Southern Superintendency." *Kansas Historical Quarterly* 39 (Winter 1973): 491–514.

Hoopes, Alban W. *Indian Affairs and Their Administration, with Special Reference to the Far West, 1849–1860*. Philadelphia: Univ. of Pennsylvania, 1932; New York: Kraus Reprint, 1972.

Howard, James H., with Willie Lena. *Oklahoma Seminoles: Medicines, Magic, and Religion*. Norman: Univ. of Oklahoma Press, 1984.

Hudson, Charles M. *The Southeastern Indians*. Knoxville: Univ. of Tennessee Press, 1976.

Josephy, Alvin M., Jr. *Now that the Buffalo's Gone: A Study of Today's American Indian.* Norman: Univ. of Oklahoma Press, 1984.

Kelsey, Harry. "William P. Dole and Mr. Lincoln's Indian Policy." *Journal of the West* 10 (July 1971): 484–92.

Kersey, Harry A., Jr. *The Seminole and Miccosukee Tribes: A Critical Bibliography.* Bloomington: Indiana Univ. Press, 1987.

Klos, George. "Blacks and the Seminole Removal Debate, 1821–1835." *Florida Historical Quarterly* 68 (July 1989): 55–78.

Kremm, Thomas W., and Diane Neal. "Civil War Controversy." *Chronicles of Oklahoma* 70 (Spring 1992): 26–45.

Krogman, Wilton Marion. "The Racial Composition of the Seminole Indians of Florida and Oklahoma." *Journal of Negro History* 19 (Jan. 1934): 412–30.

Kvasnicka, Robert M., and Herman J. Viola, eds. *The Commissioners of Indian Affairs, 1824–1977.* With a foreword by Philleo Nash. Lincoln: Univ. of Nebraska Press, 1979.

Littlefield, Daniel F., Jr. *Africans and Seminoles: From Removal to Emancipation.* Westport, Conn.: Greenwood Press, 1977.

Lollar, Wayne B. "Seminole-United States Financial Relations, 1823–1866." *Chronicles of Oklahoma* 50 (Summer 1972): 190–98.

MacHugh, R. J. *Modern Mexico.* New York: Dodd, Mead, 1914.

Mackey, Alice Hurley. "Father Murrow: Civil War Period." *Chronicles of Oklahoma* 12 (Mar. 1934): 55–65.

Mahon, John. *History of the Second Seminole War, 1835–1842.* 1967. Revised ed., Gainesville: Univ. of Florida Press, 1991.

———. "Two Seminole Treaties: Payne's Landing, 1832, and Ft. Gibson, 1833." *Florida Historical Quarterly* 41 (July 1962–Apr. 1963): 1–21.

Malone, Dumas, ed. *Dictionary of American Biography.* 22 vols. New York: Charles Scribner's Sons, 1928–1981.

Mann, William L. "James O. Rice: Hero of the Battles on the San Gabriels [*sic*]." *Southwestern Historical Quarterly* 55 (July 1951): 30–42.

Mayhall, Mildred P. *Indian Wars of Texas.* Waco, Tex.: Texian Press, 1965.

McNeil, Kinneth. "Confederate Treaties with the Tribes of Indian Territory." *Chronicles of Oklahoma* 42 (Winter 1964–65): 408–20.

McReynolds, Edwin C. *Oklahoma: A History of the Sooner State.* Norman: Univ. of Oklahoma Press, 1954.

———. *The Seminoles.* Norman: Univ. of Oklahoma Press, 1957.

McReynolds, Edwin C., Alice Marriott, and Estelle Faulconer. *Oklahoma: The Story of Its Past and Present*. Norman: Univ. of Oklahoma Press, 1961.

Meserve, John Bartlett. "Chief Opothleyahola." *Chronicles of Oklahoma* 9 (Dec. 1931): 440–53.

Miller, Robert Ryal. *Mexico: A History*. Norman: Univ. of Oklahoma Press, 1985.

Milligan, Dorothy, ed. *The Indian Way: Creeks and Seminoles*. Nortex Press, 1977.

Morton, Ohland. "Confederate Government Relations with the Five Civilized Tribes." *Chronicles of Oklahoma* 31 (Fall 1953): 189–204.

Moulton, Gary E. "Cherokees and the Second Seminole War." *Florida Historical Quarterly* 53 (July 1974–Apr. 1975): 296–305.

———. "John Ross and W. P. Dole: A Case Study of Lincoln's Indian Policy." *Journal of the West* 12 (July 1973): 414–23.

Newcomb, W. W., Jr. *The Indians of Texas: From Prehistoric to Modern Times*. Austin: Univ. of Texas Press, 1961.

Nichols, David. *Lincoln and the Indians: Civil War Policy and Politics*. Columbia: Univ. of Missouri Press, 1978.

O'Donnell, James H. *Southeastern Frontiers: Europeans, Africans, and American Indians, 1513–1840*. Bloomington: Indiana Univ. Press for the Newberry Library, 1982.

Peithman, Irvin M. *The Unconquered Seminole Indians*. St. Petersburg, Fla.: Great Outdoors Association, 1957.

Peters, Virginia B. *The Florida Wars*. Hamden, Conn.: Archon Books, 1979.

Pierce, Gerald S. *Texas under Arms*. Austin: Encino Press, 1969.

Porter, Kenneth W. "Billy Bowlegs (Holata Micco) in the Seminole Wars." *Florida Historical Quarterly* 45 (Jan. 1967): 219–42.

———. "Seminole in Mexico, 1850–1861." *Chronicles of Oklahoma* 29 (Summer 1951): 153–68.

———. "The Hawkins' Negroes Go to Mexico." *Chronicles of Oklahoma* 24 (Spring 1946): 55–58.

———. "The Seminole in Mexico, 1850–1861." *Hispanic American Historical Review* 31 (Feb. 1951): 1–36.

———. "Tiger Tail." *Florida Historical Quarterly* 24 (1946): 216–17.

———. "Wild Cat's Death and Burial." *Chronicles of Oklahoma* 21 (Mar. 1943): 41–43.

Prucha, Francis Paul. *The Great Father: The United States Government and the American Indians*. Lincoln: Univ. of Nebraska Press, 1986.

————, ed. *The Indian in American History.* Hinsdale, Ill.: Dryden Press, 1971.

———— *The Sword of the Republic: The United States Army on the Frontier, 1783–1846.* London: Macmillan, 1969.

Rampp, Larry C., and Donald L. Rampp. *The Civil War in the Indian Territory.* Austin: Presidial Press, 1975.

Remini, Robert V. *Andrew Jackson and the Course of American Empire, 1767–1821.* New York: Harper and Row, 1977.

Rippy, J. Fred. "Border Troubles along the Rio Grande, 1848–1860." *Southwestern Historical Quarterly* 23 (Oct. 1919): 91–111.

————. "The Indians of the United States in the Diplomacy of the United States and Mexico, 1848–1853." *Hispanic-American Historical Review* 2 (Aug. 1919): 363–96.

Satz, Ronald. *American Indian Policy in the Jacksonian Era.* Lincoln: Univ. of Nebraska Press, 1975.

Schmeckebier, Laurence F. *The Office of Indian Affairs: Its History, Activities and Organization.* Baltimore: John Hopkins Univ. Press, 1927.

Shearer, Ernest C. "The Callahan Expedition, 1855." *Southwestern Historical Quarterly* 54 (Apr. 1951): 430–51.

Smith, Ralph A. "Indians in American-Mexican Relations before the War of 1846." *Hispanic American Historical Review* 43 (Feb. 1963): 34–64.

Spoehr, Alexander. "Oklahoma Seminole Towns." *Chronicles of Oklahoma* 19 (Sept. 1941): 377–80.

Syrett, Harold C. *Andrew Jackson: His Contribution to the American Tradition.* New York: Bobbs-Merrill, 1953.

Trees, May. "Socioeconomic Reconstruction in the Seminole Nation, 1865–1870." *Journal of the West* 12 (July 1973): 490–98.

Trickett, Dean. "The Civil War in the Indian Territory." *Chronicles of Oklahoma* 18 (Sept. 1940): 266–80.

Tyler, Ronnie C. "The Callahan Expedition of 1855: Indians or Negroes?" *Southwestern Historical Quarterly* 70 (Apr. 1967): 574–85.

Utley, Robert M. *The Indian Frontier of the American West, 1846–1890.* Albuquerque: Univ. of New Mexico Press, 1984.

Van Every, Dale. *Disinherited: The Lost Birthright of the American Indian.* New York: William Morrow, 1966.

Walton, George. *Fearless and Free: The Seminole Indian War, 1835–1842.* New York: Bobbs-Merrill, 1977.

Ware, James W. "Indian Territory." *Journal of the West* 16 (Apr. 1977): 101–13.

Washburn, Wilcomb E., ed. *The American Indian and the United States: A Documentary History.* 4 vols. New York: Random House, 1973.

Webb, Walter Prescott. *The Texas Rangers: A Century of Frontier Defense.* With a foreword by Lyndon B. Johnson. Austin: Univ. of Texas Press, 1935, 1965.

Weisman, Brent Richards. *Like Beads on a String: A Culture History of the Seminole Indians in North Peninsular Florida.* Tuscaloosa: Univ. of Alabama Press, 1989.

Welsh, Louise. "Seminole Colonization in Oklahoma." *Chronicles of Oklahoma* 54 (Spring 1976): 77–103.

Welsh, Michael. "The Missionary Spirit: Protestantism among the Oklahoma Seminoles, 1842–1885." *Chronicles of Oklahoma* 61 (Spring 1983): 28–47.

Wickman, Patricia. *Osceola's Legacy.* Tuscaloosa: Univ. of Alabama Press, 1991.

Williams, Walter L., ed. *Southeastern Indians since the Removal Era.* Athens: Univ. of Georgia Press, 1979.

Wilson, Minnie Moore. *The Seminoles of Florida.* New York: Moffat, Yard, 1910.

Wilson, T. Paul. "Delegates of the Five Civilized Tribes to the Confederate Congress." *Chronicles of Oklahoma* 53 (Fall 1975): 353–66.

Wright, J. Leitch, Jr. "Blacks in British East Florida." *Florida Historical Quarterly* 54 (July 1975–Apr. 1976): 425–42.

———. *Creeks and Seminoles: Destruction and Regeneration of the Muscogulge People.* Lincoln: Univ. of Nebraska Press, 1986.

———. *The Only Land They Knew: The Tragic Story of the American Indians in the Old South.* New York: Free Press, 1981.

Wright, Muriel. "Seal of the Seminole Nation." *Chronicles of Oklahoma* 34 (Autumn 1956): 262–71.

———. *The Story of Oklahoma.* Guthrie, Okla.: Co-Operative Publishing, 1929.

Theses

Bittle, George Cassel. "In the Defense of Florida: The Organized Florida Militia from 1821 to 1920." Ph.D. diss., Florida State Univ., 1965.

Buice, Sammy David. "The Civil War and the Five Civilized Tribes—A Study in Federal-Indian Relations." Ph.D. diss., Univ. of Oklahoma, 1970.

Carter, Bruce Gilbert. "A History of Seminole County, Oklahoma." Master's thesis, Univ. of Oklahoma, 1932.

Chaney, Margaret A. "A Tribal History of the Seminole Indians." Master's thesis, Univ. of Oklahoma, 1928.

Wells, W. Alva. "Osceola and the Second Seminole War." Master's thesis, Univ. of Oklahoma, 1936.

Welsh, Michael E. "The Road to Assimilation: The Seminoles in Oklahoma, 1839–1936." Ph.D. diss., Univ. of New Mexico, 1983.

Wilson, Osburn Carolyn. "The Development of the Florida Territory, 1821–1845." Master's thesis, Vanderbilt Univ., 1932.

Woodward, Sara Alice. "The Second Seminole War with Especial Reference to the Attitude of Congress." Master's thesis, Columbia Univ., 1929.

Index